A Good Send-Off

A manual of funeral practice

Coping before, during and after a funeral

Dorothy Richards

Dorothy Richards

Published in Great Britain by
Pen Press Publishers Ltd
39, Chesham Road
Brighton
BN2 1NB

ISBN 1-905203-86-1

INTRODUCTION

One must take all one's life to learn how to live, and…
one must take all one's life to learn how to die.
Marcus Annaeus Seneca c. 55 BC – 40 AD

Someone has died – a child, husband, wife, partner, parent, friend. You are responsible for arranging the funeral but have never done this before. Where to begin? Everything you need to know when someone dies is mentioned in this book – registering the death, arranging the funeral, and coping before and afterwards both emotionally and practically.

I have buried both my parents and two husbands. I felt therefore that the knowledge I have acquired was something I could pass on to others. After arranging a funeral for a friend, I found myself saying, 'Well, I think we gave him *a good send-off,* didn't we?' And so, after many attempts, the final title for this book was chosen.

As I talked to clergy, members of other faiths, funeral directors, and those in charge of burial grounds and crematoria, I began to realise there was a dearth of knowledge in each field about the other parties involved in the death of an individual. I hope this book will help to inform everyone of the part played by others when someone dies.

The book is non-denominational, and is concerned with all religions, because we now live in a multi-faith society; and people from all religions, and those who are not religious, need to dispose of the earthly remains of their loved ones with care and dignity.

The last chapter suggests preparing for one's own death, making a Will, the pros and cons of prepayment funerals, and help for the dying.

There are prayers in *Appendix I* and readings in *Appendix II* that could be read at funerals or meditated on at home, from the various denominations and faiths, and some for those who do not believe in a god at all. The biblical readings are given in full, relieving the reader of trying to find the exact passages, if they are not familiar with the Bible.

Examples of music and hymns suitable to use at funeral services are suggested in *Appendix III.*

There is also a brief mention in *Appendix IV* of pet funerals and cemeteries. Children may first get to know about death when a favourite pet dies and this begins to prepare them for the death of a loved family member or friend thereafter.

There are useful addresses of people and organisations that can help at this difficult time in *Appendix V. (Telephone numbers and addresses, both postal and Internet, are correct at the time of publication of this book, as is all the information given.)*

Do contact me c/o the Publishers if you have any suggestions or comments.

Dorothy Richards, August 2005

i

Acknowledgements

Many people have assisted in the production of this book.

I interviewed a number of priests of many religions and denominations, hospital chaplains, a bishop, some funeral directors, hospice and hospital medical directors, etc. all of whom I thank for their time.

One senior bishop, who I shall not name, declined to be interviewed. When I met him socially and complained that he was the only refusal I had received, he said 'Perhaps I was the only one humble enough to think that he had nothing to say on the subject!'

Several people offered to read various bits of the book. I am particularly indebted to Peter Applewhite whose expertise was accuracy and consistency; to the Revd Frank Brown, the Revd John Job, the Revd Canon John Tibbs, and the Revd Dennis Mihill, retired vicars, all of whom suggested alterations and corrected my spelling and grammar.

I am also grateful to Paul Edwards, eminent organist who oversaw the music for funerals in Appendix III

I am grateful Geoff Smith, who is CEO of TocH, who has written a foreword, but is also a Revd Canon and Church of England curate.

And I am also indebted to the publishers who had the foresight to get involved with a subject like this.

To Curtis Brown to reproduce the poem by Sir Winston Churchill on page 139. To The Society of Authors Literary Estates for permission to reproduce the poem by Laurence Binyon on page 130, and the poem by Walter De La Mere on page 163. To Pan MacMillan for permission to reproduce the poem by Wilfrid Wilson Gibson on page 159. The Sheil Land Association for the poem by Minnie Louise Haskings on page 134, and the poem by Joyce Grenfell on page 133 copyright © The Joyce Grenfell Memorial Trust 1980. To Paul Berry of Winifred Holtby Estate for permission to reproduce the poem by Winifred Holtby on page 125. To Carl Spadoni for permission to reproduce the words by Bertrand Russell on page 121 copyright © The Bertrand Russell Peace Foundation Ltd. To A.M. Heath & Co Ltd for permission to reproduce a few words by Anne Tyler in Chapter 11. To Methuen Publishing Ltd for permission to include the poem by Noël Coward from Collected Verse on page 163, Copyright © The Estate of Noël Coward. To Pauline Webb for permission to reproduce a poem and two prayers on pages 112, 113 and 131; To A P Watt Ltd for permission to reproduce the poem by W B Yeats on page 120 from The Countess Cathleen in Paradise. To Guzelian for permission to reproduce the photograph of coffin covers in middle section.

Every effort has been made to trace the author and copyright holders of the poems used in Appendix II.

Dorothy Richards

Foreword

If the Victorians didn't consider it proper to talk about sex, we new Elizabethans find it almost impossible to talk about death.

A book about death and dying therefore may not be the most attractive of propositions to modern sensibilities, certainly not a book for a Christmas stocking or a teenager's birthday.

Reading this book, however, I found myself thinking how useful it would be in helping anyone affected by death, from the recently bereaved to the minister taking a funeral, to understand and deal with the many complexities of arranging a funeral and facing up to the loss of a loved one.

As clergyman and as CEO of a national community work charity, I am conscious of the impact of death on those who have to cope with both the practicalities and the loss of a close family member or friend.

The author explores the many facets of the funeral itself – the Will, executors' responsibilities, the memorial and the memorial service, considers the question of cremation or burial, and explores the beliefs and approaches of both Christian and other faiths.

It is a book concerned equally with the practicalities and the prayers.

As such it is both a useful compendium and a source of comfort and humour in the face of the final adventure each of us has to take in life, the adventure of dying.

More than that though, it is a book which will help its readers face up to the fact of their own mortality, and planning their own funeral, with the chapter robustly entitled 'Preparing for death'. Is this a modern parlour game for those long winter evenings, when there is nothing on the telly?

Revd Canon Geoff Smith
Chief Executive Officer
TocH The Community Action Charity.

Quick checklist of things to do when someone dies

Chapter 1   Call a doctor and get a medical certificate showing cause of death

Inform the next of kin

Call vicar or minister of religion, if appropriate

Solicitor – find the Will

Contact the Bank – freeze any sole accounts

Register the death and get a death certificate

Choose a funeral director, or if doing it oneself, get in touch with the local church or crematorium to book a date and time.

Place advertisements in the local, national and/or trade papers as appropriate

Comfort the bereaved

Take care of any pets

Chapter 2   Plan the rest of the funeral

Choose a coffin and type of hearse

Chapter 3   Choose the music

Get the service sheets, if any, printed

Arrange for flowers to be in the church

Arrange for wreaths or sprays from the florist

Arrange venue, refreshments and flowers for the wake

Chapter 7   Thank everyone

Choose headstones

Chapter 8   Make an appointment at the Probate office if not using a solicitor

Contents

Chapter 6   Funeral rites for different faiths
(in order or origin)

Chapter 7   After the funeral

Chapter 1

BEFORE THE FUNERAL

Though it be in the power of the weakest arm to take away life,
it is not in the strongest to deprive us of death.
Sir Thomas Browne 1605 – 1682

WHO TO INFORM WHEN SOMEONE DIES

Doctor

By law, a doctor must be called to come to examine the person who has died, to determine the likely cause of death and to produce a medical certificate. If there is a family doctor, someone from the practice will come. If it is in the middle of the night it may not necessarily be the doctor the deceased generally sees, but the doctor from the same practice who is on duty on that occasion.

In Great Britain dialling 999 would produce the name of a doctor who could be called. Or one can be found from the Family Practitioners Committee (see telephone directory). In a hotel the general manager will know of a doctor who can be summoned. At sea the captain will know what to do.

However, around 80% of people today (2005) die in hospital in Great Britain, and a doctor will usually be on hand or on call. Once he has certified that the patient is dead, the deceased is removed to the mortuary until it has been arranged for the body to be collected by the funeral director (undertaker).

Another 10% of people die in old people's homes or in sheltered accommodation. The warden in this case will call the doctor.

If someone dies in a hospice, one of the first things they will want to know is whether it is to be a burial – which requires one doctor's signature, or a cremation – which will require the signatures of two doctors.

The doctor will certify that the person has actually died and will give a signed medical certificate and a note giving details of how to register the death. After this anyone can call the funeral director asking him to collect the body for preparation. If the person dies at home, in the middle of the night, the doctor may offer to call a funeral director to come and take the deceased away to their premises.

Some people still prefer to have the deceased at home until the funeral, as was always the case in times past, when the local midwife usually did the laying out. If this is the case, the funeral director could be asked to send someone to prepare the deceased at home.

Some religions stipulate that only certain people are allowed to prepare the deceased (see *Chapter 6*).

The next of kin

The close family members are the next people to be informed. If the person dies in a hospital, the next of kin or a friend is informed and asked to collect the deceased's belongings as soon as possible. If the person dies in an old people's home, one is usually given longer to clear the room or flat.

Local vicar or other religious authority

If the person who has died was religious, it would be important to inform their priest, pastor etc. Church of England vicars are responsible for all the people within their parish, whether they are churchgoers or not. If one dies within a Church of England parish one is entitled to be buried there, whether one is a churchgoer or not, believer or not.

If someone dies in his parish, whether a religious service is wanted or not, the minister will often visit the family, in order to offer comfort.

For other than Christians, the appropriate person for the religion concerned should be approached.

Solicitor – finding the Will

Any solicitor known to hold the Will needs to be informed. It is necessary to find out whether a Will has been made, stating a preference for burial or cremation, and where the funeral should take place. If not at a Solicitor's the Will may be found among the deceased's private papers, safe, metal deed box or file. It is often marked 'Last Will and Testament of...' or 'To be opened in the event of my death'. Sometimes it is with the deeds of the house, with certificates of birth, marriage, or divorce, other relatives' death certificates, share certificates, or other relevant documents. Or it may also be lodged with a bank (who may have been named as executor). If nothing can be found, an advertisement in the *Law Gazette* may produce a solicitor out of the area, who has made a Will for the deceased. Or The Probate Registry (formerly Somerset House) can be consulted, as sometimes Wills are lodged there. One must also consider whether the Will was the last one made, particularly if the Will is very old. The person may have belonged to a cremation society or purchased a prepayment funeral. If so, these details ought to be with the Will. On making a Will see *Chapter 11*, and for getting probate (confirmation of the estate) see *Chapter 8*.

Bank or building society

Any bank or building society needs to be informed promptly, so that they can freeze any account belonging solely to the deceased, and cancel any standing orders or direct debits from the date of death. If there is only a joint account, there is no need to do this.

The value of shares on the stock market at the date of death can be ascertained even some days afterwards.

Public health department

People dying of notifiable diseases such as cholera, plague, fever, smallpox, typhus, HIV and AIDS, must be reported to the local public health department. The hospital will wrap the body in a cotton sheet and perhaps a plastic body bag, and the staff from the funeral director will need to be informed of the position and take extra precautions, e.g. by wearing rubber gloves, etc.

The police

If there are suspicious circumstances, like the death of a young person who had not been seen by a doctor for some months, or someone dying from a gunshot wound, the police would have to be informed and nothing should be touched until the police have arrived.

The Coroner (Procurator Fiscal in Scotland) – Inquest

If it is a sudden unexpected death, an accident, if the person dies of an industrial disease, a murder, a suicide, or if there are any other suspicious circumstances, the coroner will have to be informed, as he may wish to do a *post mortem* or *autopsy* – an after death examination of the corpse to determine the exact cause of death.

If a person dies during a surgical operation or before recovering from an anaesthetic, or is in police custody or in prison at the time of death, the coroner will also need to do a *post mortem* and the next of kin will be informed.

When the *post mortem* has taken place, the coroner will provide a pink form (form 100), which will enable registration of the death to take place. If there is to be a cremation he will issue a Certificate for Cremation (form E), which will enable cremation to take place. For a burial he will issue an Order for Burial form (form 101).

In suspicious circumstances there may also be an inquest and anyone may be called as a witness. This will delay the funeral arrangements. The coroner will then provide a Certificate After Inquest form (form 99 [rev]) so that the death can be registered. A jury may be involved and compensation may be claimable if someone was responsible for the death.

ORGAN DONATION AND MEDICAL RESEARCH

The Will may stipulate that the organs or any part of the body of the deceased, after death, have been left to help others waiting for transplants. The deceased may carry a donor card or be on the NHS Organ Donor Register, which will help relatives to make the right decision at a difficult time.

The family still has to give permission for any organs to be removed. However, nothing can be removed from the body before there is a medical certificate. It may only be practical for organs to be removed for donation if the person dies in hospital. Once the person has been certified brain stem dead, a ventilator in an intensive care unit may maintain the body, thus preserving any organs for a longer period. Otherwise it may be too late, except for corneal donations. Someone in the same hospital may urgently require the heart, kidneys, lungs, liver, pancreas, skin, bone, heart valves or corneas. Some people feel that the death of their loved one has not been in vain if another person can benefit from their death in this manner.

The Will may state that the body of the deceased has been left to medical research. This may save the cost of a funeral, but only healthy bodies are accepted, without pacemakers or any other radioactive components. No one with cancer, a notifiable disease, who has had a heart by-pass, or any transplants, hip or knee replacement, or who is obese, will be accepted.

For how to donate organs after death or to leave one's body to medical research see *Chapter 11*.

REGISTERING THE DEATH

By law all deaths must be registered with a registrar in England and Wales. This must be done within five days of the death (eight days in Scotland), preferably in the local county or borough where the death has occurred, although a declaration of death can now be given in any registration office in England or Wales. The death however can only be registered in the registers of the district where the event took place; this would be done via the postal system and so there is always a delay in the issue of documents in this case.

The next of kin or their representative usually does the registration, or it can be any person present at the death, the occupier of the house where the death occurred, or the person arranging the funeral. The address will be found in the local telephone directory under 'Registration', with sometimes the hours of opening. It is best to make an appointment at the register office to avoid too much waiting. The registration is likely to take 30 minutes.

The medical certificate given by the doctor must be taken to the registrar along with the deceased's birth certificate, if available, marriage certificate(s), divorce certificates(s), any pension book, and their National Insurance number or medical card, anything in fact which exactly identifies the person who has died. The registrar will want to know the date and place of birth, the date and place of death, their usual address, sex, date of birth of the surviving widow(er), any previous spouses, occupation, and whether receiving a pension from public funds. If it is a woman, her maiden name or previous names and her husband's name (if any) and occupation, will be required.

If the coroner (in Scotland procurator fiscal) has been involved, the death cannot be registered until the coroner has completed all his work.

For burial at sea an out of England form (form 104), will be required from the registrar to send to the coroner.

For death and burial whilst at sea, or subsequent burial or scattering of ashes at sea, see *Chapter 4*.

Babies and children

The birth of a child has to be registered within 42 days of birth but if a child dies soon after birth (within five days), the birth and death can be registered at the same time. A stillbirth after the 24th week of pregnancy must be registered and a Medical Certificate of Stillbirth obtained from the midwife to give to the registrar. The registrar will produce a green form (form 9) Certificate for Burial or Cremation and a Certificate of Registration of Stillbirth. The mother may be entitled to statutory maternity pay or maternity allowance.

Prior to the 24th week of pregnancy, it is considered a miscarriage.

THE DEATH CERTIFICATE

The registrar will enter the death in a register, for which there is no charge. But there is a charge for a copy, which is a white death certificate. This will be needed to secure probate or funds from a bank or from elsewhere.

The registrar will also produce a green form (form 9) Certificate for Burial or Cremation, free of charge, which must be given to the funeral director or crematorium, so that the funeral can proceed (unless the coroner has been involved).

The registrar will also provide a white form (form BD 8), free of charge, which has to be given to the local Department of Social Security (DSS), to alter pension benefits, arrange a widow's allowance, or widow's pension (if over 40); or widowed mother's allowance (form BW 1) if under 40 and there are children under 19, or the survivor is expecting a child; and to claim assistance with the funeral expenses if needed. There may be other payments due to meet various circumstances, where the DSS will be able to help.

The death certificate will cost £3.50 (2005). If more are required there is a charge of £3.50 at the time for each, or whilst the registrar is using the same registration book. Once another book is opened, further certificates may cost more because a search will be involved.

Various organizations may need to see the death certificate but they usually return them promptly, so for most purposes one or two will suffice. Those likely to want to see a death certificate are: insurance companies (there may be a payment to come on death or a refund of any premiums paid); employers; pension providers (pensions will stop at the date of death unless arrangements have been made for the spouse or partner to continue receiving it or part of it); local authorities (council tax may be affected by a death in the family and the person will have to be removed from the electoral roll); mortgage providers, banks, building societies, National Savings, and any companies in which shares are held, etc. These organizations will want sight of the death certificate before releasing any funds to the executors.

DYING IN SCOTLAND

A burial plot in Scotland is called a lair. If a person dies in Scotland and is repatriated to England or dies elsewhere and is repatriated to Scotland, no permission is required to move the body but the Secretary of State for Scotland requires a coroner's form 104 from the procurator fiscal. The death certificate is free but must be obtained before either a burial or cremation can take place. In Scotland an inquest is called a public enquiry.

If it is intended to bring the body back to England or Wales for the funeral, the transportation costs may be covered by insurance, but not the funeral itself. If the transport costs are not covered, it may be decided to arrange a funeral for burial or cremation where the person died.

When bringing a body back to England or Wales for a funeral, it will be necessary to produce a death certificate issued in Scotland and a Certificate of No Liability to Register from the registrar in England and Wales from the sub-district in which it is intended to bury or cremate the deceased.

If a death occurs in Scotland, a leaflet D49S can be obtained from the Scottish Executive Justice Department, or from a registration office or Citizens Advice Bureau.

DYING ABROAD

If death occurs abroad or on a foreign ship or aircraft, the death should be registered according to the local regulations and a death certificate obtained. The British Consul of that area should also be informed, who will send details to the General Register Office in the UK. He will issue another certificate or one can be obtained from the Overseas Registration Section of the Home Office or the Foreign and Commonwealth Office allowing the body to be repatriated (see addresses *Appendix V*). If the death occurred on a ship, the body can be buried at sea (see *Chapter 4*).

Whether bringing a body back for cremation or burial the import regulations of the country must be met. Transporting bodies from one country to another may involve a translation of any document, stating the cause, date and place of death, together with a freedom from infection certificate.

If there were complications such as a violent death or notifiable disease, and the body is returned to England or Wales, the coroner must be informed. If it is intended to bring the body back to the UK for cremation, a cremation order must be obtained from the Home Office, coroner's section, marking the envelope 'Cremation urgent'.

The funeral director will want a doctor's medical or registrar's death certificate from the place where the person died, translated from the language in which it is written, and showing the cause of death; or the authorization to remove the body from that country signed by the local authority or coroner. The funeral director, where it is intended to hold the funeral, will also need a Certificate of No Liability to Register from the Registrar in England and Wales, unless the coroner has issued a Certificate E for cremation or an Order for Burial.

Funeral directors can also repatriate a body to another country, if a person dies in the UK, and wishes to be buried elsewhere (see *Chapter 2*).

DISPOSAL OF THE BODY

If the person has left a Will, it might state whether there is to be a burial or a cremation, and whether a burial space has been purchased. If so there should be a deed of grant showing where the grave space has been purchased.

A dead body is not 'owned' by anyone and it has no 'rights' in the UK. The next of kin are responsible for seeing that the human remains are disposed of in a lawful manner (not necessarily in accordance with the deceased's wishes, although this is usually the case). Certainly in biblical days and in some societies where the ancestors are highly revered, the deceased's wishes would be strictly adhered to. Even if the person has expressed a desire for cremation, the executors can bury should they so desire; they are not legally bound by the deceased's decision in England, but are bound by it in the USA. No one, however, can be cremated against his or her wishes.

If neither burial nor cremation has been stipulated in the Will, it is up to the executors or the person arranging the funeral to make the decision.

If the deceased had no remaining family and no friends, an individual at the scene of death would inform the local social services department who would arrange a cremation or burial.

There is no legal requirement in the UK to have either a funeral, a burial or cremation. There is nothing legally to stop anyone having a body embalmed and then keeping it in the attic! A body can even be buried in the garden of a house, but to bury more than one body in the same garden may need a licence as it may then be deemed a cemetery. However, a burial outside a cemetery must first be approved by the local authorities.

The considerations for burial are that it is traditional and biblical, but it is more costly and the grave will have to be tended afterwards. Many parishes will have a churchyard. When the churchyard is full, the local authority has to provide space in a municipal cemetery for burials.

Modern crematoria have burial plots as well as an area for disposal of the ashes. The burial service may also take place in the crematorium chapel, where it can be less expensive to have an early morning booking, which is less popular.

The considerations for cremation are that it is ecological, more hygienic, more efficient, and less expensive. Less space is also required for the interment. Cremation only became legal in England in 1884. The Church of England disapproved of it until the 1920s and the Catholic Church disapproved of it until 1963. 85% of people, and rising, are cremated in England today (2005).

If it is to be a cremation, two doctors have to sign the certificates (forms B and C at £47 each in 2004), unless the body was referred to the coroner for a post mortem or an inquest, in which case the coroner will issue the appropriate form (form E). At the crematorium, a medical referee will issue a certificate (form F) for cremation, but he can refuse to allow a cremation. The fee for the referee will include the use of the chapel and the cremator.

Most crematoria allow 30–45 minutes per funeral but if the whole service is to be conducted at the crematorium it is possible to book two consecutive periods on some days. Mondays are the quietest, Thursdays and Fridays the busiest. Early morning may be a cheaper time to book the cremator; therefore it is sometimes preferable to have the actual cremation before the service. Recorded music is usually available (one can take one's own CDs), although some have an organist. See also music in *Chapter 3 and Appendix III*.

There were approximately 250 crematoria in England (2005).

It is important to realize that whether it is a burial or a cremation that the staff at either establishment will be very professional and also very caring.

DO-IT-YOURSELF OR ENGAGE A FUNERAL DIRECTOR?

For most people engaging a funeral director is the best way forward and the most convenient way to handle disposing of the body of a beloved one with dignity. Unless very confident of being able to handle everything oneself, it is better to engage a professional to deal with all the complicated procedure, at a time when one is perhaps in a very distressed state.

Some funeral directors offer to take charge of the whole event. Or one can do most things oneself, using the funeral director for specific tasks only.

Some people may want friends to carry the coffin, instead of using professionals. If choosing alternative bearers, it should be borne in mind that they should be strong and all the same height. Very few women currently become funeral bearers or even funeral directors.

The crematorium will charge a private person about £87 and the civic cemetery £255. This is only a guide and may vary from area to area, prices being higher in a large city.

ANNOUNCING THE DEATH AND FUNERAL ARRANGEMENTS

The person finding the body usually informs the immediate family of a death, at the earliest possible moment by telephone.

As soon as the funeral arrangements are known, the death may be announced in the local papers, a national paper, or a trade paper (if the person is still in, or has recently retired from, business). The funeral director can handle this matter if requested to do so, or one can do this oneself. If the person was well known, a photograph is sometimes incorporated into a trade paper or even into a local paper.

It is still the custom in some areas to draw the blinds or curtains of a house as soon as a death has occurred, and in an area of close housing, the word will soon get round the neighbourhood, if a death was expected.

News travels very fast among friends, family and work colleagues. It is a good idea to let one person know the funeral arrangements in each group – the employer (or ex-employer if recently retired), who will inform work colleagues, any important customers, clients, etc.; the vicar or pastor who will inform the congregation or church family; if the person was attending school or university, then the college or other appropriate person must be informed; for clubs such as golf, tennis, etc., the secretary; if a member of a political party, the local councillor or party secretary; if on the parish, borough or county council, the appropriate contact. Each sector will ring round with the details, so that everyone who needs to know is informed in time to attend the funeral, send flowers or perhaps a donation (see below).

A simple newspaper announcement could be something like these (fictitious names, places and dates have been used for privacy):

SMITH: Peacefully on 20th February 2007, aged 84 years, John Smith of Great Densham, Bedford. Beloved husband of Joan, father of Peter and Laura, and grandfather of Robert and Jane. Funeral service at Northern Road Crematorium 3rd March at 2.00 pm. Family flowers only. Donations in memory of John may be sent to Cancer Research, care of the funeral directors, Messrs Bloggs & Co. at 1001 Northern Road, Bedford.

JONES: Mary, died peacefully at home at The Manse, Kempshall, Bradford, on 21st March 2010, aged 96. She will be greatly missed by her son and daughter and eight grandchildren. There will be a church service at Saint David's, Kempshall, at 1.00 pm. on 28th March, followed by a short service at the Southern Road Crematorium. The family would appreciate it if everyone would return to the house for refreshments thereafter. Flowers may be sent to the funeral directors, Arnold & Scott of 1030 Norton Road, Bradford.

PROBY CLARKE: The Reverend Christopher, greatly loved priest, husband and father, died peacefully with his family around him on 30th June 2004. Aged 76. Memorial service to be announced. Inquiries to funeral directors, Jones, Brown & Co, High Street, Double Wallop, Sussex.

DIAMOND: Jenny, our lovely little girl, the light of our lives, on Tuesday, 3rd March, aged five. She was lent to us to care for, for such a short time. She will never be forgotten by Mummy and Daddy and little Peter. Funeral at St Michael's and All Angels, Coppice town, 7th March 2005 at 2.30 pm. After the burial in the churchyard, there will be refreshments for everyone in the church barn.

If the person is well known and it is intended to have a memorial service at a later date, then the actual funeral may be for the immediate friends and family only and this can be incorporated in any press announcement. e.g. 'A private funeral will be held at … (name). church at 10.00 am on Wednesday … (date) for the family only, followed by a thanksgiving service at a date to be announced.

It is not wise to stipulate 'no letters'. These may not be wanted at the time but afterwards can be a great comfort to those left behind, usually containing pleasant memories and reminiscences, and sometimes photographs of the deceased.

It is a great comfort to the bereaved, if all the members of the family and the friends can attend the funeral, showing their support. If time permits, a map can be offered to those not familiar with the locality.

FLOWERS OR DONATIONS?

Some people feel that only family flowers should be on the coffin and that other people should be asked instead to give a donation to an appropriate charity if they so wish. In the newspaper, when announcing the death and date of the funeral, one can say 'No flowers but donations to … Heart Foundation/ Cancer Research/ Arthritis Care / Great Ormond Street Hospital for Children/ Famine Relief, etc. (whichever is appropriate to the cause of death, or interests of the deceased). The notice may say, 'Cheques to … (the relevant charity) may be sent to … (the funeral directors), who will send them on to the charity in question. Later on, the charity or the funeral director will send to the next of kin a list of those who have donated in memory of the person who has died.

But some people like lots of flowers at a funeral. It is also said that London funerals and funerals for West Indians have more flowers than country funerals. Usually florists are used to people ringing up and asking for a wreath or two urgently, and being ready for such requests is part of their expertise. Floral tributes are often sent the day before the funeral to the funeral director. Some funeral directors have their own florists.

At some funerals, especially children's, the name, if short, can be spelled out in letters on several separate wreaths, one from each of the family siblings or other family members e.g. L U K E. Some wreaths may also spell out M U M, or D A D.

One funeral I attended had a wreath, in the shape of a teddy bear, made out of tiny blue and white chrysanthemums, with a blue bow round its neck. Florists will rise to the occasion and suggest something suitable if consulted.

Romanies often have wreaths, which depict animals, musical instruments or even a caravan! Many gypsies are Christians but their wreaths are often connected with nature.

COMFORTING THE BEREAVED

Bereaved people might appreciate cards and letters. These can be 'with sympathy' cards, incorporating appropriate wording, or just a pleasant rural scene or picture of some flowers, looking more hopefully to the future.

It is a good idea to say how much the deceased has meant to the sender over the years and/or to pay some tribute to their character or lifestyle. These letters and cards will mean much to the surviving family members, who will no doubt treasure them and keep them to read and reread.

Many people think that flowers are for the living not the dead, so that they send flowers to the bereaved, with or without a card or letter attached.

Until after the funeral, these tributes may be more appreciated than a telephone call or a visit, except for very close friends and family members.

ANIMALS LEFT BEHIND

An elderly person living alone may leave a pet, who has to be cared for, until after the funeral. Then if none of the family is prepared to give a home to the pet, a local pet charity may be able to find a new owner.

The pet, if a dog or cat, may also be distraught at the loss of its beloved owner and need loving and careful handling. The person's Will may have mentioned what he or she hoped would happen to the pet.

Chapter 2

THE FUNERAL DIRECTOR

Let us endeavour so to live that when we die, even the
Undertaker will be sorry. Mark Twain 1835 – 1910

HISTORY AND INTRODUCTION

In 1675 William Boyce was the first recorded funeral director (undertaker). And the first person ever to 'undertake' a funeral service in London was a William Russell in 1680. Before this, people would bury their own dead usually in body bags, sheets or shrouds, with the help of friends.

No licence is required to set up as a funeral director (in the UK 2005) but it would be wise to use an established firm or one that has been recommended by someone trustworthy.

There are a number of unique hearses and coffins one can use today to reflect the kind of life the deceased has lived, it is only necessary to make it clear to the funeral director exactly what one wants.

CHOOSING A FUNERAL DIRECTOR

If neither the doctor nor anyone else has been of help, a list of funeral directors can be obtained from the Yellow Pages or similar directory, or sometimes there are advertisements in the local press on the obituary pages. This is a service industry which everyone will eventually need unless they have the nerve to take on a 'do-it-yourself' or 'family funeral', when someone dies.

Ideally, the funeral director should be a member of a national trade organization, with a code of practice. 80% belong to the National Association of Funeral Directors (NAFD, founded in 1905). There is also a Funeral Standards Council (FSC) and a Society of Allied and Independent Funeral Directors (SAIF). 550 traditional funeral directors are members of the Funeral Ombudsman Scheme, which can be consulted free of charge if there is a complaint against one of its members.

Many companies today are part of the Co-op, SCI (USA) or Pompes Funèbres (France), although some may still be trading under their previous names. There are also some independent family funeral businesses, with a good name in their locality.

Some advise getting more than one quote (this can be done on the telephone), as one would with a decorator, plumber or electrician, although it is necessary to make sure that each one is quoting for a similar service. Most establishments will have a printed price list, which can, and should be, perused and contrasted with others. They should all provide a written estimate, before the funeral, with all details clearly explained and itemized.

After choosing a funeral director, a meeting will be necessary either at the funeral director's establishment or at one's own home because papers will have to be signed. The funeral director will need a copy of the green form obtained from the registrar in order to proceed with either a burial or a cremation.

Many funeral directors today are able to provide not only the basic things necessary but also a whole range of services listed below.

It is the funeral director who will be collecting the body from the house or hospital where the person has died and taking it to the firm's mortuary, where the body will be prepared for the family to view, and for burial or cremation. This can be done at any time of the day or night. If the body has to be collected from a distance, then a private ambulance rather than a hearse will be used. Usually there is free collection within a certain area (sometimes a 20-mile radius) and after that there will be a charge of something like 50p per mile, or so much per hour of time taken.

Staff at a funeral director's premises may be on call 24 hours a day, with no overtime pay. Some staff may be part-time, called in when required. Others are permanent members of staff, who have to know how to do all the jobs done by a firm of funeral directors. The pay is not great but according to those who have been employed for many years, there is great job satisfaction. Most funeral premises have full-time staff to cope during the summer months and employ extra part-time staff for the increased activity during the winter.

CHAPEL OF REST

Most funeral parlours have one or more chapels of rest, where, after embalming, the body is prepared for friends and relatives to come to say their last farewells.

It is a good idea to give the funeral director a photograph, clothes, dentures, glasses and even make-up, so that the person looks their best, with their usual hair style, etc.; one person reckoned it would not be 'him' if he were not reading a newspaper. So the funeral director agreed and he 'received his visitors' in the chapel of rest in his usual posture, with glasses on, reading the paper.

Children should neither be persuaded nor be denied to make their own goodbyes at the loss of one of the family. They can be invited to see grandma one more time to say 'goodbye' at the chapel of rest, if they want to, but should be prepared for what to expect, i.e. that she will not be able to talk or say 'goodbye' to them herself.

It is best to make an appointment when visiting a chapel of rest, so that the staff will be ready to welcome the visitors.

Some people prefer the body, after embalming, to be taken back to the house before the funeral. This helps some people come to terms with the death of a beloved. Until then, some family members may not have realized that they will never see the person again, at least in this world.

DATE AND TIME OF THE FUNERAL

A funeral can be held anywhere but is usually in a crematorium, a church, a hall, synagogue or mosque. The funeral director will ring the church and/or the crematorium or other venue, and between them will come up with a time, or a choice of times, that the funeral can be held, they will also book the coffin bearers, cars, etc. If people were coming from a long way away, then a funeral later in the day would be preferable to an early morning one.

In a cold winter, when there is a flu epidemic, or if there is a bank holiday, there may be a long wait between the death and the time of the funeral.

TYPE OF SERVICE

Usually a minister of religion will conduct the service but anyone can do it. There is no necessity to involve religion in either a crematorium or a church service, subject to the agreement of the authoritative body in the chosen location. Some vicars and ministers are willing these days to conduct non-religious services. This can be discussed and negotiated.

Most funeral directors can arrange funerals for every religion and also for those who are not religious, so the funeral director may be the best person to advise how the funeral will be conducted, or one can plan everything oneself. The whole family may want to be involved. Some might do the readings, prayers or give a reminiscence, others might sing a song or play some special solo or group music. Each should be given a time limit, particularly if any other service or event is to follow.

If the coroner has been involved, in cases of sudden death or unusual circumstances, the funeral may be delayed; it is then that embalming may be a necessity (see below).

COSTS

Most funerals are paid for out of the deceased's estate.

There are usually no costs from the funeral director for a child's funeral (under 16 in England, up to 5 years in the USA). One reason may be that it would be too embarrassing to have to chase the money from someone who has lost a child. A child's funeral would include a hearse and one car and a choice of one of three coffins. Any extras would incur a cost.

Costs from a funeral director will vary in different parts of the country but will have to be competitive within in a certain area. £1,800 is likely to be the lowest charge for any funeral (2005) and this can go up to many thousands of pounds if elaborate lined caskets of solid wood are chosen, or many cars are required, embalming and special clothes ordered. There will be extra costs for the disposal of the ashes after the cremation or for any headstones, containers for the ashes, etc. A proper estimate must be obtained from the funeral director, in advance, for each individual funeral.

Burial is more expensive than cremation and a churchyard burial is less expensive (£182 – 2005) than one in a municipal cemetery, where there may be separate sections for the burial of Catholics, Jews, Muslims, Sikhs, Hindus and Chinese, etc. Some also have a separate section for the burial of children, miscarriages and stillbirths.

The prices for coffins and for the funeral director's services will be dearer in large cities, where everything else is commensurately more expensive.

If an official person is engaged to take the funeral service, the fee is the same for a burial or a cremation and is £84 (2005).

Some churchyards are now closed because all the plots have been filled, although burials or ashes will still be allowed into a family grave, which is not full.

A funeral director's services will include removal of the body (more for out of hours), preparation for viewing, embalming, chapel of rest, coffin or casket, hearse, limousines (mileage if more than 20 miles or by time taken), bearers and funeral director; and if a cremation a casket or urn to receive the ashes after the event, plus a service for burying the ashes at a later date; or the preparation of a headstone and its positioning for a burial of a body or ashes; liaising with the church, crematorium, ministers, etc.

According to what is requested from the funeral director, there may also be fees for:

Doctor (cremation papers)

Crematorium fees

Cemetery fee

Church fees (organist, heating, choir, bells, verger, minister). There are no fees for the minister in the Church of Scotland. Mormons do not charge any fees to any members of their congregations who wish for a burial service.

Burial fees (plot, grave digger)

Newspaper costs (obituary, announcements of time and place of funeral, and flowers or donations, memorial service, thanks after the event)

Flowers (wreaths, flowers in church)

Printing (service sheet)

Catering (for reception)

Extra hearse to carry the flowers (if numerous approximately £100)

Collections after 5 pm or at weekends

For doves released at a funeral (see below)

Different types of hearse to reflect the lifestyle of the deceased (see below).

A horse-drawn vehicle may cost £675 compared with a motorised one at £160. If a horse-drawn vehicle is required, more time must be allowed for the funeral, because a horse-drawn vehicle is much slower than a motorised hearse. Belgian black stallions with black ostrich feathers, such a feature of Victorian funerals, may not now be available in some areas.

After the funeral, the funeral director must provide a written invoice in keeping with the estimate and itemizing all the disbursements paid out on behalf of the person arranging the funeral, only adding anything that has been formally agreed before hand. It is possible to arrange to pay in instalments, beforehand, with some funeral directors, if desired. Otherwise, there may be an interest charge for late payment, although this must be stated on the invoice and the amount of interest noted.

If a solicitor is taking complete charge of the estate of the deceased, then the invoice for the funeral should be sent to him.

GRANTS

If the deceased was still in work, there may be a death-in-service benefit or there may be an occupational pension scheme, which will supply a lump sum towards the funeral costs. If the person had a life insurance policy, this may cover the cost of the funeral. The deceased may have paid in advance for his or her funeral (see *Chapter 11* for a prepayment plan). Lump sums may also be payable from trade unions, a provident club or a professional body.

The Death Grant was abolished on 1st April 1987. If there is no money in the estate, or if there are no relatives or friends to take charge of the funeral, it is possible to apply to the DSS Social Fund for a grant – maximum £600 (2004) but any other grants due will reduce the amount available from the DSS. The registrar of deaths will be able to provide a claim form (form SF 200). It is the status of the person arranging the funeral that matters. If the person responsible for the funeral receives either supplementary benefit, income support, child tax credit, pension credit, working tax credit, housing benefit, rent or council tax rebate, or is out of work receiving job seekers allowance, a grant may be possible, but it is irrelevant whether the deceased was on income support. If it is later discovered that the deceased left any money or had insurance policies or any other assets, except those of personal belongings and a house left to the widow, the funeral grant will have to be paid back.

To be eligible for a grant the deceased must normally have been a resident of the UK but a funeral payment may be made for a funeral to take place elsewhere in the European Union but the grant would be limited to the cost of a funeral that would have taken place in the area where the deceased lived. It is possible to make a claim for a funeral payment up to three months after the date of the funeral.

If the deceased was a war pensioner, a grant may be available from the War Pensions Agency (see addresses *Appendix V*). If the deceased was a disabled war pensioner who died of the disablement condition, or was getting a war pensioner's constant attendance allowance, or a war disablement pension and unemployment supplement, any grant money received will not have to be repaid. Claims must be made within three months of the funeral to the Veterans Agency.

If there is no one responsible and there are no resources, the local council (county council in a rural area) has to arrange the funeral and dispose of the human remains. But they will only do this where a funeral has not already been arranged.

If someone dies in hospital, and there are no traceable relatives, the local health authority will arrange and pay for a simple funeral but they may make a claim from the deceased's estate, if money is later found to be available. If a hospital has to arrange the funeral, it will cost £150 including crematorium fees of £24, minister's fee of £24, doctors' certificates of £47, cemetery, a coffin and funeral director for £40.

EMBALMING

Some funeral directors nearly always embalm nowadays, whether it is requested or not, so it is best to check because bodies to be buried in a woodland natural burial site or buried at sea are not allowed to be embalmed.

Refrigeration is only used when the bodies are kept for a short time before the funeral or whilst waiting for embalming.

If the funeral has to be delayed for any reason or if many people are expected to want to view the body (e.g. if people are coming from abroad and wish to pay their last respects), it is necessary to embalm, not only for cosmetic but also for hygienic reasons to provide a natural look to the body for as long as possible. One person said, when the deceased's body was delivered to the house in an open coffin, after a long and painful illness, 'She hasn't looked so well for ages!'

Arterial embalming was introduced in the 1880s. It consists in forcing formaldehyde into the body through one of the main arteries (usually one in the groin) and removing blood from one of the other arteries (usually one under the arm on the opposite side of the body).

Embalming may cost £35 – £70 and take from 2 – 20 hours. It takes longer if the body has been damaged in an accident or if a post mortem has taken place, and reconstruction is necessary. (It is interesting to note in the Bible, that it took a full forty days to embalm Jacob in Egypt. *Gen. 50:3!*)

CHOOSING THE COFFIN

Most funeral directors will have the choice of perhaps fifty coffins. In distress, one may feel that the most expensive will be more honourable to the deceased but this is not necessarily so. It is not necessary to impress anybody. Coffins can be purchased from £50 – £375 from the manufacturer but the funeral director will probably charge in the region of £130 – £2,750. The most expensive would be of solid oak or tulipwood, beautifully lined with silks and satins with a hinged lid. This coffin can be left open at the service and the congregation can file past paying their last respects, which is normal for some religions or denominations.

For a burial, a coffin can have solid brass handles, or any other metal. Straps go under the coffin, for lowering it into the ground.

For a cremation, metal is banned, and plastic handles are used although they may be treated to look like brass or nickel plating.

A traditional coffin may be rectangular or tapered. Each has a lid, which comes off and is screwed down before the burial or cremation, or it may be hinged. Each has a nameplate with the name and date of death, and age of the deceased on it, ensuring there is no mix-up.

The cheapest coffin is one of chipboard with a wood or plastic veneer and is the usual type chosen by most people (but see cardboard coffins and coffin covers, below). When a nuclear attack was thought a possibility, some funeral premises kept a very large stock of cardboard coffins because they can be stored flat. The dimensions need to be checked for cardboard coffins because I am told some are too large to go through a door. And other people find them difficult to assemble.

Custom-built coffins

Vic Fearn, traditional coffin makers of Bulwell, Nottingham, specialize in custom-built coffins, reflecting the life, interests and achievements of the deceased. They have produced an egg-shaped coffin for a terminally ill customer who wished to be cremated, as she was born, in the foetal position. In 2001, they made a pearl-coloured coffin, painted with flowers, for T V presenter Paula Yates's funeral.

Among their recently built designs is a skateboard for a teenager killed in a skateboard accident, a cricket bat, and a skip for a person in the rubbish trade! Special coffins may take some time to build, so it is advisable to order one in advance of death if something special is desired.

Some people have a piece of furniture made that can be used as a coffin when the time comes. It may be a shoe chest or a coffee table for instance, or a stereo cabinet. Individual coffins may cost up to £1,000 each (2005), depending on the design (for unusual coffins see photos in middle section).

If the death is anticipated well in advance (for instance if someone has a terminal illness or is very old), a cardboard or wooden coffin can be beautifully painted appropriately for the deceased. Because the coffin will mostly be seen from a distance, artists need to be used to painting on large canvases. The cost of having a painted coffin would be at least £500 because it would take many hours to perfect and would have to be painted on all sides and underneath.

Heaven on Earth stencil veneered wood or MDF coffins from £199 or they will do a decorated coffin for £275. They do an adult willow coffin in a guitar shape, a Red Arrows Jet coffin, and a baby coffin in the shape of a dolphin. They are also funeral directors.

Coffins come in all shapes, sizes and materials but some people wouldn't be seen dead in a cardboard one, even if it were painted!

I recently went to a funeral where the deceased had requested a cardboard coffin but she was eventually buried in a wicker one. I had not seen a wicker one before but apparently they were popular in the Middle Ages when basket weaving was more of an activity among country folk. Today they may cost £400 and come in various colours, white, beige, green, brown or red. They are eco-friendly and can be purchased from the Somerset Willow Company. The SAWD Partnership, do bamboo coffins.

Ecopods were developed for green funerals but can be used for any kind of funeral. They are round instead of the usual shape of coffin and are biodegradable, decomposing more quickly. They are made of papier-mache, or mulberry leaf and silk paper; some are lined with feathers, and they have straps like a traditional coffin for carrying it or for lowering it into the ground. For burying ashes there is one in green and brown resembling an acorn. Ecopods can be delivered to anywhere in the UK within 24 hours, and are considered by some to be a work of art (for eco-friendly coffins see photos in middle section).

Some people may also like to drape the coffin with a beautiful piece of cloth or a patchwork quilt or some other embroidery that the deceased has made, and this is especially appropriate where it is stipulated that there are 'no flowers'. The cloth would be folded up before burial or cremation and offered to the next of kin.

Inside the coffin the deceased may be wrapped in a shroud of wool or cotton or be dressed in their own clothes.

For the addresses for all the above see *Appendix V*.

A revolutionary idea

A firm in Bradford has developed a unique 'Coffin Cover' arrangement, which helps protect the environment by reducing the number of trees that need to be cut down to make wooden coffins.

There is an inner cardboard coffin 22 in (55 cm) wide, made of 'Toughwall' double thickness corrugated board, which will take a person up to 17 stone (238 lbs or 108 kgs) in weight, but only up to 6 ft 2 in (188 cm) in height at the moment, and a coffin cover, which is reused by the funeral director.

The coffin cover is a handmade wooden casket, with a high-polished veneer finish, brass handles, and a satin lining. It carries the cardboard coffin to the burial site or crematorium, and then the cardboard coffin is slipped discreetly out of the coffin cover, before being placed in the cremator or being buried. The coffin cover can be folded when not in use, and put into a protective bag, which makes it easier to take away from a crematorium. If it is a burial, the coffin cover may be left in the hearse.

The cardboard coffin costs £50, which includes a waterproof lining, a pillow support and two plaques for identification purposes. It has a removable lid for viewing and three die cut handles on each side and one at each end.

This company has won a National Green Apple Environment award for the 'Coffin Cover' arrangement, which was presented at The House of Commons on 6 November 2003. The coffin is protected by several registered designs and patents are pending.

Some funeral directors may not be in favour of coffin covers because they would prefer to sell a standard coffin. Others will appreciate the need to protect the environment by the consumption of fewer trees using this method. It is up to the client to make the decision and it gives them the appearance of a higher quality coffin for less money (see photos in middle section).

PUTTING ITEMS INTO THE COFFIN

Some people like to put things in a coffin before it is sealed. Apparently Queen Victoria requested that they put into her coffin, a cast of Albert's hand, his dressing gown, and a photograph of John Brown (her devoted ghillie and some think her lover after Albert died).

Others may wish to put wedding rings, a book of poems, photographs, baby clothes, a lock of hair, or other shared mementos – anything precious in memory of the loved one.

REPATRIATION

People wishing to send back a body to another country from Great Britain find there are special regulations, which have to be adhered to, such as obtaining an 'out of England certificate' from a coroner (Removal Notice form104), which has to be obtained at least four days before the body can be moved.

A body to be sent back to Italy has to be in a coffin of solid wood, lined with zinc and hermetically sealed, with an extra coffin cover of hessian, which may cost £950 before there are any funeral or flight costs.

To send a body back to Pakistan will probably cost less, and some other countries (e.g. Ireland) do not insist on a metal lined coffin. The funeral director will know the procedure for each destination and will be able to provide the necessary 'certificate of sanitization'.

Phoenix International (see address in *Appendix V*) is the company who will liaise with the funeral director and make all the arrangements at the airport, to send the coffin off to another country.

DOVES OF PEACE

It is possible to release one or more white doves at a funeral, whether it is a woodland or any other kind. Doves have symbolized peace for centuries and they are trained when released to return home. A company specializing in providing doves for funerals is *The White Dove Company* (see address in *Appendix V*). An experienced handler brings the dove(s) to the grave or crematorium site and the person responsible for the funeral will release the bird at the appropriate moment in the ceremony, say at the committal. It may also represent the spirit leaving the body. Severe weather however may prevent the bird from being released.

TYPES OF HEARSES FOR FUNERALS

(The addresses of all below can be found in *Appendix V).*

The following are different types of hearses currently available (2005). The funeral cortège can represent the way the person has lived their life. Consequently if they had spent their whole lives among motorcycles, or vintage lorries, or narrow boats, etc., they might want their funeral to reflect this.

Motorcycle and sidecar hearse

An ardent motorbike enthusiast, Paul Sinclair, who is an ordained minister of the Pentecostal church, started his own company *Motorcycle Funerals Limited* in Coalville, Leicestershire, in 2000. In Australia and New Zealand someone has arranged a motorbike with a board to carry a coffin, but Paul Sinclair was the first to build a proper sidecar hearse. His customers are retired bikers who remember sidecars, and people who remember their parents having a bike and themselves being taken about in a sidecar as children. That generation developed a love for the open air and the roar of an engine. They have indicated that they are happy to spend their final journey as they remember their childhood journeys with a bike and sidecar. Funeral directors in other areas have also found there is a call for such a vehicle and therefore *Motorcycle Funerals Limited* are able to hire out a machine. Before this invention, people tied the coffin on to the sidecar, or one actually stood the coffin up in the sidecar to go to the funeral. Paul Sinclair has done 80 funerals with his motorcycle hearse in the last few years. His customers often say after the funeral 'that is exactly what he (or she) would have wanted'. The bike used is a Triumph. International patents are pending.

Motorbike hearse

Another revolutionary idea was developed in 2002 by funeral director Bill Tanner and a director, Tony Crathern, of the *Essex Chapter* of the *Harley-Davidson Owner's Group.* An Ultra Classic Electra Glide 1340 cc Harley-Davidson trike, pulls a domed shaped purpose-built hearse. Another outfit is now ready for the road – a Harley Davidson Heritage Softail Classic 1340 cc trike, which complete with Chapter flags, etc., are all available on hire.

Vintage lorry hearse

David Hall does a 1950 Leyland Beaver, another original funeral with a vintage lorry, 'King of the Road'. David says his customers include lorry drivers, mechanics, showmen and travellers, and ladies who do not like black hearses. The idea of having a vintage lorry hearse is attractive to anyone who has been associated with such vehicles during his or her lifetime. It is an ideal arrangement e.g. for multiple coffins travelling together, after a family disaster, or for burial at sea, because it is easier to lift coffins off a flat bed lorry than from any other kind of hearse. A sea of flowers can surround the coffin across the entire lorry. The flowers are carried in stackable purpose-built trays tilted to show them to their best advantage. A mechanic killed on the M5, who had been married for only two months, had this vintage lorry for his funeral. His widow arranged it and requested that a floral replica of his pet dog should overlook the coffin.

The driver, who acts as carriage master, wears a black boiler suit, white shirt, black tie and a black beret, which was the vogue of 1950s lorry drivers. David Hall is based in the South West but accepts funerals as far north as Leeds. Distance is no object but the lorry only does 32 mph. Costs are £300 plus £1.50 per mile, plus £15.75 insurance (2003).

Railway hearses

Railway enthusiasts can choose between a diesel, steam or electric train to carry the coffin and mourners to trackside cemeteries, especially in the Midlands. Ex-train drivers and other railway enthusiasts often like these.

There is a history of cemeteries being built alongside railway lines, especially when the populations in big cities increased dramatically during the Industrial Revolution. With an increase in population there was an increase in the number of deaths. At the same time the town churchyards were becoming full to capacity. The cholera epidemic in 1848 exacerbated the problem further. At this time a first class burial in a brick grave could be purchased for £1 and could be held in perpetuity.

Around London eight cemeteries were built from 1837 to 1841 to ease the problem of overcrowding; about two thirds of each was consecrated. Free tickets were issued for Londoners to inspect the new cemeteries, because there was still reluctance to use them. Special railway carriages were constructed to convey the bodies to these new burial grounds, with separate compartments for customers and staff; and special funeral stations were built, with separate waiting rooms for customers and staff, incorporating ventilated mortuaries, which could be used free of charge for bodies until the funeral. A workingman's funeral cost £1.14s. Other funerals might cost £2.5s to £3.16s in pre-decimal days.

By 1854 *The London Necropolis and National Mausoleum Company* was established on 2,000 acres at Brookwood, near Woking, Surrey. It had its own terminus at Waterloo until 1941, when it was damaged in an air raid (extracted from *The End of the Line* by Martin C Dawes 2003).

Other unusual types of hearse

Horse-drawn hearses are still available for the nostalgic or horse lovers, using either black or white horses, and dainty wheeled hearses, with glass sides and decorative tops. *T.Cribb & Sons* of Nottingham can supply a four-horse-drawn Shillibeer hearse with a place for the mourners to sit in with the deceased. This company can also provide a vintage car hearse (see photos in middle pages).

Hand-held biers with etched side panels are available from *Justine Burgess of Hatfield* and from *T Cribb & Sons as* above (see photos in middle pages).

A London bus driver was to be buried in a woodland green site 45 miles north of London. Hiring a funeral hearse and many following limousines was considered to be exorbitant. All the mourners and the coffin therefore were placed in a London red double-decker bus, which had the name of the deceased on the front, where the destination is usually placed. All travelled there and back in comfort and together.

A 32-stone man was carried in a transit van because the hearse would not take his weight and he had to have eight pallbearers, instead of the usual six to carry the coffin.

When a hearse broke down at a baker's funeral, someone had the presence of mind to go and get the baker's own van and his coffin was placed therein and the funeral was able to proceed.

CARDS FROM WREATHS

It is a good idea to ask the funeral director in advance to collect the cards from the wreaths and make sure that these are given to the chief mourner thereafter as part of the remembrance of the occasion.

For flowers at the service see *Chapter 3*.

Names of funeral directors

Some funeral directors have the surname 'Soul' or 'Sole', 'Dyer', 'Angel', 'Gabriel', 'Death' or 'De'Ath', etc. One wonders if this was their real name, which suggested to them which profession to take up, or whether they changed their names in order to enhance their businesses!

In Wales where everyone is known by what they do, there were two Ernies in one village. One was a travel agent 'Ernie the Journey'; the other was the local undertaker, known affectionately as 'Ernie the Final Journey'!

Chapter 3
Planning The Funeral Service

I can't think of a more wonderful thanksgiving for the life I have had than that everyone shall be jolly at my funeral. Lord Louis Mountbatten 1900 – 1979

The Purpose of a Funeral

The purpose of a funeral is to give thanks for the life of the deceased, and, if it has been long and successful, to celebrate that person's life and achievements; to dispose of the body; to gather together and comfort the bereaved; to help them to share memories and to come to terms with their grief, loss (and perhaps anger and guilt) and to say a final goodbye.

Holding a public funeral allows one to share in other people's private grief, showing solidarity with the bereaved.

A memorial service at a later date may be appropriate, particularly if the person is a national figure, well known or was involved in multiple or important activities locally.

If there is no actual body, for instance when bodies are blown to bits or someone is missing, presumed dead, there cannot be a funeral but a memorial service can be held, which gives the bereaved an occasion to share in their grief and loss.

Cars – One's Own or Official

Most people will order a hearse and if there are many people who do not drive, one or more funeral cars may be required, although nowadays, except for the principal mourners, people are more likely to use their own cars. The only exception would be the funeral of a very important public figure.

The funeral will often start at the home of the deceased and the funeral director may walk in front of the hearse for about 100 metres if a number of cars are involved, so that those cars following the hearse would have time to turn round if necessary and catch up with the funeral procession, but some people do not like this procedure.

Family cars will follow the hearse to the church or chapel or other venue, where the funeral will take place. It is a good idea if all the cars have their headlights on indicating that they are part of the funeral procession.

There may be a car-parking problem, if it is at a town centre location, and if many cars are expected the police should also be informed of the time and place. Maps can be provided for people who do not know the area. New cemeteries and crematoria have large car parks built into the complex.

In the case of an important local figure or state funeral, where many ordinary people may line the streets to watch the procession pass through the town, the police are also informed of the date and time of the event, so that they can organize the traffic flow.

BEARERS

Usually the funeral director will arrange four or six bearers to carry the coffin or it may be wheeled in on a trolley or hand bier, but if friends and the family want to do the bearing themselves rather than relying on strangers, then the funeral director will want to explain the procedure in advance to them to avoid mishaps.

THE SERVICE

The deceased may already have planned their own funeral service, which is becoming more and more common, or the person responsible for the funeral may have their own ideas.

A service is sometimes requested in a church, even though the deceased and the family are not believers. Many people use the local church only for births, marriages and deaths (hatching, matching and despatching). The local priest is usually happy to consent to this because within the Church of England, everyone who lives in the parish is entitled to use the church for any of these offices, and if they die in the parish are actually entitled to be buried in the local churchyard (if not already full), whether they are Christians or not.

Whether it is to be a burial or a cremation, the service can be held either in a church or in a crematorium.

In a church

If it is to be a church service the vicar in an Anglican church is the person to consult, or the curate or churchwardens if the vicar is away, or the ministers in the case of other denominations. The congregation should be in their seats, say 20 – 30 minutes before the family arrives, especially if a lot of people are expected to attend.

The coffin can be taken to the church the night before (with or without a service solely for the immediate family); or the coffin can be in the church when the mourners arrive; or most frequently the coffin can arrive after most people are in place in the church. It is important to tell the funeral director which is preferred in advance. If the coffin is brought into the church, when the majority are seated, they stand as a sign of respect. The procession is lead by the vicar or minister, followed by the chief mourners (usually the family and very close friends), who then sit in the front pews, which have been reserved for them. During the procession the vicar or minister will usually speak the introductory words of the service. After the service, the chief mourners are the first to leave the church, whilst the other mourners stand in respect.

At some modern churches an overhead projector will be available and may be used at a funeral to put the service on the screen, and to show photographs or a video of the deceased at happier times, perhaps whilst the eulogies are taking place. Sometimes a comforting rural scene is shown before the service actually starts.

At a crematorium

Occasionally the service may follow the cremation instead of the other way round, because of congestion at the crematorium and the popularity of certain hours for funerals and cremations.

If it is to be a service at a crematorium, then the person to consult is the superintendent. The coffin may only be brought to the chapel just before the service begins but there is the choice of whether it is in place on the catafalque before the mourners are brought in from the waiting room, or it is carried in after they have all been seated as in a church service. Usually the front seats will be reserved for the chief mourners. At a busy crematorium, one service may follow another every half hour. The people enter at one end or side of the room, and after the service depart at the opposite end or side. A double slot may be booked at certain times for a longer funeral.

Sometimes the minister or person taking the funeral will put his hand on the coffin when he gets to the committal stage.

One can also usually choose whether the coffin disappears from view (through a door or curtains are drawn around it), or whether it remains in situ until the end of the service when the mourners can file past it, even touching it as they go, if this is felt to be a more personal way of saying a final 'goodbye'.

MOBILE PHONES AND PAGERS

These must be switched off during a funeral, wherever it is held.

MUSIC

The organist needs to be booked as soon as possible after the date for the funeral is known.

In a church setting, the usual organist, or a replacement, will be asked by the minister to play for a funeral, for which a fee may be charged. There is also an organist available at most crematoria. Nowadays recorded music is used more and more; the organist may not have the non-religious repertoire that may be requested at today's funerals. Tapes, discs, CDs and DVDs can be given to the church or crematorium in advance of the funeral to be played at the appropriate time but it is advisable to find out beforehand what equipment is available.

Music for before the service in a church, whilst people are waiting for the service to begin, or after the service, whilst the family, friends and colleagues file out, is important for setting the mood of the event. Ideally everyone arrives and departs with music being played. The music does not have to be religious, although some people do play hymn tunes that are not being sung during the service. The music may be specially requested, or one can leave it to the organist to play something suitable for the occasion.

People may be feeling emotional, meditative, full of praise for a life well lived, or pensive thinking about their own mortality. The music is often chosen to comfort everyone and inspire them.

Those who have spent their lives on the stage may choose something different from someone who has served his country all his life in the armed services or the diplomatic corps, and the choice may be different for each chosen career.

The trouble with sentimental songs at a funeral is that they may increase the grief and tearfulness of the occasion, and are best used perhaps at the gathering after the funeral; whereas music which is calming and comforting, uplifting and inspiring may be more suitable at the actual service.

If an organist is not available and live music is preferred, musicians can be found from local amateur societies, schools or churches. The fee should be negotiated beforehand and what equipment they will need and what they will wear. They will also need to be told exactly what is required and when they have to play and for how long. When the husband or wife is a musician, there may be a soloist or string quartet instead of, or as well as, an organ, or someone with a beautiful voice may be invited to sing a solo. Someone from Scotland may prefer to have the bagpipes. A jazz lover may want to have a New Orleans style jazz band.

Hymns

According to the type of service, there may be one or more hymns. In making a choice one may want to select a hymn used at a previous wedding or a family christening, or a hymn known to be a favourite of the deceased may be chosen. What is important is to have something suitable for the occasion and representative of the person's life and those present who have gathered to say their final farewells.

It is advisable to make sure that the chosen hymns are in the church or chapel hymn book. In any case it is a good idea to print them on the service sheet, so that they can be taken away and remembered afterwards.

If there is no organist available, it is possible to buy a CD that plays 2,300 hymns, for every occasion, in any key and at any tempo. There are 128 pipe organ and orchestral sounds available. It is expensive but worthwhile for an establishment that holds funerals or church services regularly. This digital hymnal system is available from Hymn Technology (address in *Appendix V*).

The best hymns are those where the music and the words fit each other like a glove, with no contrived rhyming or syntax. The pitch should be within the range of the average singer (with notes not too high nor too low). The music should flow and the words have a deep meaning (for music and hymns suitable to be played at funerals see *Appendix III*).

It has been known that the organist stops when the service sheet shows there is another verse to sing or goes on playing when there are no more written verses on the service sheet. Also the organist sometimes plays the wrong tune to a hymn as printed, which may not even fit the words! These disasters can be avoided if the organist is properly instructed before hand.

The church choir may be available at extra cost, which would be especially suitable if the deceased had been a member of that choir, although this may be more difficult to arrange for a midweek service. The choir might sing a special anthem for the occasion without the congregation joining in. And if a church choir is present an ethereal descant may be introduced in the last verse of any hymn.

Apparently when Ralph Vaughn Williams was asked on his death bed what the future held for him, he is reputed to have said 'Music, but I shall not be doing the music, with all its striving and disappointments. I shall be being the music'. *The Oxford Book of Death – D J Enright.*

READINGS

With the agreement of the person conducting the funeral, any member of the family or a special friend could be asked to do a reading, bearing in mind that those who are asked may be too overcome on the day to complete the task. If this is likely to be the case, someone else who is generally less emotionally involved, could be asked to oblige.

If a person dies in Britain but has come from another country, a poem about the country of his or her birth can be read. If the person has a particular hobby, this may be included in an appropriate reading.

Favourite readings suitable for use at a funeral, or for bringing comfort to those who have been bereaved, or are approaching death themselves, are given in *Appendix II*. They are arranged in first line order alphabetically, to identify favourite readings.

THE ADDRESS

The purpose of an address is to present a tribute, giving thanks for the life of the deceased. It usually includes a short biographical account of the deceased, mentioning the wife, husband or partner and family left behind. And if any of their organs were donated, thanks may be given for this act of humanity.

The person who is to take the service and give the address therefore will want to meet some of the family and to know more about the deceased, and may ask for such details as his or her age, cause of death, religious or non-religious background, what special names the person was known by, what family they had, what work they did in life, their hobbies, honours given to them, and so on. They may quote from letters of condolence that have already come in and may ask if there are any potent memories.

It would help to write these down to give to the person who is going to take the service, especially if the details are very complicated, or merely to avoid mistakes being made.

It is difficult for anyone to give an address unless they know something about the person's life and activities, accomplishments and dreams. Some families will produce quite a curriculum vitae of the deceased – others can think of nothing to say about a person, who may have lived with them for sixty or more years!

The person taking the service may also point out that this is the last farewell from the family and friends to a valued member of the local community to which he belonged.

It has been known for a doctor to give the address, talking about his patient's final illness and how he coped with the adversity, as an encouragement to others.

EULOGIES

At some funerals many people may wish to stand up and say something about the deceased. A cherished memory, a little anecdote adds a very personal note to the occasion.

Sometimes a friend of the family may be invited to contribute a personal recollection, or members of the family themselves may wish to speak of their love, respect and memories of the deceased. They should be given a time limit, so that the time of the whole funeral is not extended.

Only someone who is not going to break down emotionally should be asked to do this. Anyone needs as much time as possible to prepare for taking this part in the service and should also write down what is to be said. On the day it is easy to forget what one intended to say because of the emotional atmosphere.

One often discovers something about the deceased at a funeral that one never knew, even after knowing that person for many years. For instance I had known a family in the village for 40 years and knew that the man had been born in India but I only found out at his funeral that his godfather was Pandit Nehru!

An amusing note is sometimes introduced here. A husband gave the eulogy about his wife, who had died of cancer. She was not very well towards the end, in a hospice. Well-meaning visitors had come to see her but she didn't feel up to it. As they put their heads round the door she cried out, 'B***** off!' and the husband reported this at the funeral. Everyone laughed knowing this was typical of her. No one was offended, although it is doubtful whether that word had ever been used in that church before in all its 900-year history!

PRINTING THE SERVICE SHEET

A service sheet is not necessary but it serves as a memorial of a loved family member. It will need to be prepared before the funeral. Local printers realize the importance of delivering the service sheets on time but it is courteous to give them as much notice as possible.

It is usually an A4 sheet folded to A5 size (or sometimes A6), giving four pages or more. The front cover usually contains the full name and honours (if any) of the deceased, with the years of birth and death. It may also carry a cross or other symbol of the person's faith or a family crest if appropriate. At the bottom, it may give the church, or crematorium, or other venue, the town or village and the date and time of the funeral.

A recent funeral for a toddler had his photograph on the front cover of the service sheet, which I thought was a lovely idea and one that could catch on for everyone. It is best to use a photograph that shows the person looking their best, not perhaps so old and decrepit as they may have become by the time that they died but a few years previously, more in their prime, how most people would like to remember them.

Inside is the order of service, together with the hymns (or when a hymn book is used it may just say 'Hymn No…' and perhaps the first line). It may give the names of the persons doing the address, the readings and the eulogy. It could also print the readings themselves plus any special prayers, etc., that people may want to remember and can take home with them.

On the back page can be printed the venue of the reception (if any), and whether everyone is invited to attend or just the family.

It may say 'Donations in memory of (name of the deceased) may be sent to (name of charity or society and the relevant address)'. Alternatively people can be asked to send the cheques to the funeral director (give his address), who would collect all the cheques, send them on to the charity, and send a list of the donors to the bereaved family.

The service sheets can be given out at the door by the ushers or placed ready in the pews. They can also be sent to family members and friends who for one reason or another could not attend the funeral in person.

STEWARDS/ USHERS/ SIDESPERSONS

It is a good idea to have some people to show the mourners to their seats, if a large crowd is expected. Some members of the family or close friends often do this. The front pews are reserved for the chief mourners. The family can be asked in advance how many seats need to be reserved for them.

RECORD OF ATTENDEES

It is also a good idea to have one person at the door taking the names of the people who attend and whether they are family, colleagues, etc. If the person is an important public figure, the local press usually perform this task with a view to printing it in a local or national paper.

Alternatively some funeral directors put cards in the pews asking mourners to fill them in. These are collected up by the funeral director after the service and passed to the chief mourner, so that there is a record of those who attended the service. The disadvantage of this method is that some people will not fill them in, either because they did not bring their glasses and cannot read them or have no pen with them. Sometimes the ushers hand out such slips to people on arrival, providing pens and tables, so no-one slips through the net. Sometimes there is a book and people are asked to sign it either on arrival or before they leave the service or reception.

FLOWERS AT THE SERVICE

If the service is held at a crematorium, the flowers are usually provided for all the services that are going to happen there that day or week. If it is in a church, there may be a regular flower rota, and the person whose turn it is may like to do the flowers but they are usually given extra money to provide whatever is requested by the bereaved. Alternatively one of the family may decide to do the flowers.

FUNERAL WREATHS AND SPRAYS

Floral tributes were only introduced into England in the 1860s, and in the 1890s glazed porcelain flowers under glass domes from Germany became fashionable. Nowadays it is wreaths and sprays.

One or more wreaths may be carried into the church or crematorium on the coffin (well secured), the rest are laid out in the grounds for people to view and to read the cards after the service. They often remain there for several days, especially in a churchyard.

Flowers cost more in winter than at other times of the year and those placed in vases in the church may afterwards be left for future services or be taken to old people's homes in the district. Hospitals generally do not want flowers brought in to the wards because they run out of vases, and some get knocked over and broken. The nurses also do not have enough time to arrange flowers nor to clear up any accidental damage.

I am told that in Finland the participants at a funeral bring their own floral tributes and leave them on a stand. At a particular point in the service each group brings its flowers to the front and places them on the coffin. Then, facing the chief mourners, they take up their flowers again and read out the cards. This is a charming ritual, but in England people are frequently asked not to bring flowers at all but to send a donation instead to a charity.

Another charming ritual is to give each person who attends the funeral a small pot of snowdrops, if in winter, or a primrose in spring, etc., as a keepsake.

A local man, who was a nurseryman and very interested in wildlife died suddenly of cancer. He had carved beautiful decoy ducks, so they placed one of his decoy ducks on the coffin, along with some reed mace, thistles and other wild flowers. His widow said, 'This is just what he would have wanted!' It is possible nowadays to have more or less anything one really wants.

CHILDREN AT FUNERALS

Children can be invited to go to the funeral if they want to but should not be forced nor denied. They should however be told what to expect from the service and that some people may be upset. It is amazing what children can understand, if told the truth. Clearly as they get older they will experience more and more deaths among family and friends. Funerals are a part of everyday life and should therefore form part of everyone's experience as they grow up.

The cemetery or crematorium can also be explained by saying, for example, that, 'The loved person is put into a wooden box, and after we have all said our goodbyes, they are buried in the ground or are changed into ashes, which can be buried or scattered in a lovely place, where we can come and think about them at any time. They will never be forgotten'.

PHOTOGRAPHS

Photographs are not as usual at funerals as at weddings but they are sometimes taken and sometimes it is a consolation afterwards to have a pictorial record of the event. They must of course be taken discreetly. Some will also video the whole service, by arrangement with the family, so that those unable to attend can watch the proceedings at a later date. It is wise to enquire beforehand, to avoid embarrassment, whether the use of a camera or video is allowed, either at a crematorium or a church.

WHAT TO WEAR

It is not as necessary today, as in the past, to wear black to a funeral, although muted colours are more suitable. It may seem extravagant to purchase a new black outfit but one attends more funerals as one gets older, so a black, grey or navy outfit of some sort would be a good addition to any wardrobe. The organizers may have expressly asked people to wear bright colours, 'because this is what the deceased would want'. Hats are also a matter of fashion and location. But comfortable shoes are important because there is often a lot of standing about at a graveside, and an umbrella would be useful if the weather is expected to be wet. One never knows how the emotions will react on the day, so plenty of tissues might come in useful!

THE BURIAL

Sometimes only the family proceed to the burial site in the churchyard or civic cemetery after the service, and then join the other mourners at the reception. Sometimes everyone crowds round the graveside. If many people are present it is a good idea for the person conducting the service to announce during the service, what the family would prefer. The bearers will carry the coffin from the church or chapel to the open grave. The deceased is carried feet first. The minister will then say a few words at the graveside (the committal) before the coffin is lowered into the grave. The chief mourners are asked to throw in the first handful of earth or a flower if preferred. The undertakers, if asked, will provide some dry earth or a collection of, say, single roses for this purpose, or people can be asked to bring a single flower with them.

The rest of the earth is replaced after the people have left. In some religions the men in the family backfill the grave themselves, with shovels provided by the funeral director.

The burial service may be in a churchyard or at a municipal cemetery or crematorium complex, where some have burial sites as well as a place for the burial of ashes after a cremation.

THE CREMATION

If there is a church service first, it may be decided that only the family will proceed to the crematorium for the committal and short further service. They will then rejoin the rest of the mourners at the reception.

Or the crematorium service may be the sole funeral service, which is becoming more common; then everyone goes to the crematorium and afterwards go together to the reception (wake), if there is one.

It is a good idea to find out in advance exactly what procedures are offered and what one actually wants.

It is possible at some crematoria, if requested, for a few people to view the placing of the coffin in the cremator. For some religions this is obligatory (e.g. Sikhs). However only the cremator staff are allowed actually to handle the coffin into the cremator. Others are not permitted to do this themselves.

Religious symbols, such as a cross, Jewish menorah, Muslim or Jain etc. symbols, are kept at most crematoria, so that they can be interchanged rapidly, making the chapel suitable for whatever faith the funeral is for.

Some crematoria are closed at weekends, which is difficult for those faiths that have to bury their dead within twenty-four hours.

For a cremation, any pacemaker or radioactive equipment in the body has to be removed beforehand. Bodies take about one-and-a-half to two hours at 1600 Celsius to cremate. Metal parts in the body are taken out of the ashes subsequently by a magnet, such as artificial hips and teeth fillings. These are subsequently buried in the cemetery under concrete, or more recently may be recycled and sold for charity.

Any bones, which are still unburnt, are crushed in a bone crusher. Thus the so-called 'ashes' are actually the crushed bones of the deceased. There may be no ashes at all therefore when a newborn or very young baby is cremated. The ashes or cremated remains take about 45 minutes to cool; they are then placed in a plastic bag (if due to be scattered in the cemetery), or a container with an identifying label.

The law used to state that each body should be cremated the same day. Now there is more leeway in busy times. Mondays take longer than Fridays because the ovens will not have heated up. Any large cancer tumours may also take longer. The cremator is brick lined and takes only one body at a time, although some crematoria have more than one cremator.

If the ashes are to be buried in a churchyard in an urn or casket, there may be a subsequent short service some days or weeks later. The ashes may be collected within fourteen days of the cremation but if left for weeks, there may be a storage charge.

If they are to be sprinkled in a garden of remembrance or in a favourite spot loved by the deceased, this is usually a private matter done by family or friends.

In Germany ashes cannot be scattered but must be in an urn, which must be biodegradable.

Some crematoria are now installing a filtration plant, to clean up the mercury and other metals being released into the atmosphere. Breast implants and even trainers generate a lot of smoke!

FEES

The fee charged by the minister for taking a funeral service is the same for a burial or a cremation and is fixed annually by the Church of England (£84 in 2005), plus travel expenses if out of the district.

Most other denominations follow the same scale, although some free churches do not make a charge for members of their own congregations.

When burying the ashes in a churchyard the fee would be £69 for the vicar and £89 for the funeral director for preparation of the ground and attendance (2004).

The fee for burial in an Anglican churchyard at the time of the service is £139 or on another day £166 (for instance if the funeral is late in the day, the burial would not be allowed on the same day after dusk, to comply with health and safety rules).

THE WAKE OR RECEPTION

Pagan practice also included a funeral feast, which is where some think this practice came from.

Many people like to produce refreshments for everybody who comes to the funeral, especially if they have come from far away. It can be at the home of the deceased or in a local hall or hotel, a church hall, golf club or any other premises.

Many purpose-built homes for the elderly, with wardens on site, have a special room where people can offer refreshments, after a funeral for a resident. Likewise some funeral directors' premises incorporate a room where a reception can be held.

It should be announced at the funeral whether everyone is invited or only the family, or this information may be printed on the service sheet. The vicar is usually asked to come as well, and if he knows the family, he will normally accept, continuing to comfort the bereaved. Some funeral directors are not allowed to attend a reception after a funeral.

At one funeral I organized, I put up photographs of the deceased where the reception was being held, which was much appreciated by the mourners.

When an artist died, some of her pictures were hung in the hall for all to admire. All of these things help to celebrate the life of the deceased and to give him or her *A Good Send-Off!*

CATERING

The family or a local organization of which the deceased was a member, can do the refreshments or a professional caterer can be engaged. Some funeral directors' establishments offer a catering service, either at their premises or elsewhere. A full luncheon complete with wine and coffee may be produced or just some simple refreshment of sandwiches and cakes with a glass of wine, soft drinks, coffee or tea can be offered.

If there are not many people involved, a small luncheon for those present may be arranged, if preferred, after the service, at a local restaurant or hotel.

Chapter 4

TYPES OF FUNERALS

Death is the supreme festival on the road to freedom.
Dietrich Bonhoeffer 1906 –1945

FUNERALS FOR BABIES

Funerals for miscarriages, the newly born, or cot deaths are usually fairly traumatic, as the hopes and dreams of the parents have come to nothing. They are usually fairly private family affairs, and geared to the needs of the families concerned. It may also be difficult to arrange and conduct funerals for very young children who may have met with an accident. Most funeral directors do not charge for a baby's funeral.

A hospital may also arrange a burial or cremation for a stillborn baby free of charge or the parents can arrange a funeral themselves if they so wish.

CHILDREN'S FUNERALS

Most funeral directors do not charge for a child's funeral, up to 16 years of age in England. This would include a hearse and one car. Anything extra would have to be paid for.

Young children's coffins are usually white and of course are very small. Recently at a child's funeral, it was to be a cremation but then the ashes were to be put back in to the small white coffin and the coffin interred, where a headstone could be erected, so that the other small children in the family could understand, and there was somewhere for them to go to talk to their brother 'Luke' at a later date. It was felt that they would not understand their brother reduced to a small handful of ash.

A W Lymn of Nottingham, have a silver Rolls Royce, which take passengers and a child's coffin with flowers, so that the family can travel in the same vehicle with the deceased child (see photo in middle section and addresses *Appendix V*).

In Yoruba land, in Nigeria, the parents are not allowed to attend the funerals of their children because, in the natural order of things, children should bury their parents (Nigel Barley, *Dead Good Funerals*. p.142).

YOUNG ADULTS' FUNERALS

The churches or chapels tend to be packed for funerals for young adults. They are attended by work colleagues, or masses of school or college friends and their parents, who no doubt are thinking, 'But for the grace of God, this could have been our child'.

The parents of young people feel that all the years they helped to bring this child to maturity now seem to have been for nothing. Now there will be no weddings to arrange, no son or daughter-in-law to welcome into the family and no grandchildren from this offspring. It is a time of readjustment and deep grief. Guilt may be an added reaction, for example – if the teenager had just been given a car of his or her own, in which they promptly had a fatal accident.

It is still possible to have a celebration of all that this young person has achieved during his or her life and to be thankful that they existed at all, and gave so much pleasure whilst on earth.

Funerals for young people therefore need to be where there is plenty of room. A new crematorium that seats 160 people, can relay the service through loud speakers to those who cannot be accommodated inside.

FUNERALS FOR SERVICE AND OTHER ASSOCIATION'S PERSONNEL

If the deceased had been serving in the Army, Navy, Air Force, Merchant Navy, etc. or was the wife, husband or partner of such a person, the service in question usually turn out in force complete with banners, and the last post is played. A service funeral may have a flag over the coffin, which will be folded up and given to the chief mourner after the service. Top brass (senior personnel) may be present for a full military funeral.

Likewise if the deceased is a member of the British Legion or a Masonic lodge, other banners may be present. Scouts, cubs, girl guides, life brigades and other organizations may also be asked to form a guard of honour at the funeral of someone connected with one of these organizations.

WOODLAND OR GREEN FUNERALS

Some people prefer to be buried, or for their ashes to be scattered, in a woodland setting or in a green field. One can still have a funeral service as outlined in *Chapter 3* beforehand, or not as desired.

Generally at these sites no pollutants such as embalming fluid, are allowed, and the sites are usually not on consecrated ground, although in some areas individual graves can be blessed or consecrated.

A green burial can have a cardboard, natural soft wood, ecopod, split bamboo, willow basket or other natural, biodegradable coffin or a natural fabric shroud, either wool or cotton. In fact any eco-friendly material may be used.

On greenfield sites where a tree is planted in remembrance on a grave, it is impossible to add another body, without disturbing the sapling.

A burial space may be purchased in advance and there are single plots about the size of a normal grave, or family plots for two burials one on top of the other or side by side, or even a four metre square plot to take up to ten burials of ashes.

Most will not permit cuddly toys or photographs, as this would defeat the object of a natural area. But a wooden post featuring the bare details of the person is sometimes encouraged (£150 – £250, 2004).

Most have a remembrance book, and some have an open day each year to celebrate those who have died and are buried there during the previous twelve months.

It is not possible to mention all locations but examples of two different types – a mature woodland burial ground, and an open greenfield site, destined to become a wood in the course of time are described in the following paragraphs.

There is a very beautiful twelve acre woodland burial place at Colney, just outside Norwich, in Norfolk (see photo in middle section), where people can be buried, or have their ashes scattered, in amongst mature trees in a very peaceful setting. Snowdrops, bluebells and other native wild flowers appear in their seasons. The memorials are pieces of wood (preferably oak) with a sloping face, on which a name, date and a bird, butterfly, dragonfly, etc. motif can be placed. No metal, stone or concrete memorials are allowed and no vases of flowers can mark the gravesite. Christmas wreaths are allowed made of holly, ivy and mistletoe, which are removed by twelfth night. Bird or bat boxes are also encouraged.

Attractive wooden buildings, with under-floor heating form a waiting room, offices and chapel. The latter is particularly beautiful with seats facing on to the woods and a lectern resembling a tree. There are no time restrictions here and catering facilities are also available. There is an opportunity to place a stained glass window or door panel in the Woodland Hall, which will last for the life of the building, at least fifty years.

People with limited mobility are catered for at this site by electric buggies, driven by the staff, to transport visitors around.

At Olney in Buckinghamshire, on former agricultural land on a lovely hill overlooking the town, there is a greenfield site.

A tree is planted for each person, either a burial or for ashes, and in a few years when the trees have grown up, the site will resemble the nearby ancient woodlands with bluebells, snowdrops and other woodland plants and grasses growing between the trees. One can choose between an oak, birch, wild cherry, field maple, ash, or hazel. To preserve the rural effect, no headstones are allowed, and nothing must be attached to the trees themselves. Grass walkways are cut in the longer grass whilst the site is developing.

There is only an office at present (2004), no chapel, so that any service beforehand would be carried out elsewhere, as would any reception after the burial.

The Church of England has a consecrated green burial site at Barton, in Cambridgeshire, which is currently only an open field but it has beautiful wrought iron gates with a vine and fig leaf motif in black and gold.

The Natural Death Handbook (4th edition, 2004, *Rider*) lists 182 natural burial grounds in Great Britain and one or two overseas. More are planned for the future, as this is becoming a preference for many. This enables a rural feeling rather than an urban feeling, often engendered by the traditional cemetery with its many headstones, although some new cemeteries also include a woodland or green area within a traditional complex.

Finding farming uneconomic, farmers may choose this as a good eco-friendly alternative use for agricultural land.

COSTS OF GREEN OR WOODLAND FUNERALS

In a site where headstones are not allowed, the cost of the monumental mason will be saved. The cost of burial plots can vary throughout the country but run from about £500 for a single plot to £3,000 for a double grave. Ecopods may cost about £500 or £750 for a gold leaf pod lined with feathers (2003). Ecopods carry a person up to 6 ft 2 inches (188 cm) tall.

Burial of ashes in a woodland setting may be from £26 in some areas to £500 in others. The acorn pod for the interment of ashes costs £30 from the manufacture but more from a burial ground. A tree plaque allowed at some grounds can cost £85 and upwards.

Prices can vary enormously and should be obtained from the relevant ground where people wish for the burial or ashes to be interred. In some areas there is a once and for all cost, in others there is an annual charge for maintenance.

There is an Association of Natural Burial Grounds (est. 1994) (see addresses in *Appendix V*) that has a code of practice for members. Each has to offer long-term security to clients and must accept bodies for burial whether wrapped in a shroud, or placed in cardboard, wooden or other coffin, provided they are environmentally suitable. Members must accept families to organize a funeral without a funeral director if desired, and must manage their sites ecologically. If taking money for funerals in advance, they must agree to abide by the Financial Services and Markets Act 2000 Regulation of Funeral Plan Contracts.

NON-RELIGIOUS FUNERALS

If one does not believe in a god of any description, it is still necessary to bury or cremate the dead and this is done usually by holding a funeral. *Chapter 3* 'Planning the funeral service' will cover most of the things one needs to know about holding any kind of funeral but one needs to explain to the person taking the funeral that one does not want God mentioned or to have any prayers or hymns although music may be played. There are readings in *Appendix II* that are suitable for a non-religious funeral.

Most crematoria have a person on hand who is willing to conduct a non-religious funeral but because there are not many officiators usually available a charge of £100 may be made.

In the address at the funeral of an unbeliever, it is more difficult to talk about the future and the emphasis is therefore more on celebrating the life the person has enjoyed.

One can still have a reception afterwards.

DO-IT-YOURSELF FUNERALS OR FAMILY FUNERALS

Whether for burial or cremation it is possible to do everything oneself, without the help of a funeral director, but with the help of friends. Some people think that a friend taking the deceased to the church or crematorium instead of strangers is in some way more personal. It is also cheaper. It is still necessary to contact the local church or crematorium if a service in either is requested, and there will be a charge for this. Music of any kind will be suitable and any hymns or songs can still be chosen and prayers or readings incorporated.

The death still has to be registered as detailed in *Chapter 1*, and the green disposal certificate (form 9) will be needed to complete the statutory cremation forms, or interment forms for a burial (for which at least 48 hours' notice must be given if in a municipal cemetery).

The family will be responsible for moving the body themselves and will need to contact the hospital mortuary, if the person died in hospital. If the family wishes the hospital to keep the body until the funeral a charge may be made.

If the person dies at home, a nurse or someone with experience in laying out needs to prepare the body before *rigor mortis* (stiffening of the body) sets in. A coffin may be purchased for the deceased to lie in whilst waiting for the funeral but it is advisable to turn the heat off in the room where the body is kept, to delay the effects of decomposition. Washing in salt water or packing it with dry ice is advantageous (the address of *British Oxygen* for dry ice is in *Appendix V*).

Coffins in wood or strong cardboard, or body bags can be bought from a funeral director or from specialist firms, if the local undertaker will not supply anything but a full service (for suppliers see *Appendix V*).

The deceased can be transported to the place of burial or cremation in any vehicle, estate car, people carrier or van. If the deceased has to be collected from the hospital, the staff there may help to move the body into the coffin, but an appointment will be necessary.

Once the funeral party reaches the church or crematorium, it is necessary to arrange for enough strong able-bodied people (usually men) to carry the coffin into the building, or to place it on to a wheeled bier and later to transport it from the bier to the catafalque in the crematorium chapel.

If it is to be a burial, then the bearers may have to carry it some distance to the church and later from the church to the grave. They will then lower it into the grave, with the help of strong cotton webbing.

There will still be the cost of a gravesite or a place for the disposal of the ashes at a later date, unless it is intended to scatter them in a private garden or hillside.

If all of the above seems too daunting, it is better to employ a funeral director.

There is actually no legal requirement to have a funeral at all; one can just bury the person in the garden, having first obtained permission from the local authorities. However, more than one grave in a garden may constitute a cemetery and need a special licence.

If one has an estate with acres of land, and one wants all the family to be buried in it in due course, it may still be possible. In some areas it may be necessary to get planning permission for 'change of use' from farmland or forest or moorland or meadow to private burial ground, even if it is a non-commercial site, i.e. for the family only.

It is wise to inform the Environment Agency, who may have some views on the matter (address in *Appendix V*). In any case, if the land is ever sold, it would be wise to inform the buyer that bodies are buried on the land in private graves, with a detailed plan of where they are and at what depth.

Under the Registration of Burials Act 1864 all burials must be recorded at each burial site together with the forename, surname, dates of birth, death and burial dates, an entry number and a plan reference number, together with the name of the officiating officer, if there is one.

PERSONS WITHOUT FRIENDS OR FAMILY

More and more frequently, elderly people die without either friends or family, as they have outlived them all, and no one comes to the funeral. If the person dies in hospital or an old people's home, perhaps the matron or other official will attend the funeral as a sign of respect. I once attended a funeral at Elstow Abbey, a very big church, of someone who had worked for me many years earlier. To my surprise only my husband and I and one other couple were in attendance. How can one go through life with so little human contact? It was very sad. If one is so old and has had no children, however, this could be the result.

FUNERALS FOR FAMOUS PERSONS

When a famous or well-known person in the community dies, people turn out in droves to 'see them off'. This happened in Glasgow when Jock Stein, a popular football manager, died. It was to be a 'family only' funeral but ten thousand people lined the streets on the way to the crematorium to pay their last respects.

In the case of Princess Diana, in 1997, millions of people lined the streets and left flowers in front of Kensington Palace, Buckingham Palace, Althorpe (the Spencer family home) and elsewhere. It was probably the best-attended funeral of all time and viewed on television by millions of people worldwide. Clearly the whole nation, if not the whole world, was affected by the early demise of this lovely young woman.

When the Queen Mother died, in 2002, many people, including tourists who happened to be in London at the time, lined the streets to view the pomp and ceremony of a royal funeral.

Statesmen often have a very well organized state funeral, especially if in office at the time of their demise. They may be carried on a gun carriage, with a flag draped over the coffin, and followed by a contingent of those in the same profession.

There were apparently 7,000 people at St Paul's Cathedral for Nelson's funeral in 1805, and none of them were women.

FUNERALS FOR SUICIDES

The prevalent feeling at a suicide funeral is one of shock and dismay. There is no need for the mourners to feel guilty or frustrated, or to feel deep regret, because they did not do enough to help the deceased while still alive. In practice it is almost impossible to help those who are clinically depressed and feel that suicide is the only way out.

Some ministers will stress the point that one should not judge the deceased, not knowing the pressures that may have been upon that person, and that one should respect the person's choice of how they decided to cope with those pressures.

The minister may also add that whatever they have done, 'there is a God who is able to forgive'.

Until the 1960s, suicides, were not allowed to have a funeral service in church or to be buried in consecrated land i.e. churchyards. They used to have to be buried, along with unbaptised infants, in unconsecrated ground. In the early nineteenth century they could be buried only between 9 pm and midnight. Or they might be allowed only on the north side of the churchyard (considered the devil's side in medieval times, as the north door of a church was considered the devil's door). Since then this rule has been relaxed. There is an organization called Survivors of Bereavement by Suicide (SOBS) who may be able to help (See addresses *Appendix V).*

FUNERALS FOR MURDERERS

Until the 1960s, murderers were not allowed to be buried in a churchyard, because it was consecrated ground. It is now at the discretion of the incumbent (vicar/rector/priest in charge).

FUNERALS FOR MURDER VICTIMS

When a person has been murdered, the police usually attend the funeral in order to discover something that may help them to solve the crime, if the perpetrator is not already known. There is an organization called Support for Victims of Murder and Manslaughter (SAMM) (See addresses *Appendix V).*

When children are murdered, there are usually hundreds of people in the congregation.

BODIES THAT HAVE BEEN USED FOR MEDICAL RESEARCH

After three years (maximum), the teaching hospital that used the body is responsible for burying or cremating it. It will be cremated at the South London Crematorium, Streatham (if in the London area), between the hours of 8.30 am and 10.00 am, at the medical school's expense. The family can attend and have the ashes if they so wish.

Or if requested the body can be returned to the family to be disposed of by burial or cremation, at the family's expense.

DYING AT SEA AND BEING BURIED AT SEA

If a person dies whilst at sea on a passenger-carrying vessel, whether he is a passenger or from the crew, or if anyone in the Merchant Navy dies, the details must be sent to the registry of Shipping and Seamen, at the Maritime and Coast guard Agency, Cardiff (see addresses *Appendix V).* There is one form for UK registration for British ships in British waters, and a foreign registration for foreign ships in British waters. There may be two doctors on board a passenger ship, who can issue a death certificate after a post mortem, if necessary. There is not usually a doctor on board smaller ships or fishing vessels.

Sometimes fishermen and others are washed overboard in rough weather, or a suicide may choose this way to exit the world. If a body is lost overboard, a death enquiry is held. If foul play is expected or the death is not due to a medical condition, then the police are involved and the body (if any) is taken to a coroner. If there is no body, a funeral cannot be held but a memorial service can be arranged.

The bodies of those who have died at sea may be buried at sea, if required, wrapped in a body bag weighted with metal bars. In olden times on merchant ships the body would have been sewn into a tarpaulin and the last stitch would go through the nose of the body to make sure the person was actually dead!

On a cruise ship, the funeral party would consist of the captain, staff captain, ship's doctor(s), nurse, purser, and the widow or widower or a member of the travelling party. The service would take place at 6.30 am or at sunrise or even at sunset, whilst the ship's decks were relatively empty, and would take about eight to ten minutes. The captain would normally follow the Christian prayer book service, committing the body to the deep, rather than to the earth. There are usually some flowers on board and one or more would be offered to any surviving next of kin or friend to throw after the body. The captain would give a longitude and latitude reference to the family, and enter it in his official log, and the deck log of the ship, along with the date of death. There is not normally a charge for a burial at sea if the person has died on the ship, nor for ashes thrown overboard, but a bottle of rum to the boatswain (bosun) might be an acceptable gesture!

Apparently a number of people died on British ships during the era of assisted passages to the commonwealth (1954 – 1972), or when elderly parents subsequently visited these emigrants.

On a cruise ship, part of the fare paid by the passenger may actually be reimbursed.

The writer Eleanor Hibbert (who wrote under the names of Victoria Holt, Philippa Carr, Jean Plaidy) died on a cruise ship between Piraeus, Greece and Port Said, Egypt in 1967, and was buried in the Mediterranean.

If the person were not a Christian, the body could be taken back to the homeport. Most cruise ships have a morgue on board, where two or three bodies may be stored until a port is reached.

BURIAL AT SEA FOLLOWING A DEATH ON LAND

Permission and a licence has to be sought from the relevant authorities for people who have died on land, but shown a preference for a burial at sea, whether by boat, aircraft, hovercraft, or marine structure. An out of England form 104, will also be required from the registrar to send to the coroner (Food and Environment Protection Act 1985). A freedom from infection certificate from the appropriate medical practitioner is also necessary.

The licence, which is free of charge, can be obtained from the Marine Consents and Environment Unit of the Department for Environment, Food and Rural Affairs in England *(DEFRA)*, or the National Assembly for Wales, which are the relevant licensing authorities. The licence will state where the burial will take place, the date, and specifications of the design and materials that must be used.

The body must be taken outside the three-mile limit from the shore. A special coffin of iron, concrete or wood with holes in it must be used, securely weighted to 200 kgs. No plastic is allowed. The body must not be embalmed.

There are various sites, one in North East England, nine miles from Newcastle upon Tyne, one off The Needles to the west of the Isle of Wight, and one at Newhaven, East Sussex (Marine Volunteer Reserve). There is also one off the Pembrokeshire coast in Wales. The *Britannia Shipping Co*, Devon can also arrange for a burial at sea.

The relevant port authorities have special boats, which are used for burials at sea. Due to tides, the funerals have to take place at a suitable time. Up to six people can attend, when a short service is held and flowers are placed on the water. The commanding officer will give a grid reference to the next of kin. The cost could be £4,000.

Many people were buried at sea during World War II. Since then many, especially service people, have requested to be buried or to have their ashes scattered at sea.

Some famous people who have chosen to be buried at sea in the US are John F. Kennedy, Rock Hudson, Ingrid Bergman, Robert Mitcham, Steve McQueen and Vincent Price. Lord Louis Mountbatten was buried in the Irish Sea.

All relevant addresses are in *Appendix V.*

SCATTERING OF ASHES AT SEA

Because of the danger of bodies being trawled up by fishing nets, the relevant authorities prefer the scattering of ashes to a burial at sea and for this no licence is required.

If a sailor or anyone else dies on land but wishes his ashes to be scattered at sea, the captain will take them out to the stated place, perhaps where the sailor stipulated in his will, such as the English Channel, and he will pour the ashes from a container, from the lee side of the ship on to a (hopefully) calm sea, because otherwise the ashes might blow back on board. It is not possible to stop a ship nowadays, perhaps doing 25 knots, to perform such a task. No plastic or other containers are now allowed to be jettisoned from a boat. The captain will also give a grid reference, and give a water sample from the site to the next of kin.

SCATTERING OF ASHES IN TIDAL WATER

Some religions insist on the ashes being scattered onto tidal waters (see Hindu funerals in *Chapter 6).*

Chapter 5

CHRISTIAN FUNERALS

Tis death is dead, not he! Percy Bysshe Shelley 1792 – 1822

God Himself took a day to rest in, and a good man's grave is his Sabbath.
John Donne 1572 – 1631

Billy Graham, the well-known American evangelist in the latter half of the twentieth century, made a point of being a non-denominational Christian appealing to everyone from Catholics, Orthodox, Anglicans and the free churches to know God.

Many theological differences between Christian denominations centre on issues that are not essential to the Christian faith. I too believe that everyone who accepts Jesus Christ as their Saviour and believes what he says about the Kingdom of God is a Christian and is part of the body of Christ, whatever else they may believe about the virgin birth, transubstantiation, the trinity, purgatory, etc., even though many churches cut themselves off from others by making themselves exclusive.

The different funeral rites of the denominations are described in this chapter.

THE CHRISTIAN DIMENSION

Most Christian funerals follow the pattern in *Chapter 3* with the added dimension of putting God more fully in the centre of things, the God in whom all Christians believe; incorporating more biblical passages, Christian readings and prayers.

A Christian funeral is the last rite of passage, and an act of worship, marking the end of this life. It will start with one or more opening sentences as outlined in *Appendix I*, such as 'In the midst of life, we are in death' Anglican funeral service, *The Book of Common Prayer 1549*.

For a true believing Christian a funeral is a celebration, not only of the life lived but a rejoicing that the deceased is on the way to another life, either immediately (some think), or only at the resurrection (say others although this may well be the next conscious moment, even if years later), where there will be no pain; one will be reunited with family and friends, and live forever with God and others (in a place called heaven, which may be on a renewed earth), in harmony and happiness.

> The final heartbeat for the Christian is not the mysterious conclusion to a meaningless existence. It is rather the grand beginning to a life that will never end. *Dr James Dobson*

> Death is part of the future for everyone. It is the last post of this life and the reveille of the next. Everywhere men fear death – it is the end of our present life. It is parting from loved ones, it is setting out

into the unknown. We overcome death by accepting it as the will of God, by finding him in it. Death, like birth, is only a transformation, another birth. When I die I shall change my state, that is all. And in faith in God, it is as easy and natural as going to sleep here and waking up there. *Journey for a Soul – Bishop Appleton.*

BURIAL OR CREMATION FOR CHRISTIANS?

The symbolism of burial for Christians, of the seed being planted (dying) before the new plant (with a new body) can be resurrected, is still important. Cremation was for centuries anathema since many of the pagan nations around the early Christians burnt their dead (including the Philistines). Resurrection would be easier if the body were intact from burial, they thought, forgetting that the resurrected body would be a new incorruptible body, not the old one full of illness and decay, which had gone from dust back to dust again,

See *Chapter 1* for the current considerations between burial and cremation.

MUSIC (See also *Appendix III*, and *Chapters 1 and 3*)

Hymns and Psalms

As well as some hymns, in a liturgical service one or more psalms may be sung or chanted and would be appropriate if the majority of the congregation attended an Anglican church. The metrical version of a psalm such as the 23rd Psalm to Crimond is a favourite one to be sung at funerals and is generally known by most churchgoing people of all denominations.

BELLS

Some people still ring the minute bell before a funeral, one unmuffled toll for each year of the person's life. If the deceased were a bell ringer or part of a hand bell group, bells may also be requested or a hymn or psalm played on the hand bells.

PRAYERS

The minister usually discusses the prayers with the bereaved before the service. They may include a plea for the mercy of God, a commending of the deceased to God, the hope that the soul of the deceased will rest in peace until the resurrection.

Prayers may include a request that those left behind will find strength to cope with their loss, or any guilt or anger that they may feel, and be aware of any shortcomings in their own lives.

They may give thanks that the deceased was a hard worker, a loving husband or wife and father or mother, or grandfather or grandmother, who loved golf, fishing, dogs, stamps, who was affectionate, witty, generous and gave a lot of his or her time to charity and serving others. He or she may have been a Sunday school teacher or Churchwarden or sang in the choir, etc.

They may refer to the fact that the person had died too young or lived to a ripe old age.

There are set prayers, both biblical and others, in *Appendix I.*

READINGS

Bible verses about death and the life hereafter are read at a Christian funeral.

Readings suitable to be read at funerals, both biblical and others, may be found in *Appendix III*.

The non-biblical ones are in alphabetical first line order, to find a favourite reading quickly. The biblical ones are written in full in order of their appearance in the Bible, first from the Old Testament and then from the New Testament.

See also the section on readings and who would be suitable to read at a funeral in *Chapter 3.*

THE ADDRESS

The minister, who will seek the guidance of God for what to say on each individual occasion, normally gives the address.

During the address, some ministers feel that it is not fair to preach to non-churchgoers during a funeral.

Others feel that it is their duty to do so and that this may be the only chance one is given to reach such people. They may therefore seek in some way to encourage all to think about their own lives and inevitable mortality, and what preparation they may need to make before it is too late. They may like to take the opportunity to tell of the love and mercy of God, and that Jesus died for them personally, and told them, before his death, about the hope of a future Kingdom that was to come. Or he may decide to question whether some of those present know God, and are ready to meet him.

At a funeral for a believer, they may like to proclaim the triumph of the gospel in the life of the deceased.

THE EULOGIES

Until quite recently the Church of England frowned upon eulogies. It was felt that the emphasis at a funeral should be on God not on the deceased.

But nowadays they have become the norm and are usually done by the family or friends (see *Chapter 3).*

They also seem to include more humour than in previous times. At a recent funeral of a minister another minister giving the eulogy was reminiscing about the time when all of them were at theological college together. 'We are all getting on a bit now,' he said, 'some of us have gone ahead, like our dear friend, others have become bishops or been defrocked!'

EUCHARIST – REQUIEM MASS

There is sometimes a Eucharist at a Christian funeral, or a requiem mass just for the family the evening before, or at a later memorial service. Those who request a Eucharist at a funeral take the view that it is only natural to be celebrating together with the deceased and all the saints who have gone before and those who are left, coming together as one body. It symbolizes the death and resurrection of the Lord, and his triumph over death.

THE COMMITTAL

At a Christian funeral the vicar will say a few extra prayers at the graveside as he commits the human remains to the grave. He commends the deceased to God and requests mercy for him. The official committal prayers may be recited, which will end the official act of worship. In a crematorium as the committal prayers are said the minister may decide to put his hand on the coffin at this point in the service. It is a personal touch much liked by some Christians.

Many Church of England parishes have churchyards but these may be full, although still open for adding a spouse or partner to an existing grave or adding ashes to a family grave.

In a churchyard bodies are buried with their feet pointing east, with the exception of a minister, who even in death still faces his congregation, both in the church and in the churchyard! If it is a metal coffin, throwing the soil in can be very noisy, so a layer of carpet tiles may cover the coffin before it is backfilled. For the committal prayer, see *Appendix I*.

West Indians culturally have the longest funerals. There is likely to be a one-hour service at a church or a crematorium followed by a two and a half hour service at the graveside, singing hymns and gospel songs. They also like their own family or friends to be the bearers and they also like to backfill the grave themselves, for which the funeral director will provide shovels.

THE WAKE OR RECEPTION

'Practice hospitality to one another'. *1 Peter 4:9*

Traditionally the reception represents the feast to be enjoyed in the Kingdom of God, together with Christ at the resurrection. Cinnamon bread and mulled wine were traditionally offered. *Chapter 3* offers more information or suggestions about holding a wake after a funeral service.

DENOMINATIONAL DIFFERENCES IN FUNERAL RITES

Catholics

The Catholic catechism states that the deceased has passed beyond sacramental economy, and that any funeral celebration comprises four principle elements – the greeting of the community, the liturgy of the Word, the Eucharistic Sacrifice, and a farewell.

There is always a requiem mass at a Catholic funeral. Catholic churches also have a vigil between death and the funeral, which can be at home, in a hospital, funeral home, or church. There may be a reception before or after the vigil or one after the funeral. Sometimes there is a service the night before the funeral in the church, which is often a mass. Italian churches may have a service the evening before the funeral for the immediate family. There is also a service on the anniversary of the death, or on the seventh or fortieth day after death.

Catholics traditionally believe in purgatory as an intermediate state of punishment and purification before the dead pass on into heaven, although recently some have begun to see that this belief is a contradiction of Christ's death being sufficient.

In the eighteenth and nineteenth centuries cremation was regarded by the Catholic Church as an anti-religious statement, but by Papal decree in 1963, Catholics could be cremated.

Orthodox

Greek Orthodox:
The Greek Orthodox Church does not permit cremation. The deceased must be buried in the tunic in which they were baptized, and buried in the earth from which the Creator took mankind. Most orthodox churches have a vigil between death and the funeral.

Prayers for the departed are of great effect as are prayers of the departed for those still on earth.

They do not believe in purgatory but believe in eternal life, either in God's Kingdom or in hell. The departed already have a foretaste of their final destiny (spiritual) resting as it were in Abraham's bosom, but the entirety comes only at the resurrection and last judgement at Christ's second coming (both spiritual and physical). Man's soul has had no previous existence.

There is no salvation outside their trinitarian church. It is exclusive.

Russian Orthodox
For the Russian Orthodox funeral, the open coffin is placed in the centre of the church and everyone stands around holding candles. At the end of the service everyone (including the children) give the departed a last kiss. Often the uncovered coffin is left in the church during other services, waiting for burial, so that embalming is essential. A Eucharist is always held. Burial follows.

Those who have gone before, those present on earth and by inference all those Christians still to come are part of the body of Christ.

Free churches

Many free churches such as Baptists and Methodists follow the Anglican form of funeral service.

Some nonconformist churches have a cemetery but this is unusual. A nonconformist cemetery was opened in London at Bunfields in 1665 and functioned until 1854, when the last interment, of a 15-year-old, took place. 120,000 people were buried there in 180 years, including John Bunyan (1628 – 1688), and John Strudwick in 1697 in whose house Bunyan had died. There is now no further room for burials. Most non-conformist churches allow either burial or cremation but Strict Baptists do not allow cremation.

Reformed churches

Reformed churches follow the teachings (and order of worship) of Calvin. They may be Presbyterian, Congregational, Calvinistic Methodists, or Independents, and hold funeral services similar to Anglican ones.

Quakers – Society of Friends

The Quakers hold a normal unstructured worship meeting for a funeral, where people who knew the deceased stand up and speak encouragingly about them. There is no ordained ministry, no sacraments and no creeds. Instead authority derives from the Holy Spirit, the 'inner light of the living Christ' in each believer.

Moravians

The funeral service takes the form of praise, thanksgiving and with accent on the resurrection.

Some Moravian churches have their own burial grounds and gardens of remembrance but only members are permitted to be buried there, although worshippers and people in the parish can have their funeral services in the church and their ashes scattered in the burial grounds. The service and burial are free to members; they do not buy a plot though they have to pay for any headstones. A small fee may be charged to outsiders who wish to hold a service and each congregation decides this.

Traditionally the minister would give the eulogy (but since Princess Diana's funeral, when her brother gave it, the Moravian family is encouraged, more and more to do the eulogy themselves).

Moravians distrust traditional creeds.

The Salvation Army

At Salvation Army funerals, the coffin is draped with a Salvation Army flag and the deceased's hat or bonnet (women) placed upon it. This corresponds to other service funerals. The Salvation Army considers itself to be a fighting force, albeit in a spiritual battle. The person whose funeral it is has been 'promoted to Glory', so the prayers are mainly for the bereaved.

Pentecostals

Pentecostals allow both burial and cremation. Their funeral services follow those of the protestant community, with hymns, prayers and readings.

Jehovah's Witnesses (from 1870s)

They believe all sleep in the grave until the resurrection. 144,000 will reign over the earth with Christ from heaven. The rest will be resurrected to live everlastingly on this renewed earth.

There is only one God, the Father. Jesus was the man God sent to be his messiah.

Witnesses do not accept blood transfusions, even in the face of death, nor post mortems. Abortions are unacceptable but organ donation is allowed.

Christadelphians

Christadelphians prefer burial but do allow cremation. The funeral service is simple and is held in one of their halls of worship or a local chapel. There are hymns and prayers and readings like a usual Christian service. On a fine day there may only be a service at the graveside. There is no funeral service fee, because there are no paid nor ordained ministers in the church. They do believe in resurrection and judgement and are very interested in prophesy. The Bible is infallible.

Seventh Day Adventists

The funeral service for Adventists is similar to the normal Christian service with hymns, readings and prayers. They believe that at death the body rots in the grave if buried, or at cremation returns to dust, but the spirit goes back to God who gave it. They believe in eternal life at the resurrection, when Jesus comes again. The funeral can be any day except the Sabbath (Friday evening to Saturday evening).

Christian Scientists

There are no specified last rites for Christian Scientists. The individual or family decides such issues and questions relating to care of the body. In general, Christian Scientists request that, whenever possible, the body of a female should be prepared for burial by a female.

They normally prefer cremation. There is no set funeral service; the individual or family decides what to include. A service would usually be conducted by a church member and/or relatives at the local crematorium or cemetery chapel, not in their own church.

If there are Bible readings (King James's version) there may also be linked passages from *Science and Health with Key to the Scriptures* by Mary Baker Eddy, which may include the Lord's Prayer, and what Christian Scientists understand its spiritual sense to be (see *Appendix I*).

Christian Scientists believe that all will experience Christ Jesus' promise of eternal life and therefore they have no mourning rites.

BEREAVEMENT FOR ANY CHRISTIAN

If one believes and trusts in God and in Jesus Christ as one's Saviour, faith can be a real comfort at this stressful time – somehow one is upheld when others fall apart. Divine help does not take away the pain; it just makes it easier to bear.

'The Lord is close to the broken-hearted and saves
those who are crushed in spirit.*' Ps. 34: 18.*

'I am with you always, even unto the end of the world
(or this age)' assures Jesus. *Matt 28:20*

And 'no one shall snatch them out of my hand'. *John 10:28.*

LOSS OF FAITH

Bereavement can challenge one's faith. If someone announces that they have lost their faith because God let their child, spouse or partner die, this may be perceived as unanswered prayer. It may also suggest doubt as to how real their faith was before tragedy struck.

It is good to pray for such people, for a restored faith, and for encouragement to seek God in their distress. The minister is there to help.

WHAT IS LIFE AND WHAT IS DEATH?

The Lord God formed the man from the dust of the ground
and breathed into his nostrils the breath of life and the man
became a living being. *Gen. 2:7 NIV.*

Life is not just flesh and blood, there is another component, a life force (breath of life), which when it departs brings on the state called death. According to the Bible, man and the animals have differing flesh. *1 Cor.15: 39* but they have the same life force and the same fate, when it is taken away.

Death may be the answer to prayers for healing, when prayer for a cure does not come. Jesus's command 'Take up your bed and walk' may mean, for some, the walk from this life into the next.

The Bible says that death is an enemy of mankind. Hope in a future eternal existence makes death bearable and takes away the sting.

AN AFTERLIFE FOR CHRISTIANS

Christians believe that there is another life after death because their Saviour, Jesus the Christ (the Messiah) told them that it would be so:

> There are many rooms in my Father's house. I wouldn't tell you this unless it was true. I am going there to prepare a place for each of you. After I have done this, I will come back and take you with me. Then we will be together. *John 4:2 CEV.*

And the only remedy for death is resurrection. We cannot earn eternal life; it is a gift from God. Only God can bestow eternal life. We do not obtain eternal life because we are good, but because God is good, and because Jesus died in our place.

> 'Such is Christ's power that he can raise the dead more easily than we can arouse the sleeping.' (St Braulio of Saragossa, Letter 19, from the Office for the Dead in the Roman Breviary).

The fact that God raised Jesus to life on the third day meant that all (because he died for the whole world) would also be raised from death to life on the Day of Judgement – because Jesus is the Resurrection and the Life.

> 'But Christ has indeed been raised from the dead, the first fruits of those who have fallen asleep. For since death came through a man, the resurrection of the dead comes also through a man. For as in Adam all die, so in Christ all will be made alive. But each in his own turn, Christ the first fruits; then, when he comes, those who belong to him' *1 Cor. 15:20–23, 51–54.*

The Bible declares that Jesus will come again (Parousia or Second coming of Christ), when the righteous (those who believe in him), will be resurrected.

> 'For this we declare to you by the word of the Lord, that we who are alive, who are left until the coming of the Lord, shall not precede those who have fallen asleep (died). For the Lord himself will descend from heaven with a cry of command, with the archangel's call, and with the sound of the trumpet of God and the dead in Christ shall rise first; then we who are alive, who are left, will be caught up together with them in the clouds to meet the Lord in the air; and so we shall always be with the Lord.' *1 Thess. 4:15–18.*

> Jesus said 'I am the resurrection and the life. He who believes in me will live, even though he dies, and whoever lives and believes in me will never die'. *John 11:25–26*

The Bible seems to indicate a resurrection to judgement for everyone eventually, with the outcome of being with God, Jesus and his angels; or to hell, without

God but with Satan and his demons (fallen angels) as the two alternatives, the latter to be avoided at all costs.

'When the Son of Man comes in his glory, and all the angels with him, he will sit on his throne in heavenly glory. All the nations will be gathered before him, and he will separate the people one from another as a shepherd separates the sheep from the goats. He will put the sheep on his right and the goats on his left. Then the King will say to those on his right, "Come, you who are blessed by my Father; take your inheritance, the kingdom prepared for you since the creation of the world. For I was hungry and you gave me something to eat, I was thirsty and you gave me something to drink, I was a stranger and you invited me in, I needed clothes and you clothed me, I was sick and you looked after me, I was in prison and you came to visit me… I tell you the truth, whatever you did for one of the least of these brothers of mine, you did for me".' *Matt 25: 31– 36, 40.*

Some will ask, 'What about Hitler, Idi Amin, Saddam Hussein, Myra Hindley, etc.' The parable of the men working in the vineyard explains *(Matt 20)* that even if people have committed extreme genocide or other gross sins, they will still get the same reward as Mother Teresa, if they truly repent, even at the eleventh hour. Some will say, 'That's not fair.' No. But it is Christian. It may not be justice but it is love, it is grace, it is unearned but freely given by a loving, merciful God. And Our Father God is like that, loving and merciful and full of grace.

Chapter 6
FUNERAL RITES FOR DIFFERENT FAITHS

Now that the world religions are spreading to all countries in the world, people from all faiths will need to bury or cremate their dead in their own way, wherever they now reside. The religions mentioned are placed in approximate historical order.

HINDUISM

(From 5000 B.C. or B.C.E.)

Death is not the extinguishing of the light, but the putting out of the light, because dawn has come. Rabindranath Tagore 1861 – 1941

Hindus believe in the need for cremation after death (in order to release the spirit so that it is free to enter another body i.e. rebirth). The only ones allowed to be buried are non-viable foetus's and children under the age of five.

Until the early part of the nineteenth century, widows were burnt on the funeral pyre of their husbands (*suttee*) in India. It is now illegal (the British suppressed it in 1828), but in 2002 there was an incident in India when a wife jumped on to the funeral pyre of her husband.

If the person dies in the daytime, the body is ideally cremated the same day. If the person dies after dusk then cremation will be the following day.

At death the Hindu body is lowered to the floor, washed (preferably a male body by a male and a female body by a female), preferably in holy water from the Ganges and water is poured into the mouth. The body is then touched with five metals, silver, gold, iron, copper and a mixed alloy. Sweet smelling incense is burnt to bring clean spirits into the area. Sandalwood and a red powder are applied to the face. The body is then wrapped in clean clothes and covered in a white sheet, over which flowers are strewn.

The mourners will generally wear traditional Indian garments. White being the traditional mourning colour. Flowers or sweetmeats may be offered. The male mourners may shave their heads as a sign of respect.

In India the body is placed on a bamboo stretcher and carried head first to the burning ghat (the place of cremation), where it is burned feet first, which symbolises looking ahead to a future life. The son or other male member of the family, nephew, or brother lights the funeral pyre.

After cremation the ashes are taken to a holy river such as the Ganges, where they are sprinkled for purification. This Hindu funeral rite is an offering to the gods, such as *Shiva* (God of destruction) and Lord *Yama* (God of death) and is considered a good sacrificial death. The sacred city of Varanasi, on the

Ganges, has ghats (landing steps at a riverside) leading down to the water from the cremation site and is favoured for this reason.

In Great Britain the cost prohibits most Hindus from returning to India for the cremation and ashes service. Also a number of Hindus in Great Britain have never been to India, having arrived from East Africa or were born in Britain. It is often desired therefore to cremate in Britain and to submerge the ashes into running water, preferably a tidal river, so that eventually they can reach the sea, and ultimately the Ganges in India, but permission should be obtained first from the relevant environment authority. The service must also take place on an auspicious day at an auspicious time.

In London, there is only one cremation site on the Thames with steps leading down to the river, at Mortlake. *City Cruises*, for twenty years, has offered a much-valued service to the Asian community by hiring out boats to Asian families on the tidal part of the river. Each boat, which runs from Cherry Garden pier, is for the sole use of one family and provides a captain and crew to operate the vessel. The boats run ashes services seven days a week, in six hourly slots. The return trip takes about half an hour.

After the 2004 tsunami, where hundreds of thousands of Hindus and other people died in the greatest natural catastrophe for centuries, it was not possible to arrange funeral pyres for everyone and many dead bodies were buried in mass graves.

On the 13th day after the death a ceremony known as Kirya is held. The family priest will pray for the departed soul and also ask for rebirth into a good family. Everyone is invited to take food with the family.

On a fixed day every month the soul is remembered and prayers are said until the annual Remembrance Day that takes place eleven months after the death. The family priest again says prayers and the bereaved family donate food and clothes to the priest.

At the annual remembrance – *Shradh* – the family again give food and clothing to the priest on the assumption that these goods are reaching the departed souls, via the priest.

There are 8,000 Hindu and Sikh cremations in the UK each year, of which 5,000 take place in London. 50% of the ashes are taken back to India and 50% are scattered or submerged in the River Thames or other watercourse. Any religion can take advantage of *City Cruises* vessels (address *Appendix V*).

There is an Asian Family Counselling Service at Southall, Mddsx.

The biggest Hindu temple in Europe, and in fact the world, outside Delhi, is at Neasden, north London.

Reincarnation

From ancient times, the Dravidians in southern India and northern Sri Lanka believed in an immortal soul and purification being a separation of the soul from the body. If the soul could exist separately at death, it could also exist separately at birth. This led to a belief in reincarnation, the transmigration of souls from one life to another *(samsara)*. All Hindus believe in reincarnation. One's Karma (one's good and bad deeds) determines one's next reincarnation. This continues indefinitely unless the individual attains the final goal of *Nirvana* – a state of non-existence, a state of oblivion.

One thing is not explained by reincarnation and *nirvana* and that is the continuing increase in world population.

JUDAISM

(From 3,600 B.C.E.)

No one is allowed to touch a Jewish person who dies in hospital or a hospice. The body must be treated with honour. Each Jewish community has a *Chevra Kadisha,* which is a Jewish burial society, which prepares the body and arranges the funeral. At death, the body is ritually washed and wrapped in a shroud and put in a coffin. A man is also wrapped in a prayer shawl *(tallit).* The body is never left alone, and autopsy is not generally acceptable.

On hearing of a death, people in the past rent their clothes. Nowadays it is more usual to pin a piece of cloth to the lapel, the left one (nearest the heart) for a close relative or the right one for others.

It is Jewish tradition that people are buried within 24 hours of death (but not on the Sabbath [Saturday] or Day of Atonement). This practice is still maintained throughout the world if at all possible, even though Jews do not all now live in a hot country. Any limbs that are severed are buried with the rest of the body.

Cremation is generally frowned upon because in the Jewish scriptures it is associated with pagans and human sacrifice. Ashkenazi Jews (from North and East Europe) and Sephardi Jews (from Spain and Portugal) may only bury. Reform, Progressive or Liberal Jews may now be buried or cremated, but it still has to be within 2–3 days or as soon as possible. Ashes cannot be buried in an official Jewish cemetery but can be buried in a municipal cemetery. Since the holocaust some people feel that there should be no more cremation.

Being buried near other members of the family is important. To be buried in Israel is desired but elsewhere earth from Israel may be put on the head or under the body.

The body stays at home or is brought home from hospital and lies with a candle at the head and the foot. The Rabbi may come to the home before the funeral, or may meet the family at the prayer hall at the burial place. The mourners walk behind the coffin for a while before entering into the funeral cars. No money is charged for a funeral and no flowers are allowed. Instead friends are asked to plant a tree in Israel.

At the service, which can be anywhere, and which anyone can take, because there is no priesthood as such, men sit on the left and the women on the right (or upstairs in the gallery). Ten males (Orthodox) have to be present for a religious service to be complete or ten adults (Reform and Liberal). The fiercely monotheistic prayer is said 'Hear O Israel, the Lord our God, the Lord is one'. Prayers (called the *Kaddish* – in Aramaic doxology) and psalms are said, and a eulogy given *(hesped).* Then everyone shakes hands. After a burial, male relatives back fill the gravesite. Graves are not tended but are allowed to deteriorate for eternity.

A funeral at a synagogue is rare and is usually reserved for an important person (such as Hugo Gryn a few years ago).

At home, after the funeral, the family and friends come and go for seven days, traditionally without washing or shaving. Visitors bring all the food. They sit and eat on low chairs (which can be hired from the synagogue), with the chief mourner. Candles are lit (nowadays they may even be electric candles). A service is held every morning and evening for a week (Sitting *Shiva*), praising

God. They meet for a further service a month after, when the beards are shaved off, and there is another meeting a year after that.

Jewish tradition emphasises respect for the dead and the dying, and deference and adherence to the last wishes of a dying man. In the Bible, the final requests of Jacob *Gen. 49:29,* Joseph *Gen. 50: 25* and David *1 Kings 2: 1–9,* are all faithfully recorded, heeded and observed. When Jacob died in Egypt, his son Joseph had him embalmed and taken back to Canaan to be buried, because his father had made this request *Gen. 49: 29–50:14.* When Joseph died, his sons also embalmed him and placed him in a coffin in Egypt *Gen. 50:22–26.* But Joseph had made his sons swear that his bones would be taken back to Canaan too, and this was done by Moses *Exod. 13:19.*

Some say that there is no eternal damnation for the Jews, although rabbinic descriptions of hell are as galling as any depicted in Islam or early Christianity. In history there has been as much discussion about what happens after death as was expounded on the minutiae of the law.

But Jews believe in a world to come. At death or after the resurrection the righteous go to a Garden of Eden, a paradise or *pardes*, an orchard, and live with God. The evil go to *Gehinnom,* a place of punishment outside Jerusalem, which is remote from God. Jews have an ongoing hope for a Messiah, who when he comes will not be God.

There is a Jewish Bereavement Counselling Service (See *Appendix V*)

PARSIS (PARSEES)

ZOROASTRIANS

(1200 B.C.E.)

Parsis are Zoroastrians from Persia (Iran). Historically they neither bury nor cremate their dead because this would pollute nature. The corpse is washed and dressed in old clothes (wastefulness is a sin), and then when everyone has seen the corpse for the last time, a few prayers are said. Death is a major rite of passage where the soul goes to join its ancestors.

In India (and formerly in Iran) the body is carried to the desert on a metal bier, the same day and placed in a Tower of Silence. Because the journey into the desert may be long, there is a team of bearers *(Nassesalars),* dressed in white and wearing white gloves. The priest will recite *Vesta* prayers at the tower,

The Towers of Silence have high walls open to the sky and may measure100 feet across. There is a well in the middle of the tower, then an inner ring for children to be laid, then a ring for females and an outer ring for males. Here the bodies are placed, stripped of all their clothes and left to the mercy of the sun and for vultures and other birds of prey to devour (in India this may only take 30–60 minutes). Large bones turn to powder in the sun and wind. All bones are eventually put into the well, which is cleaned out once a year.

There is currently a great shortage of vultures in India due to the practice of giving veterinary drugs to farm animals, which die and are eaten by vultures, which then develop kidney failure. It is thought to be the fastest decline of any animal species worldwide.

Because this practice would not be allowed in the UK, the bodies of Parsis are usually repatriated to India, although there has been a cemetery plot for Parsis at Brookwood, Surrey, since 1863, where bodies may be buried above the ground in stone coffins, preferred by Parsis because stone does not permeate evil, or where their ashes after cremation may be buried.

A communal meal follows of bread, eggs and herbs. Then the mourners announce a gift to charity in memory of the deceased, which is considered a better use of money than providing a gravestone.

After three days prayers are said again whilst the soul, which is immortal, prepares to leave the body. It is led by conscience to the Bridge of the Separator or Judgement. Those whose thoughts, words and deeds are predominantly good cross over the bridge to paradise, where they are tested in molten metal. To the good it is like a bath in warm milk. The wicked fall from the bridge and live in torment. Punishment must be corrective however, so hell cannot be eternal.

There is a resurrection *(Frashkart)* of the body and spirit later, for everyone (sinners are released from hell), where they are judged again. When the Saviour comes, he will slit the throat of the serpent or dragon. Thus when the whole man, both soul and body in its prime has been corrected, he can live with God. That is his final destiny.

Meantime hands and faces are washed before worship. Hospitality is shown to strangers and there is active concern for the under-priviledged. Life is black and white; there are no grey areas. Promiscuity and prostitution are unacceptable.

Their fire temples are bare with no artificial light, the fire alone, which may be six feet high, symbolizes God, who is pure eternal light. A good Parsi prays five times a day. Pessimism and despair are considered sins.

The European headquarters of the faith (Zoroastrian Trust Of Europe) is at West Hampstead.

JAINISM

(580 B.C.E.)

The ideal death in old age is by self-starvation. The soul is important not the body.

Jains believe in cremation and reincarnation, and at death rebirth is instantaneous, unlike Hinduism and Buddhism. The soul enters a new foetus when it is three months old. A human soul would not go into a lesser body or plant or animal. They believe that *nirvana* is only attainable through asceticism.

Every soul is potentially divine. Jains are atheistic, and they reject the caste system. There is no creator God, and all objects such as stones, metal and earth as well as all traditional living things are alive and have feelings. This leads to non-violence in every aspect of life; therefore abortion is unacceptable. Jains also avoid some violent professions, such as farming, butchery and military careers.

Their prayers include all faiths and all those on the spiritual path. Individuals are expected to conquer their inner passions of greed, anger, ego and deceit.

Mahatma Gandhi was said to be greatly influenced by the Jain religion, with their non-possessiveness and non-violence. Jains are also vegetarians.

The only Jain temple in Europe was built inside a disused non-conformist chapel in Leicester in 1973. Their temples are plain on the outside but very elaborate on the inside, like Jains should be. This was a protection when the Muslim moguls destroyed Hindu and Jain temples. Monks and Nuns shave their heads like the Buddhists.

BUDDHISM

(From 563 B.C.E.)

The Buddhist believes that he is dying from the moment he is born. Whilst in the womb the body is being prepared for life in this world and whilst in this world the soul is being prepared for eternal life in the next; meantime there is rebirth.

Monks, who always have shaved heads, must be informed of a death and stay with the dying person. The body is brought out of the house. Homage is paid to Buddha. Candles are lit, incense is burnt, lit by the eldest son; there may be wreaths and coloured lights. It should be three to seven days before the body is disposed of, because some Buddhists believe that consciousness remains in the body for a while after death.

Buddhists in Tibet have what they call a 'sky funeral'. They take the body up to the top of a mountain, cut it up and let the vultures clean the bones. This may be because there is a shortage of wood. This shows compassion to the birds. In other countries cremation is most usual, although bodies may be buried (except monks) possibly in a woodland setting depending on the family.

In the UK the funeral would take place at a Buddhist temple, or a church (if the incumbent agreed), or at any crematorium.

The five precepts are recited (how a Buddhist promises to live). A sermon is given on death and transience and the dead person is referred to. The coffin is closed and buried or cremated and the mourners go on to a funeral meal. On the seventh day the monks are given alms.

Rebirth follows. The eight-spoked wheel, which goes on turning, symbolizes life that goes on forever.

In Japan the body is washed and covered with a white sheet and a knife is placed on the chest to ward off evil spirits. Candles and sticks of incense burn round the bed and *sutras* (prayers) from the Buddhist canonical books are recited. The deceased is given a posthumous Buddhist name, for which a large sum must be paid. The body is placed in an unpainted coffin, which is taken to the altar, with a picture of the deceased.

The law requires cremation but incense and candles are still burnt until the soul has lost its influence over human affairs and joins the ancestors in universal nature.

The Buddhist believes that death is inevitable for all. The body is cherished, fed, clothed, and washed but it is treacherous, completely deserting its owner at the time of death. Death itself occurs when all bodily functions cease and even one's consciousness has left the body (which may be sometime after other bodily functions cease).

Buddhists believe that at death each human being and animal has indefinite reincarnation (rebirth or metempsychosis) into another human or animal form (some sects even say plants). This is decided by whether one has positive or negative actions in this life (Karma). One does not usually remember a previous life because of the trauma of death and rebirth.

One must not willingly kill any living thing, because in a previous life one might have been another human being or animal, fish or insect. Therefore abortion is unacceptable. If one does accidentally kill someone or something, one generates negative thoughts and must compensate by having positive thoughts and actions, or one will be reborn next time into a lower form of life.

The constant uncontrollable cycle of death and rebirth into this life of suffering and sorrow is known as *Samsara.* The only way out is to escape to the Pure Land of Buddha and attain Enlightenment *(Nirvana).* This is done by meditation and clearing the mind of all the sin and sorrows of this world, which are brought on by attachments to things and people (craving after gratification of the senses, prosperity, or the future life). When one has become a Buddha one is able to help others to attain enlightenment. There is no belief in an all-powerful creator God.

There is belief in an immortal soul, even though everything material is impermanent. Purification comes from the separation of the soul from the body.

JAPANESE RELIGIONS

(From 550 B.C.E.)

Shintoism is the indigenous Japanese religion but Confucianism, Zen Buddhism, Taoism and Christianity are all present among the Japanese.

Shintoists fear the spirits of departed souls, so they have to appease them with gifts and food. A departed soul still has a personality but is stained because of death. It is purified by the memorial rites, eventually rising to the position of an ancestral deity or guardian (ancestor worship). The family is very important. Zen Buddhist priests largely conduct their funeral rites.

CHINESE RELIGIONS

(From 500 B.C.E.)

Confucianism has formed the main Chinese philosophy for the last 2,500 years along with Taoism, but there is also Buddhism, and Christianity present in China and there are also some Muslim Chinese. The Chinese who come to Britain may belong to any one of these religions.

The Chinese today will be remembered in their family forever, because of the practice of ancestor worship. At death the soul is split three ways – one part goes to heaven, one part stays in the grave and receives sacrifices of food (often rice which is a large part of any diet), and the third part resides in the ancestral shrine.

Death is accompanied by ceremony and ritual. The coffin is bought well in advance of death as a sign of respect. It is left open for viewing by friends and relatives. At the funeral family members chant prayers and burn paper money. They are buried with food, money, and personal effects put into the orifices. The siting of the grave is very important. Loud mourning to demonstrate grief is common.

The Chinese like a funeral procession with a band leading; on one occasion when none could be found, in England, they settled for six bagpipers and everyone came out on to the street to watch this strange, very loud event pass by.

There is a memorial service after 100 days at the home of the senior male heir. Here joss sticks are burned. An ancestor tablet contains the name and status of the deceased and a photograph.

Later the body is disinterred and the bones put into a pot in the open air and then the pot is buried. They are remembered thereafter with incense at family shrines. Sometimes the bones or ashes are sent back to Hong Kong.

Pagodas illustrate Mahayana Buddhism in China.

Taoists believe in a simplicity of, and harmony with, nature (Tao). The system is philosophical and their rituals are similar to Confucians and Buddhists.

Reburials

There is a growing trend among the Chinese, especially in California (home to four million Asians), for bringing ancestors over from China or the Philippines, for reburial in America, where the descendants can take care of them better. As part of ancestor worship, it is necessary to visit the graves of one's forebears bringing flowers, incense and offerings during the holidays, but this is not easily done if the ancestors are half a world away. From *The Daily Telegraph* 31 Aug. 2002.

It is usually the bones or the ashes that are transported. To exhume a body or even ashes in Britain, a license has to be obtained from the Home Office except from a Columbarium (a place for the storage of ashes above ground).

ISLAM

(From 600 C.E.)

Muslims do not allow cremation. They believe that the soul departs from the body at the moment of death, which is an act of Allah, so there is no need to get unduly emotional. Post mortems are generally avoided. The last words a dying Muslim should hear are 'There is no God but Allah'.

A member of the family of the same sex as the deceased washes the body. It is put in a clean unsewn white shroud and placed on a stretcher, although some countries specify burial must be in a coffin. If so the family will put the body into a brand new coffin, which is buried, within 24 hours of death or as soon as possible, with the body lying in a north-west – south-east direction with the head at the south-east end and the face turned toward Mecca.

A Muslim grave has to be brick lined or in concrete, and they only allow one body per plot as they will not disturb a grave once a body has been interred. Gravestones and monuments are not allowed.

Muslims also like to carry the coffin themselves. If professional bearers are used, they must wear gloves.

Salat (ritual prayer) is said, always in Arabic, in the mosque, including a prayer for the happiness of the departed soul. The funeral service is very short, perhaps three minutes unless it includes a sermon by the Imam.

Forty days after the funeral there is a family commemoration.

Muslims believe that all suffering in this world will be rewarded in the next. There is a last day of judgement, when the books will be opened, and everyone will be judged by what they have done. There is a resurrection and a heaven of worldly delights and a lurid hell. All who live good lives will achieve paradise but those infidels who openly reject Islam will receive no mercy.

The five pillars of Islam include the proclamation that God is One and Muhammad is his prophet, offering prayer five times a day, almsgiving, fasting during Ramadan, and going on a pilgrimage to Mecca at least once in a lifetime.

A Muslim may have four wives as long as he treats them all equally.

There were no mosques in Great Britain until the end of the nineteenth century, when the first one was built in Woking.

The first in London was built in Regent's Park in the 1960s. Now almost every city in the country has a mosque or one is planned.

Armadi Muslims, a minor sect from India have completed the largest mosque in Europe in 2003, to hold 10,000 people in South London.

SIKHISM

(From 1480s C.E.)

Death is nothing but a gateway to Divinity and Eternity.
Guru Gobind Singh Mansukhani AD 1666 – 1708

Sikhs permit only cremation, within 24 hours in India, but in Great Britain they may have to wait for a crematorium slot, particularly in winter or at times of epidemics.

At the death bed prayers of peace are read in Punjabi. Unlike Hinduism the body must not be placed on the floor, nor must a lamp be lit beside the body. If the person dies in hospital, the body is taken home before the funeral where the family washes it themselves. Sons will wash the father's body and daughters the mother's body. Clean but normal clothes are put on; and people come and pay their respects, then the coffin is closed and the funeral director takes over the rest of the arrangements, booking the crematorium, etc. The funeral service is a celebration. There is no sorrow, and no fear of death; it is a time of rejoicing. Mourning is discouraged particularly when there has been a long life.

30–40 people can watch the body in some crematoria whilst the son or nearest male relative to the deceased lights the funeral pyre, or turns on the gas as the coffin enters the furnace. They are allowed to watch behind a barrier until the flames surround the coffin and then the doors are closed. The ashes are collected on the other side of the cremator, when cooled, and are immersed in running water or the sea (in England this must have permission from the relevant environment authority). Some prefer to take the ashes back to the Punjab. They may also be buried but no monuments or memorials may be erected at the place where the last remains of the deceased were strewn. If cremation is not possible the body may be consigned to the sea.

For scattering of ashes in the tidal River Thames, see the section in Hinduism (above) and address for City Cruises *(Appendix V).*

Prayers continue to be read in the *Gurdwara* (Sikh temple) for 48 hours, day and night. The whole *Adi Granth,* their holy book, is read on a Friday.

The scriptures are then read for nine days. On the tenth day, the relatives and friends of the family gather for a ceremony, which includes hymns, prayers and reading. Sometimes food is offered. Presents are sometimes distributed to the grandchildren and donations announced for charities or religious organizations. There is no further ceremony after the tenth day.

Sometimes this is followed by a turban-tying ceremony where the eldest member of the family is declared the new head of the family and given a turban ceremonially, a token of his new responsibility for looking after the family and estate of the dead person.

The evil person however will dread death because he is condemned to the unending cycle of birth and death. There is judgement and a record of all one's good and evil deeds written down by scribes. The God of justice cannot be bribed or influenced. Man is responsible for his own actions and cannot escape punishment through the intervention of a spiritual leader, unlike Christianity.

There is no actual heaven or hell. They are merely conditions of the mind. Hell is to be out of the presence of God. The virtuous man is happy and contented, as if he is living in heaven.

Sikhs believe in an immortal soul. After death they can merge with God (Akal Purakh), or *Nirvana,* if by spiritual effort they have amassed enough Holy Spirit (the Name), thus being released from the continuous rebirth cycle.

Sikhism was meant to unite Hinduism and Islam.

The main Sikh temple is the Golden Temple in Amritsa, India. There are many Sikh temples and adherents in the UK.

MORMONISM

(From 1820 C.E.)

Mormons favour burial rather than cremation and are buried in their temple robes (white and symbolic), which they wear to go to their wards (churches). They do not have their own cemeteries and they do not charge fees for funerals.

Mormons call themselves Latter Day Saints and believe in a resurrection. They also baptise for the dead. Those who have been baptized can decide at the resurrection whether they wish to go God's way or not, even if they did not know God when on this earth. It is necessary to live according to God's way of life in order to be able to live in God's presence. God's way is orderliness, not confusion.

They believe that all humans were spirit beings before they were sent down to this earth as freewill human beings to be tried and tested as to whether they would accept good or evil as a way of life and philosophy. They believe that people work towards good or evil throughout their lives. Those who have chosen to do right become fully mature sons and daughters of God. In heaven they are reunited with their wives and create spiritual children who are sent down to earth as they were.

Women can only attain heaven through their husbands; so all women must be married. Some breakaway Mormon churches still accept polygamy but the mainstream Churches of Latter Day Saints do not. They would be excommunicated today for adultery or polygamy. However, when they have repented they can be taken back into the church, which is one of love, not condemnation.

Today the headquarters of the Mormon faith is in Salt Lake City, Utah, USA but there are wards or churches throughout the world and stakes (= dioceses).

BAHA'I FAITH

(From 1850s C.E.)

'Death, the tender messenger of joy, opens the door
to eternal life in all the worlds of God.'

When a Baha'i dies they are carefully washed and put in a white shroud of cotton or silk and a wooden coffin. The body should decompose naturally. The body is never embalmed unless it is required by law. Cremation is not allowed. Organs may be left to medical science but the rest of the body must be buried as soon as possible and within an hour's journey from where it dies. Death is reunion with God. The body is the temple of the soul and is therefore to be respected.

In the UK, they use the chapels of the local cemeteries and allow a local funeral director to make all the arrangements. There is no priesthood and the family will organize the service. There may be various readings, done by the local Baha'i community, music, hymns, eulogy etc. The service is short, simple, dignified and uplifting. There is only one obligation for the funeral of anyone over 15 years of age – to include the special Prayer for the Dead (shown in full in *Appendix I*).

It is not a mournful occasion. There will be praising of God and celebrating the life of the deceased. A memorial service, which is longer, may be held (about 30–40 days) after the funeral.

Baha'u'llah, the founder of the faith insisted that all Baha'is make a Will, and that their instructions are carried out exactly. They fast and are usually teetotal.

Children who die before 15 years of age (the age of discretion) or before the appointed time of their birth are 'considered to be under the shadow and favour of God; and as they have not committed any sin, and are not soiled with the impurities of the world of nature, they are the centres of the manifestation of bounty, and the Eye of Compassion will be turned upon them'.

A reading for those who die before 15 or before birth is to be found in *Appendix II*. It commences with the line 'The master says...'

Baha'is believe that all religions come from the same source. They totally reject reincarnation but do believe in an afterlife. They believe that life on earth is a preparation for the life of the soul or spirit. Everyone has an immortal soul, which comes into being in the womb, where it is prepared for this life. After death the disembodied spirit without the body, for which it has no further use, is free to move into another dimension, gradually moving towards God but never actually becoming divine. The purpose of life is to know and to love God and to acquire virtues and spiritual qualities.

There is a daily obligation for prayer and regular fasting and feasting. They meet in each other's homes but there are local and national centres in major big cities and one Mother Temple in each continent, the one in Europe being in Frankfurt, Germany.

There is one overall Universal House of Justice, which has extensive buildings and is located at Haifa on the lower slopes of Mount Carmel. Some make pilgrimages to the shrines at Haifa and Akka, both in Israel.

Dr Kelly, a government scientist working on the investigation of Iraq's weapons of mass destruction, who was alleged to have committed suicide in 2003, was a Baha'i.

HUMANISTS, ATHEISTS AND FREE-THOUGHT SECULARISTS

These people do not believe in a god, which they see as something invented by man in his own image. But I am told there are no atheists in a shipwreck!

'When times are tough, people often make promises to a god in whom they do not believe.' John Nicol – 'It's Your funeral.' Night and Day, supplement to The Mail on Sunday 10 November 2002.

They usually hold funerals in a church, and cremation or burial is allowed, but not in consecrated ground, only in a wood or similar green site. There is no resurrection. They feel that this life is all there is, therefore one should make the most of it. Thereafter there is only oblivion. The only way they may live on is in their children, or in their works. Some may have been famous as an author, composer, inventor, or have been acknowledged as experts in some other field.

Some people may think that humanism, atheism (not agnosticism which is 'not knowing') and secularism are not religions at all, but it requires as much faith to believe that there is no god as to believe in one. Therefore they can be called faiths but it is doubtful whether anyone has had their life 'changed' by becoming an atheist!

There is a British Humanist Association (see addresses Appendix V).

'Here lies an atheist all dressed up but with nowhere to go!'
Dylan Thomas AD 1914 – 53

C.S. Lewis AD 1898 – 1963 added: 'I bet he wishes that were so!'

SPIRITUALISM

Spiritualist funerals take the form of most other people in the UK.

Spiritualism is the attempt to communicate with spirit beings (those who have died), using mediums. They have séances using table turning and automatic writing. People are most likely to be interested for the first time in spiritualism, when they have been bereaved.

All mainstream Christian churches denounce these practices because the Bible is adamant that God has prohibited humans from trying to contact the dead in any way. e.g. Lev. 19:31 and Lev. 20:6.

Chapter 7

AFTER THE FUNERAL

*We should all be concerned about the future, because we will
have to spend the rest of our lives there. Charles Kettering*

OTHER PEOPLE TO INFORM

Contacting everyone else can usually be left until after the funeral (except the
solicitor to see if he or she holds the Will), and the bank manager (who will
freeze the account(s) on the date of death and cancel standing orders, etc. (See
Chapter 1). Others may include any landlord (who will want to know when the
house or flat can be vacated), the tax office, private pension providers (pensions
are paid up to the date of death), life insurance companies (there may be a sum
payable on death), National Insurance office if self-employed or if receiving a
state pension or are on other government benefit, motor and private insurance
companies (there may be a refund to come), National Savings certificates,
premium bonds, financial adviser if any, (if there is no financial adviser a bank or
solicitor will be able to ascertain the value of shares at the date of death),
passport office (return deceased's passport), DVLA Swansea (return deceased's
driving licence and counterpart and advise change of ownership of vehicle), and
any clubs or known associations (there may be a subscription refund). If a
season ticket for travel is held, there may be a refund. If the person was
receiving meals on wheels, these will have to be cancelled. Royal Mail may
need to be contacted to redirect mail. It will be necessary to cancel any hospital
or dentist's appointments, and return any hospital equipment that may have
been borrowed. Library books should also be returned.

A solicitor can handle many of the above, if he is going to be handling the
whole estate.

BEREAVEMENT REGISTER

The Bereavement register launched in 2000 is a service solely designed to
remove from databases and mailing files, the names and addresses of people
who have died. Coming to terms with the loss of a loved one takes time and the
last thing one wants is to receive mail addressed to a loved one who has
recently passed away. Registering with the Bereavement Register is free and
whilst a complete stop to all direct mail cannot be guaranteed, there will be a
significant reduction within six weeks in the amount of mail one's loved one
would otherwise have received. (The address is in *Appendix V and see also
advertisement in the middle section).*

THANKING EVERYONE

Everyone needs to be thanked after the funeral for their support at such a difficult time. The minister, the funeral director, those who sent flowers for the funeral, those who sent cards, did the flowers in church, did the catering, were stewards, lent cars or whatever. A printed card, suitable to be sent to everyone, can do this or it may help those left behind to respond to each person individually. If a printed one to suit all is decided upon, this can also be put into those newspapers that printed the notice that the service would take place.

Example:
Mary Jones, of Little Pangbourne, and her family wish to express their sincere thanks to you and to the many other friends, whose letters, cards, thoughts and prayers were a great comfort to them when John died in May earlier this year.

DISPOSING OF THE CLOTHES AND EFFECTS

Sometimes this is a very difficult task. One cannot bear to part with a favourite piece of clothing. The walking shoes always left beside the back door. An old dressing gown, a favourite sweater, a panama hat.

The family may be asked first whether they would like any of the clothes of the deceased. I remember one man who had six brothers; his suits and even his shoes fitted them all perfectly. They were soon distributed among the survivors.

Another man eight years after his wife had died still had all her clothes. When asked, however, he willingly donated them to a Samaritan jumble sale. Some of the articles had never been worn.

If no one in the family is interested, the clothes can be given to a charity shop, organization, or nearby hospice, to make money for their charity. If necessary, most voluntary organizations will collect.

Other close friends could be asked whether they would like a memento.

INTERRING OR SPRINKLING THE ASHES

Sometime after the cremation, if the ashes are to be buried with a headstone or a plaque engraved for a columbarium (a memorial above ground for interring the ashes of many people), a separate service may be held at the cemetery or churchyard. It is usually only the family who are invited to attend this ceremony.

If the ashes are to be sprinkled or kept in an urn at home or elsewhere, the ashes are handed over to the chief mourner, who will arrange to do whatever is required privately. The funeral director will be able to supply a variety of urns or boxes, if one is required. Everything from a cut-glass Waterford crystal bowl to urns beautifully made in wood, metal, etc. are available.

One funeral director given the job of sprinkling the ashes from a helicopter tied the urn to his wrist so that he didn't drop it! He said the turbulence made it difficult to shake out the ashes.

One person had his ashes put into a firework, which was let off with great aplomb and all the family present.

I heard recently of a friend whose father died first and she kept his ashes in an urn at home, then when the mother died the ashes of both of them were intermingled and buried together into the same grave, so that they would 'always be together' having enjoyed a long loving marriage.

Some people want the ashes sprinkled over a golf course or in a river. It is an offence however to sprinkle ashes in a public place or on a waterway without the relevant permission from the landowner or environment agency. But I believe there is nothing to stop the sprinkling of ashes on one's own land, in Great Britain.

Ashes may not be sprinkled in Germany but must be in a container and buried.

HEADSTONES

The chief reason for a headstone is to mark the location of the grave. The Romans introduced memorials and inscriptions to Britain. 'Thus churchyards may contain a priceless heritage of vernacular art, mirroring the contemporary social scene throughout the centuries.' (Geoff N Wright, *Discovering Epitaphs* Shire Publications).

Headstones are usually ordered after the funeral and placed in the ground when the soil has settled. The Church of England has specific conditions for headstones erected in churchyards, which may be different in each diocese. The vicar, rector, stonemason or funeral director will know exactly what is allowed in any given location.

A headstone for the cremated remains is usually smaller than that for a burial but is still restricted as to type of stone and lettering in Church of England churchyards. Welsh cemeteries are less restrictive.

There will be more freedom of choice in a municipal cemetery, where it is still possible to erect angels with wings or other figures, providing one can afford it, but the superintendent of the cemetery still has to give his permission for the desired design and wording.

A very heavy and elaborate memorial will mean waiting for six to twelve months for the ground to settle first. I remember seeing, in the last decade of the twentieth century, in an East London cemetery, a cement floor as large as a room, with a sculpted woman at one corner, dressed in modern clothes and hairstyle, and carrying a handbag. Her children set it up for an Italian mamma. Presumably there was room to inter the whole family in the years to come in this massive grave. Funeral directors often consider themselves memorial consultants, taking commission from a local stonemason, rather than making the headstones themselves.

The price of a grave usually gives one the use of it for no more than 100 years or sometimes for only 50 or 75 years.

One may choose to give a memorial seat instead of or as well as a headstone in memory of a loved one. This may be a good idea in the churchyard itself, on a village green or beside a village pond, along a river, or anywhere where people walk, or take their dogs for a walk, and may appreciate a rest along the way.

MAUSOLEUMS

Wealthy families in the past would build a mausoleum to house members of the family for generations to come. These mausoleums would be built either in the church or in the parish churchyard, which was often next to the stately home where the family lived.

One of the most spectacular was built at Castle Howard in 1731, so much so that Horace Walpole described it as 'a mausoleum that would tempt one to be buried alive'.

Some took up to half the area of the church, such as the Grey mausoleum at Flitton in Bedfordshire, built to house the Dukes of Kent, who lived at nearby Wrest Park.

A mausoleum surrounded by iron railings lies in a corner of Blunham churchyard, in Bedfordshire, (where the poet John Donne was the incumbent, and a Dean of St Paul's Cathedral, during the seventeenth century). This was to hold the bodies of the Thornton family who lived at nearby Moggerhanger Park (a Grade I listed building reordered by Sir John Soane from 1780 to 1820 with grounds laid out by Humphry Repton). Godfrey Thornton was at the time the Governor of the Bank of England and his son Stephen was also a director of the bank.

In the vaults in mausoleums, coronets for those entitled to wear them were often left on top of the coffin although in some an iron replica would be substituted for the original.

If there is room, current family members can still be interred in these buildings.

Modern mausoleums

Modern mausoleums in municipal cemeteries are made of concrete and look like a wall of very large pigeonholes. Each space is big enough to take a full-sized, lead-lined coffin and is sealed at the front with a marble plaque giving the name and birth and death dates of the person interred. When all the pigeonholes are filled a marble pediment is put on top (see photo in middle section). Spaces in this kind of mausoleum can cost £4,000 and they are very popular with some communities.

MONUMENTS

Many sculptors were engaged in the past to build monuments inside churches. These may take the form of marble plaques or life-sized models of people, either lying on their coffins (singly or as man and wife), or sitting up surrounded by angels and garlands of flowers, etc. The nearer the altar they were placed, the more important the family.

But burial within a church was condemned by sanitary reformers Southwood Smith, Walker, Chadwick and others in the nineteenth century as being an unhealthy practice.

Some of the grandest buildings in the world are tombs or monuments to the dead – the Pyramids, the Taj Mahal, the Castle of St Angelo, the Tomb of Cecilia Metellae to name but a few.

Many famous cemeteries have wonderful monuments, such as Père Lachaise in Paris, Arlington in the US, Glasgow Cathedral in Scotland and Highgate Cemetery in London.

There are other fine monuments in many of Britain's churches and cathedrals. Some of the finest in England that I've seen are in a small country church at Warkton, in Northamptonshire, where there are four by Roubiliac and van Gelder, the latter in an apse by Robert Adam. They are for the family of the Dukes of Montagu, and cover the period of the eighteenth and nineteenth centuries.

After the Victorian era, monuments were more restrained.

But even in this generation (first decade of the twenty-first century), a Cotswold builder, Roger Franklin, erected a 43-foot (13.11 metres) obelisk in his garden to commemorate his wife who committed suicide. It can be seen by all for miles around and is a monument to commemorate his grief in losing the woman he loved (reported by Bel Mooney in the *Daily Telegraph,* July 2000).

STAINED GLASS WINDOWS

In medieval times the stained glass windows in a church illustrated the parables and other biblical events, because most people could not read. Later some windows were designed as memorials or monuments to important people in the parish. This is still sometimes done in parish churches, and many churches installed a stained glass window to commemorate the passing of the millennium in the year 2000.

EPITAPHS

Inscriptions on headstones today in churchyards are quite restrained. Just the name JOE BLOGGS – the years of his birth and death 'held in affectionate memory by his wife – JANE and his children, EMMA, ASHLEY, SUSAN and PETER' for example is enough, or 'JOAN FORSYTH, darling wife of Roger. You died as you lived, everyone's friend.'

There is not usually room for long poems as was fashionable in previous centuries, and possibly not permission for this from the relevant authorities today. Neither are sentimental phrases such as 'Til we meet again' or even RIP (*Requiescat in Pace* – Rest in Peace) in fashion.

My own grandfather put this poem on my grandmother's grave in 1929; at least it showed his depth of faith in the resurrection:

Rest dear wife in gentle slumber, 'til the resurrection morn.
Then awake to join the number who its triumph shall adorn.

It was also common to have a moral theme:

As you are now, so once was I;
As I am now, so shall you be;
Therefore prepare to follow me!

An exception may be made today for a child's grave, in a civic cemetery, where I have seen:

Baby daughter, little sister,
Happy little angel be;
run and play in heaven's sunshine,
live and laugh eternally.

There is an interesting one at St Mary's, Witney dated 1789:

Released at length from cares and lingering pains,
Here peaceful sleep Maria's loved remains.

In her, the great Creator sweetly joined
the fairest body to the purest mind.
In charity she lived; in peace she died;
her husband's joy; her children's friend and guide.
Religion's path together here they trod:
together humbly hope to see their God.

Epicurus *(c. 341 – 270 BC)* wrote: I was not. I have been. I am not. I do not mind.

Sir Christopher Wren, who built St Paul's Cathedral in London, is buried in the crypt there. His son wrote 'If you would seek his monument "Look around you" '. This is inscribed in the floor of the Crypt.

Because Field Marshall Goering during World War II was reputed to be a stranger to the truth, there was a rumour going round at the time that his headstone just said 'Here LIES Goering'.

Lord Hailsham when asked what he would like on his tombstone, thought of his time as a defence lawyer and said, 'What about "The defence rests"? '

Robert Burbidge, an actor from Norwich, has 'Exit Burbidge' on his tombstone.

Jack Lemmon, another actor and film star has decided to have 'Jack Lemmon IN.'

Many an author may wish for Hillaire Belloc's: 'When I am dead, I hope it may be said "His sins were scarlet, but his books were read".'

DISINTERMENT AND REBURIAL

Once a body has been buried or the ashes interred, they may not be dug up again except by obtaining a Home Office licence and a Bishop's faculty (diocesan permission) if in consecrated ground.

If ashes are placed in a columbarium, or a body is placed in a mausoleum above ground, no licence is required for a retrieval.

PLANNING A MEMORIAL OR THANKSGIVING SERVICE

To live in hearts we leave is not to die.
Thomas Campbell

'Memorial services are the cocktail parties of the geriatric set'
said *Sir Ralph Richardson – Ruth Dudley Edwards – Macmillan 1983*

And it is true that memorial services can be great opportunities for people of like minds and experiences to meet together again for a reunion.

If someone is missing, presumed dead, it is difficult to have a funeral but there can be always be a memorial service.

If someone has been an important person in the eyes of the local or national community, it is appropriate to hold a memorial or thanksgiving service for them. The venue can be anywhere – a church, a school (if a teacher) or a hall or hotel, as appropriate. It usually takes place sometime after the funeral, so that colleagues and others who wish to pay their last respects can have more notice to arrange to attend. Notice of a month or more may be necessary in order to plan exactly what is required. The announcement for it would again be put in the local or national press, as appropriate.

The more important a public figure, the longer it may take to arrange, and the wider the circulation of the announcement will need to be and the larger the venue. August is not usually chosen because so many people are on holiday then. It is best not to have a winter remembrance service if the weather is likely to limit attendance.

The service itself will have more readings and eulogies. A number of people may be requested, or may ask, to talk about their memories and give a few anecdotes. Often there will be hymns and prayers and the relevant school or association song as well.

When Holly Wells and Jessica Chapman were murdered by the school caretaker, even Ely Cathedral could hardly contain those who wished to attend their memorial service in 2002.

At a recent memorial service the eldest grandchild read out the thoughts and memories from all the grandchildren who were living in Australia. 'When we were in England,' said the second youngest, 'we bought fish and chips wrapped in paper, then we took them back to the house and ate them off porcelain china with silver cutlery'! 'The youngest child said 'I think grandma is more English than the Queen.'

At the last thanksgiving or memorial service I attended, for a local minister, photographs were shown on an overhead projector of the deceased during his life from when he was a baby, through his teen age years, Bible college, marriage, etc. Several people spoke about how he had affected their lives both here and abroad, and a video was shown about his work in India and Kenya. Then a piece of Peter Sellers in *The Pink Panther* was shown, apparently one of his favourite films, and in between activities and at the start and end a silent film was shown of waves crashing on the sea shore. About half way through the service the widow announced that her husband's secret addiction was liquorice allsorts and so she had put a bowl at the end of each pew so that we could all enjoy some, and these were passed round. I felt very much that we had now moved seriously into the twenty-first century.

Refreshments usually follow the memorial or thanksgiving service, because people may have come from far and wide. Anything from a glass of wine to a full buffet would be appropriate but most people appreciate knowing in advance what has been prepared.

ANNUAL REMEMBRANCE SERVICE

Some hospitals have an annual memorial service for babies or children who have died at the hospital during the year or during the last two years. At one, a number of coloured helium balloons were released outside, one for each child, before everyone went inside for the ceremony.

Hospices (founder Dame Cecily Saunders) or the Sue Ryder homes often have a service once a year for those who have been bereaved during the previous 12 months. This helps those who have lost a loved one to come to terms with their loss and to move on.

Some gardens of remembrance have an open day and memorial service once a year for those whose family members are laid to rest there. One can visit and meditate on the loved one in peaceful and beautiful surroundings.

In France, and some other countries, on All Souls Day, many people go to the cemetery and place chrysanthemums on the graves, remembering all those souls who have already died. This is a countrywide practice, bringing much comfort to some.

I am told that it is becoming increasingly popular in churches to hold a memorial service on or about All Souls or All Saints Day each year for those who have been bereaved during the year. One Reader told me that she preached on these occasions about the journey of bereavement. It was essential to go through it and recognize the help that people have given them and with hope to come out the other side and move on.

Other countries have a 'day of the dead', where they celebrate in a way particular to their culture.

The Natural Death Centre in England has nominated a National Day of the Dead in April, with a co-ordinated open day at UK natural burial grounds, and a central London event.

There is an annual Remembrance Service at the Albert Hall in London attended by the Queen and members of the royal family, on the eve of Remembrance Sunday. It is in memory of all those who gave their lives for their country in all wars since the 1914–18 First World War. Most of the services and most denominations take part. At the end of the service a poppy for each person who died is released from the ceiling, taking some few minutes to float down to the floor. Someone from every Christian denomination takes part and recently different faiths are also included in the ceremony.

Remembrance Sunday

On Remembrance Sunday (the nearest Sunday to 11 November), there is a commemoration at London's Whitehall for those who died in war. Most regiments march past to the services bands, each laying a wreath of poppies on the Cenotaph. This ceremony is attended by members of the royal family and leading politicians from most parties.

WAR MEMORIALS

In the UK in most villages and many towns there are memorials with the names inscribed of those from that area who died in the First World War (1914–18). The names of those who died in the Second World War (1939–45), and the Falklands war have been added to some of these. These are remembered on Remembrance Sunday every year, when the local people hold a service round the memorial and place a wreath of poppies on it, 'lest we forget' those who gave their lives as a sacrifice for us all.

WAR GRAVES AND CEMETERIES

During a war numerous people are killed abroad. It has been the practice since the 1914–18 war to bury them on or near the site where a fatal battle took place. Rows of identical crosses identify those who have died and a chapel is often provided giving the history of the services to which the men buried there belonged. Many such chapels are works of art containing beautiful stained glass windows, statues, and engraved lists of those who have died and are buried there.

There is one in North Africa where 38,000 servicemen who fell at El Alamein are commemorated. Many others have been sited in Europe and Hawaii. Individuals come from all over the world to visit where their loved ones fell, and to commemorate their sacrifices. Often this is of great benefit to the bereaved, who find consolation in meeting others who have suffered in a similar way. It is comforting to know that the casualties of war have not been forgotten. There are organizations that arrange annual trips to visit these war cemeteries (see addresses in *Appendix V*)

The only cemetery in Great Britain for American servicemen and women who died in the 1939–45 second world war is a 30.5-acre (75 hectare) site near Cambridge, donated by Cambridge University. There are 3,811 headstones with either a Latin cross or a Star of David and these are laid out in great arcs across the landscape. The names of 5,127 people missing in action are inscribed along a wall 427 feet (130 meters) long. The magnificent memorial chapel is built of Portland stone. The cemetery was completed and dedicated in July 1956.

The last military funeral with full honours to take place there was in 2003. It was for a 23-year-old bomber pilot, 57 years after he was shot down and killed. His remains were found near the river Stour in the plane's wreckage (see photo in middle section).

REMEMBRANCE

Remembrance album

Some people will write letters or cards to the bereaved either before or after the funeral. Some will be of the 'with sympathy' type; others will be bright and cheerful looking to the future, according to the sender's view of death. All will be valued by the recipient and a great consolation in their hour of need.

Many people find it helpful to have these communications, together with the cards that came with the flowers, press cuttings, any photographs taken at the funeral, or photographs of the deceased, put into an album. To this can be added the names of those who came to the funeral, and those who donated in memoriam (a list is usually sent from the relevant charity). This album can be a source of great comfort in the months and years to come.

Gardens of remembrance

Gardens of remembrance may be in a churchyard, crematorium or elsewhere. Ashes may be sprinkled or buried in a 'garden of remembrance' with permission from the relevant owners, but there will be no headstones or individually marked graves. There may however be a space on a wall or on the ground to place a small memorial plaque (like those for naming rose bushes) at some establishments. It may also be possible to buy bulbs, shrubs or trees, which will be planted in accordance with the general layout of the garden.

One crematorium has a garden of remembrance divided into Spring, Summer, Autumn and Winter, so that on the annual visit a family may make to remember a loved one, the flowers there are at their peak.

The fee for dispersal of the ashes in a garden of remembrance may be something like £26 or if the cremation took place at another crematorium the fee might be £52. These figures may be increased if it is desired to witness this event.

Memorials (if allowed at these gardens) may be in the form of vases, wall plaques, or kerbstones and can costs hundreds of pounds in granite with gold lettering. A donation for bulbs could be a cheaper option and very attractive. Each site will have its own system of costs, so it is advisable to visit the site and view the options, so as not to be surprised at a later date.

After the funeral of a friend called Meg, a Meg rose was sent to each household as a thank you from the family for their support at a difficult time, and as an ongoing remembrance of the person who had died.

Book of remembrance

A 'book of remembrance' is available at most cemeteries and may be the only memorial for cemeteries where there is just a garden of remembrance. There is usually a one off charge for each insertion, priced according to how many words or characters are used.

After the person's name and other details they may say something such as 'A beloved wife, mother, grandmother and sister' or 'Treasured memories, always', or 'Lived and remembered always,' or 'Peace after pain, rest after weariness.'

I have seen even short poems:

'Your tears held the sweetness of summer and spring,
for you were our world, our everything.'

and

'Sad are the hearts that loved you,
silent the tears that fall,
living our lives without you
is the hardest thing of all.'

Many churches have a book of remembrance where those who have died in the parish are recorded. The book is then left open at the appropriate month each year, so that mourners can see that their loved ones are not forgotten. There is not usually a charge for this but a donation may be appropriate.

Memorial forests

Originally launched by the late Queen Mother in the north of England, 'Life for a Life' charity involves planting a tree to commemorate a loved one. There are already memorial forests in Cumbria, Lancashire and around the Greater Manchester area. Bedfordshire and Buckinghamshire are expected to be next. The money raised will go to help hospitals, hospices and other health charities. The scheme is for all people regardless of creed, race or status. People can bury the ashes of their loved one under a tree in a memorial forest.

With more woodland, our oxygen levels will be renewed and those trees with berries will feed the birds in winter.

Other forms of remembrance

Keeping photographs, a box or book of remembrance with all sorts of mementoes in it of a past life together can be comforting, and should be encouraged, especially for children (see *Chapter 7*).

Another way of remembering someone, who has been a good cook, is to publish a recipe book of his or her favourite recipes. This can be handed down the generations for the family to cherish as they remember family occasions when these recipes were used and enjoyed.

But to keep a room 'just as it was' when someone has died is considered not very good for the mental health of the one who is left. Life is for the living, not remaining in the past with a beloved who has 'gone ahead', 'passed on' or 'died' however much that person meant to the one who is left.

'They spend their time looking forward to the past!' John Osborne says in *Look Back in Anger* 1956.

Chapter 8

THE LEGALITIES

*For we brought nothing in to the world and we can
take nothing out of it. 1 Timothy 6:7*

THE WILL

A Will is a legal document, which stipulates what the deceased wants to happen
to his/her estate (property, money, possessions) after his/her death. It must have
been made by someone over 18 years old and of sound mind. It must also be
validated (i.e. dated, signed and witnessed by two people at the same time, the
witnesses not being beneficiaries of the Will). If at some future date the Will is
disputed, it may be necessary to find the signatories and ask them to swear that
the Will is genuine and has been witnessed in the correct way, i.e. that they
actually saw the person sign the document in their presence.

The Will usually gives the names of one or more executors (see below), who
will be responsible for seeing that the wishes in the Will are carried out. It may
also include a list of the person's assets (possessions), and a list of the
bequests (the gifts to be made to relatives and friends).

Any change in marital status can invalidate an existing Will. Therefore, after
marriage, remarriage or divorce, a new Will should have been made, dated and
signed in the proper fashion.

If no Will can be found, it may have to be assumed that the person has died
'intestate', which means without having made a Will.

INTESTACY

If someone dies who has not made a Will, or the Will is not a valid one (i.e. has
not been signed and witnessed by two people over 18), this may cause great
complications for the survivors

Any surviving spouse is currently entitled to the first £125,000 (2004) if there
are children, and £200,000 if there is no issue but parents and brothers and
sisters.

In Scotland, the wife or husband and any children have a right to one third of
any estate, excluding that comprising buildings or land.

In the case of intestacy, letters of administration are issued. These can be
obtained from the probate office and the fee will be the same as if there had
been a Will (£90 in 2005 or nil if the estate is less than £5,000).

Then the Personal Representative can share out the estate according to the
rules that cover the rights of a surviving spouse, children, parents or any other
dependants or close family. Verbal promises may not be honoured without going
to a court of law.

If there are no blood relatives, or dependants, the Crown may have the right to the whole estate. The Treasury Solicitor's Department (BV) will deal with this (see addresses *Appendix V*).

READING THE WILL

At some point after the funeral, the Will is read. This is done either informally if everything is left to one person e.g. the surviving spouse with small bequests elsewhere, or formally by a solicitor if a lot of money and several people are involved. If a solicitor is handling the whole estate, he will do everything necessary after this, keeping the family or other executors informed.

For finding the Will when someone has died see *Chapter I*. For how to make a Will see *Chapter 11*.

EXECUTORS

It is the executors' job to find out the value of the estate, by liquidizing all the assets i.e. turning them into cash unless specifically donated to a specific person, or obtaining their value on the day of death in the case of stocks and shares and property; paying any outstanding bills (electricity, gas, water, telephone, tradesmen's bills), and paying for the funeral. Subscriptions will have to be cancelled and any moneys due back on cancellations of insurance, club fees, etc., received.

Tradesmen usually expect to have to wait a while before being paid from an estate, once a person has died; but when a death has been notified in the local papers, there may be a rush of bills that come in so that their claim is not forgotten.

The executor is also responsible for getting probate and for paying any inheritance tax (see below). Income tax on earned or unearned income whilst the deceased was alive will have to be paid, and any capital gains owing from the same financial period will have to be accounted for. If the deceased were an employee paid by PAYE, there may be a refund of income tax.

Once all the tax and outstanding bills have been paid, the executors (one of which may be a solicitor or bank) are in a position to distribute the bequests, whether money, furniture, paintings, jewellery, etc. If some beneficiaries wish to obtain any of the other assets before they are sold, as part of their share, this can be agreed with the executors and the other beneficiaries.

PROBATE (GRANT OF REPRESENTATION IN SCOTLAND)

When a person dies, it is necessary, by law, to go to a probate office, in order that the validity of the Will can be proven (get confirmation of the estate in Scotland) and that the government can decide what tax and inheritance tax if any is due to it.

It is not necessary to engage a solicitor for this, particularly if the estate is small, but if no one else is able or willing, a solicitor will take on the task for which service there will be a charge. It is quite in order to obtain an estimate from one or more solicitors, before engaging one, and the fee usually comes out of the deceased's estate. The solicitor's fee is based on the time taken to obtain probate, and is therefore likely to be more if the deceased's affairs are very complicated.

If one does it oneself, the current fee for getting a grant of probate in 2005 is £90 (unless the estate is less than £5,000 when the fee is waived). But the probate office will only charge a solicitor £40. Certified copies of the grant are £1 each. These must be obtained before anything can be distributed to the beneficiaries. Normally an executor will perform this task but if none is available then a widow, widower, child, parent, brother or sister, other more distant relative or someone with an interest in the residuary estate can apply. Illegitimate offspring and their relatives may not apply for a grant of probate or representation, except sons and daughters of the deceased, if there is no one else. Form PA2 from a probate registry, or from the Citizens Advice Bureau, will explain the procedure if a solicitor is not engaged. It could take several weeks and entail more than one visit to the probate office.

A personal visit is necessary – probate is not something that can be done entirely by post, but forms can be obtained by post from the probate registry (not a probate office) nearest to the probate office of one's choice. These should be returned to the probate registry together with a death certificate, any written Will (keep a copy yourself and send the original by registered post) along with the completed forms. No other bankbooks, share certificates, etc., should be sent at this time. If a probate registry is nearby, the forms can be handed in personally. On receipt of the completed forms, notice of an appointment will be sent to the applicant. It will take place at the probate office requested by the applicant on the forms, which can be nearest to where the applicant lives, not necessarily where the deceased was living.

At the appointment, one needs to have on hand a **list of the assets** of the deceased, including property (at the full current market value), house contents, jewellery, cash, bank balances, building society balances, stocks and shares (at value on date of death), any amounts payable on death from insurance companies, arrears of wages or pension, any arrears of rent if a landlord, any other money owing to the deceased, over payments on household bills if paid in regular amounts by direct debits or standing orders, National Savings certificates held (showing date of purchase and value at date of death), etc.

A corresponding **list of liabilities** of the deceased must also be ascertained and will include the cost of the funeral; any household bills outstanding (gas, electric, water, telephone, newsagents, milk), mortgages due, taxes due, including inheritance tax (if estate is over £275,000 [2005] see below), and other money owing, etc. Some items may be on hire purchase. If more than a third of the purchase price has been paid, the item cannot be repossessed without a court order, but the balance of the purchase price will have to be paid out of the estate.

To arrive at the **value of an estate**, the liabilities are deducted from the assets.

Donations to registered charities, or to a political party, in a Will are free of inheritance tax.

The applicant will have to swear at the probate office on the Bible if a Christian, or the Qur'an (Koran) if a Muslim, that the Will is the last Will and testament of the deceased and that all the information that has been given is true. If of no religious faith the applicant is asked just to affirm that what they have said is true.

The required fee, if any, will have to be paid before the grant can be issued. The grant will be sent to the applicant by post, after the interview.

The grant of probate or grant of representation is issued to the person named in the Will as the executor(s) and proves that the person(s) so named is/are entitled to receive the assets of the deceased for distribution according to the Will.

If there is no executor, letters of administration are issued by the probate office to the personal representative or administrator such as a solicitor, who is prepared to deal with the Will and its distribution. After a divorce, the previous spouse is not able to be the personal representative. After remarriage, the former Will is null and void.

Usually before an insurance company, bank, stockbroker, or any other asset holder will release goods or money, he will need to see the grant or letters of administration and sometimes the death certificate. The same will be necessary before a house or other property can be legally transferred to another party or sold. Companies expect to see an original grant, a copy is not acceptable, but they usually return it promptly, so not many original grants need to be obtained. The grants are not valid unless they bear the impressed seal of the court.

INHERITANCE TAX

I am told that most people die with an estate not in the inheritance tax band, despite the fact that house prices have gone up. If there is no inheritance tax to pay, each person mentioned in the Will, would get the full amount or proportion due to them, after all bills, tax and solicitor's fees have been paid.

For the tax year 2005/6 inheritance tax at 40% must be paid on an estate over £275,000. In the tax year 2006/7 this will go up to £285,000 and in 2007/8 to £300,000.

The amount can vary with each successive budget produced by the Chancellor of the Exchequer. In August 2004 it was rumoured that inheritance tax was going to be only 22% for the first £25,000 over the nil tax band and that it would be raised to 60% for estates worth over £750,000 but this has not yet come into force (2005).

If inheritance tax is applicable, this will have to be paid within six months of a grant of probate or of administration being issued. For this reason it is often necessary to sell shares, if there are any, at an inconvenient time (such as when at their lowest level), because these can be disposed of more readily than say property or some other assets.

There are ways to limit the amount of inheritance tax payable if thought of whilst making a Will (see *Chapter 11*, Preparing for one's own death).

EFFECTS OF INHERITANCE TAX ON A WILL (2005)

This is an example of a Will of a widower with assets of £350,000 (after all debts and legal fees have been paid), three children, six grandchildren, an old housekeeper, a younger sister, a mother-in-law, and who gives regular donations to four charities, who stated in his Will that his money was to be distributed in the stipulated proportions as follows:

	Balance
Total assets to be distributed	£350,000
Donation to four charities in equal proportions of £7,500 each = £30,000 leaving	£320,000

(Note this £30,000 would otherwise go to the government, not to one's family)

Tax on £320,000, less £275,000 i.e. on £45,000 @ 40% = £18,000 leaving	£302,000

Dividing £302,000 into six equal portions = c. £50,333 each
    1 portion to Child 1 outright
    1 portion to Child 2 outright
    1 portion to Child 3 outright

2 portions divided equally between the six grandchildren = c. £16,777 each

1 portion divided between the sister 50% = (£25,166.5)
the mother-in-law 30% = (£15,099)
and the old housekeeper 10% = (£5,033)
the remaining 10% = (£5,033) to allow small bequests to household staff, gardener, friends and colleagues in the percentages stipulated in the Will.

N.B. When the time comes, if the estate is worth double this amount, the recipients would get less than double (because the inheritance tax would be much larger) but if the estate is only half the amount, then everybody would get more than half the above because there would be no inheritance tax to pay.

Chapter 9

GETTING IT RIGHT!

Life is a great surprise. I do not see why death should
not be an even greater one. *Vladimir Nabokov 1899 – 1977*

AVOIDING SHOCKS AND SURPRISES

Announcements

Obituaries are prepared in advance for famous people by writers familiar with
their lives, and kept in reserve for the day of their death. In order to be first with
the news, some media people have in the past not taken enough care to check
the details. As when Lord Colyton was announced dead, when in fact it was Lord
Coliston who had died.

Time magazine in 2000 published an obituary of Lord MacKay and showed a
picture of an entirely different Lord. It was supplied erroneously by a picture
agency.

One should not be too flippant, like the man who sent a telegram to his
siblings when their mother died 'Regret to inform you, hand that rocked the
cradle, kicked the bucket!' Anon. Ned Sherrin *in his Anecdotage 1993.*

A man died and the remaining brother asked the local paper to put in 'Forsyth
of Berkhamstead, dead'. The girl taking the notice said, 'you can have six words
for the same money'. He thought for a bit and then added, 'Volvo for sale'!

'The thought of death has now become a part of my life,' said Neil Simon
(Last of the Red Hot Lovers, 1970). 'I read the obituaries every day just for the
satisfaction of not seeing my name there.'

Mark Twain was reported dead in 1897. He immediately replied in print: 'the
reports of my death have been greatly exaggerated'.

Bob Hope's death was also announced whilst he was still alive, but
prematurely publishing someone's death is considered to be unforgivable. It is
enough to give them a heart attack and carry them off!

Hearses, limousines, cars

A friend of mine was executor for someone who had died in Cornwall. The only
stipulation was that the hearse should be a Rolls Royce. Apparently his mother
had gone in a Rolls Royce to the hospital to give birth to him, but he had actually
arrived early and been born on the way. So having entered the world in a Rolls
Royce he requested that he go out the same way. There were none to be
obtained in Cornwall at the time and one had to be brought from Devon for the
occasion.

The funeral director usually knows the way from the church to the
crematorium as it is followed very often. However, if the funeral director has had

to take the deceased from his own region to another, less well known area, because the family want to have him buried in his own home town, then it is a good idea to give the undertaker a good street map of the new town. Once a procession of twelve or so mourning cars went in and out of a Tesco's car park, to the amazement of the shoppers, because the lead driver took the wrong turning at a roundabout. Many shoppers may have thought that it was the manager of the supermarket that was being buried.

Sometimes one funeral will be late, due to a road accident or other adversity, which causes a delay in all the funerals following that day.

When my husband died, the funeral director luckily discussed the route with me, 'We shall go along Bromham Road and then down Gold Lane to the church' he said. 'Oh No!' I replied, 'we always went to church down Day's Lane and through the village' and so the route was changed at the last minute. I would have been mortified if he had not said anything and we had proceeded to the church in the 'wrong' direction. It is important to make sure everyone who is involved gets the whole picture to avoid surprises. (Day's Lane was a private road but as we had a house there at the time, we were allowed to use it.)

Another shock was to see my husband's car on the way to the church, as though he had come to his own funeral! As it was a company car, some of the staff had arrived in it and had parked it before the service near the village church.

I heard of one mourning car which went into the back of the hearse in front of it on a motorway exit road, because the hearse had stopped unexpectedly without warning (as some cars do). The mourners were thrown into the glass screen behind the driver. Hearses nowadays have aluminium bodies, so that not much damage was done but the mourners were a bit shaken.

The late Dave Allen has pictured in his TV comedies a coffin sliding out of the back of a hearse on a steep slope, and this, I have reliably been told, has actually happened on more than one occasion.

Cars are known to have punctures (more so in the past). Funeral cars are no exception, and all carry mobile phones today in order to summon help, and to give advance warning of any delay to their destination (church or crematorium). Modern hearses may have a built-in jack to facilitate changing a wheel. At a VIP funeral, there may be a back-up hearse in the procession, in case anything goes wrong.

At one funeral the hearse backed into the following limousine early on in the day, so that the rear door could not close properly. The funeral director had to tie the rear door of the hearse together with string. On arrival at the church he had to untie the string again, with as much dignity as he could muster.

On another occasion, the funeral director had a heart attack during the procession. As it was a family-run firm, the wife continued with the funeral as though nothing had happened, whilst her husband was rushed to the hospital.

Some hearses have 'SAD' 'RIP' or similar letter number plates, which some people may think adds to the tone of the whole event. One firm has 999 as part of all the number plates on cars and hearses, although you might think that it is a bit late for 999 once the person is dead!

Flowers

The flowers should be anchored to the coffin, if being taken into the church. When my father died, I ordered a wreath in the shape of a bird, because my father was a bird-watcher. The florist produced an owl. It was not anchored on to the coffin and 'flew' into the lap of my mother, the widow, who was following the coffin into the church in a wheelchair!

Floral tributes may not carry the name that everyone recognizes for the deceased. The person may be called by one forename by the family, another by his wife and a further name by his work colleagues. This can create a problem for the funeral director, with wreaths arriving in different names for several funerals on the same day. My own husband throughout his life had been known as Robert, or Bob or Dickie (short for Richards). The service sheet said Robert (Dickie) Richards.

Mistaken identity

On the morning of the funeral, when the funeral director came to our house, he said, 'Mrs Hurn'? No,' I replied, 'I am Mrs Richards, the deceased's wife.' As my friend, Mrs Hurn, had gone to register the death for me and had signed the form, the funeral director thought that we must be a couple living together, rather than being married, because the names were different. This caused a temporary shock.

One officiate was asked to take a funeral at the crematorium for a family he did not know. When he began the service he talked about a man who had died and one of the mourners called out, 'she was a woman!' He was given the wrong papers at the crematorium (although the right body), which caused a delay and was very embarrassing for all concerned.

It is most unlikely, but it has happened, that there are two 'Smiths' (or any other common name) being buried or cremated on the same day. Once a coffin with the wrong 'Smith' was taken to the church for a funeral. The unscrupulous funeral director said, 'Lets just take the name plate off and bury him, then change the name on the other coffin when we get back. No one will know.' However the bearers insisted that this was not good practice and there was a considerable delay whilst the right coffin was fetched. This is another reason for going to a reputable firm of funeral directors.

A previous vicar in our village arrived to take part in a ceremony at the local crematorium and he saw that the previous funeral was for a Dorothy Richards. He said to the churchwarden, 'You didn't tell me that Dorothy had died.' 'Well,' she said, 'I saw her this morning, so I assume that this was not her. It must be someone with the same name.'

Premature burial or cremation

There is a condition where a person goes in to a coma. There is no pulse and the person is pronounced dead, only to wake up in the mortuary! This has happened to one woman more than once and is the fear that most people have – being buried alive. This is less likely to happen when the body is kept for a few days before burial, and I am assured that this cannot happen nowadays.

Some people feel they would like to take a bell with them into the coffin, in case they 'wake up' – they can then draw attention to their plight by ringing the bell. This was sometimes done in previous centuries.

Some want to take a few coins with them into the coffin, in case they really do have to pay the mythological Greek ferryman!

Thomas à Kempis, who wrote the Christian classic *The Imitation of Christ*, when exhumed to be made a saint, was found to have scratched his coffin lid all over in a desperate bid to be rescued. He was clearly buried whilst still alive. They never made him into a saint!

Premature death

Doctors usually know when someone has died but one doctor was examining a patient and decided that he was too late. 'I am afraid he is dead,' he said to the man's wife, whereupon the man whispered, 'No, I'm not, I'm still alive'. 'Keep quiet,' said his wife, 'don't contradict the doctor. He knows best!' (reported in *The Reader's Digest*).

Burials

Once the wrong grave was opened up for the husband's burial to follow some years after the burial of his wife. It was only after the family had departed that it was noticed that this was the wrong grave. The minister rang the funeral director and arranged for it to be transferred to the proper grave the following day. Fortunately it was discovered before the grave was backfilled after the committal.

Another girl, who was claustrophobic, was buried in a glass coffin, so she could 'look out'.

A couple were known to be dying within a few months of each other, so the children naturally assumed that they would be buried in the same grave. However, the mother who would likely die first screamed through the morphine 'I've not had your father on top of me for 30 years and I'm not having him on top of me for eternity!' The children felt obliged therefore to bury them side-by-side, a much more expensive option. (From *Home Truths,* Radio 4, 21.4.2001.)

At the funeral of a young person, a dog was allowed to be present as they had been inseparable in life, but someone fell over the dog at the service and fractured his own skull.

Occasionally a bearer or minister has fallen into the grave because after rain the soil is wet on the edge. This can be avoided by making sure the edges of the grave have wooden supports covered with artificial grass.

Once there were two open graves close together, one was left ready to receive the body, the other covered over with grass and nothing else. One of the mourners fell through the grass into the other grave, much to the amusement of the other mourners but, needless to say, the person who fell in was not at all amused.

On one occasion the coffin split when a heavy person fell on it.

It is advisable for the funeral director to make sure that the grave is large enough for the coffin that has been ordered. Probably more than once the wooden shuttering had to be removed and the grave enlarged before the coffin could be lowered into place.

On another occasion when it came to the burial, the grave was found to be full of water.

Crematoria

The coffin had been placed on the catafalque and the people had filed in to the chapel. Then a knocking was heard and a voice calling, 'Let me out.' Everyone, including the minister, was shell-shocked. Had they imagined it? It came again, a knocking and then a voice calling, 'let me out.' There was no mistake. The coffin was lifted off the catafalque and a head came up from underneath, 'thank goodness for that,' said the workman, 'I was just fixing something under there which had come adrift.' Everyone breathed a sigh of relief and the funeral proceeded.

Catholics often put Mass cards onto the coffin before it goes through the curtains to the cremator. Once a man came rushing back having already reached his home to say 'by mistake I left an envelope containing £50 for the priest on top of the coffin, with my mass card, 'is it too late?' Unfortunately it was and the envelope had been burnt along with the corpse! (From *It's You Minister* by James Martin, Nuprint, 1990.

Once the wrong body was cremated, which theoretically is impossible, but it is recorded as a fact.

Others have not wanted to have the lid on but coffins without a lid are not accepted at a crematorium. Having a hatch so that the face was visible but when removed to the cremator, the hatch was slid across, it made a suitable compromise.

It was recorded in the national press that at one crematorium, when the service went on too long, the people were turned out in the middle of it, because their time was up and several more services were to follow that day. It is important to know what time is allotted and to stick to it, or to book a double slot.

When the curtains are drawn before the coffin is moved out of sight, it is necessary to stand clear. Once the curtains wrapped round the priest as well.

Cremated remains – ashes (known in the US sometimes as 'cremains')

A coffin is usually 6 ft x 2 ft (182 cm x 61 cm), so it is often a shock to see the ashes being delivered in a smaller box only 9" x 3" (22.5 cm x 7.5 cm). How could he or she have shrunk so much?

Often people keep their loved one's remains at home. I once called upon a woman whose husband had died the same day as my own, 'There's Bob,' she said, pointing to an urn in the fireplace. She subsequently married again. Then he died. She now has two urns, one on each side of the inglenook.

And a bishop once showed me the remains of his grandmother kept in a jar in his filing cabinet!

You can scatter the remains from an aeroplane. One funeral director said you should be careful if you go for a walk and get a speck of dirt in your eye. You won't know who it is!

It is reputed that one woman made her husband's ashes into an egg timer. 'He was a lazy so-and-so when he was alive, he might as well do something useful now he's dead! ' she had said.

During the war, people in England were used to getting food parcels from abroad. Something arrived at one family that looked like soup powder, so they made it in to soup and consumed it. The next week a letter arrived saying, 'we hope you received Aunt Maud's ashes, which we sent by airmail last week.'

The service sheet

If there is time, the proofs should be corrected. One sheet had 'Lead us LOT into temptation'! Another had *1 Cor. 5*, which is about immoral sexual behaviour, instead of *2 Cor. 5*, which is much more suitable to be read at a funeral or thanksgiving service.

Calling on the bereaved

Ministers usually call at a house where they know someone has died, to offer comfort and a listening ear and most people are happy to talk lovingly about the deceased. Occasionally however there is an exception. One called at a house saying, 'I am so sorry to hear of your mother's death,' only to be told, 'Well you're the only one who is!'

Another widow when called on by the vicar to know what to say at the funeral was told, 'I hope you're not going to say anything good about him. He was an absolute bastard'.

Career prospect

When someone went to a careers advisor, they fed into the computer that the girl was strong, sympathetic, serious and sensitive. The advice came out that the girl should become a funeral director! Was this considered a 'dead end' job?

Double families

More than once a second family has turned up at a man's funeral, unknown to the first wife and family. Bigamists don't usually let either family know about the other. In the 1950s there was a stage production called *The Amazing Mr Pennypacker*, who it turned out had a family in New York and a family in Pittsburgh, neither of whom knew of the existence of the other. He was a travelling salesman. The play was based on a true story.

Not updating a Will

It is important to update a Will every so often.

A friend died at 94, she had no immediate family left, they had all predeceased her. She told everyone that she wanted the person who had looked after her for the last three years to have the house, and she indicated that certain friends were to have a picture, mirror, etc. The month before she died she spent some time closeted with her solicitor and everyone thought she was updating her Will. However, when she died only an old Will was produced, leaving nothing to the person who had looked after her to the end. Bequests were left instead to her helpers who had left her service years before and not visited her since.

COMPENSATION

At one London funeral the bearers arrived late and obviously drunk. The priest in charge advised the family not to pay for the funeral and indeed they were given a refund.

I am reliably informed that if anything goes wrong with a funeral, wrong announcements, flowers or service sheets late, etc., then financial compensation is usually paid, either by the funeral director or the person ultimately responsible.

COMPLAINTS

The Office of Fair Trading says that 96% of people are satisfied or very satisfied with the service they receive from funeral directors. If for some reason something does go wrong with the funeral arrangements, one should first contact the funeral director. It may have been his mistake or the caterer's, or someone else's. He will usually be able to sort it out. If not, the Citizens Advice Bureau may be able to help.

There is a National Association of Funeral Directors Conciliation Service (80% of funeral directors belong to this organization). But if all else fails, one can consult an independent arbitrator. Names can be obtained from the Chartered Institute of Arbitration (see useful addresses in *Appendix V*).

SUMMARY

Things can go wrong when planning a funeral, as evidenced in this chapter, but the great majority of funerals progress beautifully and are a fitting tribute to the deceased person everyone has come to pay their last respects to and to bid farewell.

Chapter 10

FACING THE WORLD AGAIN

Grief is not forever but Love is. Anon.

The future is that period of time in which our affairs prosper,
our friends are true, and our happiness is assured.
Ambrose Bierce 1842–1914 – The Cynics Word Book (1906)

COPING WITH BEREAVEMENT AND GRIEF

There are approximately 640,000 deaths a year in the UK out of a population of over 58 million.

To lose a family member or friend may be a very traumatic, numbing experience, even when, after a long illness, death is expected. Sudden death can be even more traumatic. There is the feeling 'I didn't even have a chance to say "Goodbye".'

There are recognised stages that one may go through at these times and it may help to realise that these are normal reactions for most people. Denial, anger, guilt, depression, loneliness are all normal although not everyone may feel all of these. We may feel disbelief – 'I just cannot take this in. It cannot be happening. Not to me!'

Perhaps one will be angry with God or with someone else one thinks was responsible, rightly or wrongly. 'How can God let this happen?' Or 'how can God do this to me?' may be a frequent response. I remember one widow in our village being very angry because having sent all her children off to college, she was now able to go on exciting business trips with her husband, and she was looking forward to this enormously, after having been housebound for years. Then her husband had a heart attack and died suddenly, whilst still quite young. She felt absolutely cheated out of what she considered to be her just rewards.

Some are incapacitated by guilt, 'Could I have prevented this? Was there more I could have done for that person?' Or by regret – 'If only I had gone to see her.' 'If only I had told him that I loved him.' 'If only we hadn't quarrelled last time we met'. In families there are usually faults on both sides. It is too late to ask forgiveness from the deceased but one can still ask God or others for forgiveness where appropriate. And we can determine to love more those who are still with us.

There may be feelings of despair – we will miss them so much! Or we cannot possibly go on living without them. There may also be a feeling of numbness and loneliness – 'I miss him or her so terribly.' 'The central point and purpose of my life has gone.' And 'I cannot cope by myself.' Many people feel that the death of a loved one is akin to amputation.

When we hear of the death of someone we love, our feelings of loss are coloured by the realization that we shall never see that person again in this life.

We have to cope with an unwanted change in lifestyle, one we would never have chosen for ourselves.

Taking time to grieve, to realize that one has gone through the mill emotionally and that the body needs to come to terms with it all is very natural. Take one day at a time. It is not a sin to weep; in fact crying has great healing power and helps to release tensions. Grief should not be stifled. It is all right to weep, despite the stiff upper lip some of us have been brought up to display during adversity. We are told that it is better to grieve than to repress one's feelings. 'To weep is to make less the depth of grief.' *William Shakespeare.*

But circumstances affect different people in varying ways. Some feel that some things are just too deep for tears. If someone does not weep, it doesn't necessarily mean that they do not care.

Grief is not a disease requiring a cure but a temporary state of mind. Most people recover in due course. It is not helpful to the healing process to leave a room 'just as it was when he or she was alive'.

Constructive thoughts can be acceptance, hope and thankfulness. Remember the good times – some things have been lost – but be thankful for what remains. If religious, spending time with God can bring much consolation.

It is a good idea to share how one feels with a sympathetic friend or neighbour. It will not bring the beloved back, nor take away the pain but it does help. 'A trouble shared is a trouble halved'. One should try to guard against bitterness and self pity. 'Why me?' But 'why not?'

Once one can gather up the confidence to go out – one may see the back of a loved one and be sure it was all a mistake and there he or she is! Same figure, same clothes, same hat! Hallucinations like this or in dreams soon fade but are troubling whilst they last.

At home, one may continue to lay the dining table for two, before remembering. This is quite natural – one isn't going mad.

Occasionally, even months after, a memory will be kindled that reduces one to tears. This is to be expected. Personally I was deeply moved if I found a piece of paper with my husband's handwriting on it. Was he still writing me letters?

When we lose a loved one, our relationship has been severed but it is somewhat restored through the grieving process. One has to work through it; there is no magic formula for getting rid of the pain. Family and friends may rally round at the beginning but when the funeral is over and they have all gone away, it may take some time for the realisation to sink in that there is a new but different life to be lived.

People may say 'time will heal' or 'if there is anything I can do'. Do not resent them – they are only trying to help. Their attitude should be 'I will stay if you want me to or I will go if you want me to, just tell me what you want'. Let them know you need their help and their friendship at this time. Let them cook, shop, walk the dog, change the beds, meet the children from school, or do any of the things that need doing but that one cannot face one's self. Everyone will feel the benefit, not least the helpers. And remember no one is perfect. The helpers may get it wrong. Try to be patient, loving, forgiving, and thankful.

If a couple are too self-sufficient and keep out all other friends, it will be harder for the one who is left, than if they had had a larger circle of friends. In the twenty-first century a man left on his own is more fortunate in one way because people are always looking for a man to make up numbers, whereas most areas have a surfeit of lone females.

When someone dies it is the end of an era – life will certainly never be the same again but life does go on and one can be happy again, even though perhaps in a completely different way and in a way that one may not otherwise have chosen. Often by comforting someone else at this time, one feels better oneself. Keeping busy is another help in disguise. It takes one's mind off oneself and one's own troubles, whilst the process of invisible healing is taking place.

It is a good idea to get in touch with old friends, to take up a new interest that one has not had time for before but always wanted to do. To join an evening class, learn a language, learn to paint, to play bridge, play golf, go to bingo, invite someone in for tea, for a drink or even a meal, go to church.

People's reactions to the bereaved vary. Some avoid meeting them because they do not know what to say. C S Lewis in *A Grief Observed* puts it:

'I am an embarrassment to everyone I meet. At work, at the club, in the street, I see people as they approach me, trying to make up their minds whether they'll "say something about it" or not. I hate it if they do and if they don't... Perhaps the bereaved ought to be isolated in special settlements like lepers.'

The Turkish people, when there has been a death in the family, say '*Basinitz sag olsun*' or 'May *your* life be spared.'

GRIEVING FOR A BABY

In miscarriages (before 24 weeks of pregnancy) and in still births (after 24 weeks of pregnancy), the parents' hopes are shattered, especially the wife's because she has carried the baby for months within her and the bonding with the child has suddenly come to an end. The husband has not bonded with the child so much before birth but it is necessary for them both to share their grief at this time. At either stage, the parents may want a naming ceremony, to help them cope with their loss. If it is a still birth, it may be a good idea to remove the pram and baby clothes and toys from the home, before the mother returns from the hospital, or at least to put them out of sight.

GRIEVING FOR A CHILD

Death devours lambs as well as sheep. *English Proverb*

In the natural order of things, children should bury their parents. For a parent to bury a child is much more of a tragedy and not something we expect.

Some parents never get over the shock of losing a child and all that it means for the future, it affects their lives forever after. They may be feeling very depressed or desperate. They have both loved the child for months before he or she was born but now it means there is no future for that child, such a waste, no wedding, no son or daughter-in-law, no grandchildren, it is the end of so many dreams. This can be hard for the parents to bear. They have lost a part of themselves, regardless of how many other children they produce. That one child will always be remembered and loved. It is unique.

One father whose two children were burnt to death in a fire describes his grief:

'I think I was actually mad then – crazed with grief and filled with a blind despairing anger at the knowledge that what had been taken from me could never be restored.'

'You wake each morning filled with absence; with the sensation that all of your existence has evaporated except for an immense heaviness, which is both yourself and the crushing weight of your loss. For relief you begin to cry. In time you get up, shower, dress – eat even; but all the time with the feeling that none of these things is possible any more. You wander through the house picking up objects at random and putting them down again. You weep intermittently, perhaps for a few seconds, perhaps for ten or fifteen minutes.'

'You wring your hands because there is nothing else to do with them. From time to time you have an attack of trembling. Then the house becomes claustrophobic, so you drag yourself out in to the garden; and from the heart of the vast emptiness you now inhabit, you see the material world looking just as it always has but somehow transformed, somehow beyond – a world in which (it seems) you no longer have any place. (John Tittensor, published in *The Guardian*.)

The special poem in the readings in *Appendix II 'I'll lend you for a little time a child of mine'* is a great comfort to some people at this time. Children are only on loan to us for their lifetime.

Parents are vulnerable at this time. They may be drawn together more after sharing the loss of a child. Alternatively they may begin to blame each other, and the marriage falls apart, ending in separation.

DEATH OF A SCHOOL FRIEND

If a young school friend has died, one's own children can be encouraged to write to the parents, saying how much they valued their child's friendship. Or if a school friend has lost a parent, one's own children can be asked to be especially kind to the bereaved child. It is a chance to explain that sorrow and sadness are a part of life. Most children can accept anything as long as they are sure that somebody loves them.

LOSING A PARENT

If children have lost a parent, they may not to want to go out, in case the other parent disappears too. They should not be kept in to keep the other parent company. Eventually they must be persuaded to return to a normal routine, and to become independent adults.

If a child has lost one or both of its parents, the grandparents, or another sibling or cousin, may be called upon to take over the bringing up of this child. It should be someone who will show a great deal of love and concern for the child, who will be in a very vulnerable state.

Even if one is an adult when a parent dies, there will be a sudden unwelcome change, 'they have always been there'. It is the end of an era.

Sometimes a mother and daughter can be life partners, if the father dies very early when the only child is a baby, and the daughter never marries. I remember such a case. The mother and daughter had lived together for 60 years, longer than many marriages. The daughter was 60 when the mother died but there was no corresponding support from friends and family like there is when a man or woman loses their other half. People thought she was making too much of her grief. 'Everyone buries their parents in due course!' was the general unsympathetic opinion. This poor woman eventually succumbed to ME for a number of years, unable to cope with the grief and loss that others were unable to understand. The same could happen with a father and son or daughter.

WHAT TO SAY TO CHILDREN WHO ARE BEREAVED

It is important for a child to understand about death. It helps to point out that all living things die, such as plants and animals. After so many years the body just wears out. No one knows when this will be. Some people get sick first, some just go suddenly. Not everyone who gets sick dies. It is all a mystery. Most people live a long time but occasionally a young person may die.

Winston's wish (a child bereavement association) suggests that one should throw any question back at a child when they ask a question. 'Well what do you think?' This helps them to think about what has happened and be clearer in their minds.

Children need to know that everybody is born into this world and that sooner or later they will also depart from it, and then they won't feel pain anymore. It is not necessarily anybody's fault when someone dies, least of all the child's, although some feel guilty about this because of something they said or didn't say or did or didn't do, just before the person died.

They need to know that the person who died was loved and will be very much missed. And that he/she loved those who were left behind. Of course it is sad to have to say goodbye to someone we love, but this sadness will not last forever.

If one says, 'We've lost Grandma,' they may expect Grandma subsequently to be 'found'. If one says, 'Grandpa is gone', the child may also expect him to 'come back' at some time in the future.

If one says 'Mummy has gone to sleep', this may make them afraid to go to bed at night. It may be the reason many people say, 'Mummy is now with Jesus', even though some people believe that we sleep in the grave until the resurrection (which may be the next conscious moment, even though many years hence). It would be hard for a child to take this in, because they cannot imagine being outside time and space, as we know it.

Children may feel abandoned by the person who is no longer there, so it is important to say something to the effect that he or she would never have left them, had it been their choice. Even if it were a suicide, one can say that 'Daddy truly thought that they would be better off without him'. The time of death is something none of us have any control over.

After the funeral, children may find it helpful to make a 'memory box' about the loved one (see Winston's wish below).

Doris Stickney has written a lovely little book *Water Bugs and Dragonflies*, explaining death to children. By using the analogy of the water bug's short life under water as man's time on earth and their emergence as dragonflies into the bright sunlit world above the water as man's life after death, she conveys her belief that life's most basic truths are found in a simple story.

Other books recommended for children are *When Dinosaurs Die* by Marc Brown and Michael Rosen's *Sad Book*, illustrated by Quentin Blake.

DEATH OF A SPOUSE OR PARTNER

According to the *Holmes-Rahe Social Readjustment Rating Scale,* losing a spouse or partner is the most stressful thing that can happen to anybody. It has a value of 100 in life changing units. Compare this to the addition of a new family member at 39, and change in residence at only 20.

In addition a person may find they have lost their cook, housekeeper, laundress, children's nanny, chauffeur, gardener, odd-job man and friend, as well as their lover. These amount to major losses and will be difficult to handle.

One should not feel disloyal when one begins to enjoy one's self again. This is what one's spouse or partner would have wished.

LOSING A PATIENT

If someone has nursed a patient through a long illness, no longer having to do this can be a real difficulty for some, 'I am not wanted by anyone anymore.' The answer may be to find someone else to look after, who needs plenty of care and attention. There is an association of Care for the Carers, which may help (See *Appendix V*).

ROAD TRAFFIC ACCIDENTS

If there has been a fatal road traffic accident, there is an association called Roadpeace, that may be able to help. (See *Appendix V*).

KEEPING UP ONE'S HEALTH

Many people have reported that they have felt physically unwell for as long as two years after the death of someone close to them. Any disease that is latent may be brought to the fore by shock. Hence people report the onset of arthritis or diabetes, headaches, dizziness, chest pains, backache or depression, which never troubled them before, or that come on in a more concentrated form. If the symptoms persist, a doctor should be consulted.

Most people feel very tired for some time; others may feel hyperactive and feel they must be doing something. Some want to sleep all the time or cannot sleep at all – or dream a lot – either bad dreams, or dreams in which the loved one is still alive and they are enjoying life together again.

It is important to eat properly at this time, although the effort to do so may seem insuperable. One may lose all appetite, but not eating a balanced diet will bring on further complications. Resorting to drugs or alcohol instead is tempting but is not a good idea.

It helps a woman's self esteem to make her face up, have her hair done and to dress well each day.

'There is no cure for birth and death save to enjoy the interval.'
George Santayana

One needs to exercise but also to take plenty of rest. They used to say 'if you cannot sleep, start counting sheep' but Christians say, 'don't count sheep – have a word with the Shepherd'!

SHOULD ONE MOVE HOUSE?

Decisions on whether to move house, or to go and join another part of the family in another part of the country, or abroad, should not be taken lightly or quickly, but be left until a balanced decision based on all the relevant facts can be made. One has to think very carefully about moving in with relatives. They may only want a built in babysitter. This could end up making one feel used as well as unloved.

Moving house immediately means taking one's grief with one. It is better to remain where friends can call and help through the worst of the grieving period. Inviting someone to stay as a guest will mean that certain regular chores will have to be done, which will form part of the healing process, and help to alleviate any depression.

If the mortgage was not paid on the death of the spouse, or if the remaining spouse or partner was left unprovided for, or cannot pay the rent, then in some circumstances it may be necessary to move. The local council has to provide accommodation if anyone, or a family, is actually homeless.

GETTING A JOB

Younger people may decide to alleviate loneliness by getting a job. It is a start to decide where one's talents lie. Perhaps for example in cooking, flower arranging, sewing, secretarial work, book-keeping, child minding, hairdressing, computing, selling, nursing, cleaning, carpentry, gardening, window cleaning, driving, decorating, washing, ironing, looking after old people, writing, teaching, etc.

I knew a girl who was left with three young children to bring up and she put all of them through public school by making and selling cakes and opening teashops.

Starting a business from home may require a licence. The Citizen's Advice Bureau will give advice. If one works, will one lose some state benefits? The advantages and disadvantages have to be considered. Will one earn enough to cover engaging a child minder? And what about the school holidays? Someone else I knew took a job as a school secretary and so she was able to have most of the school holidays at home with the children.

If one wants to work but cannot get a job, then one may be entitled to a Jobseeker's allowance.

It may be a better idea to let one or more rooms in the house, on a 'bed and breakfast' basis, if space is available. £3,000 per year can be earned in this way without paying tax on the income (2004). One can also charge for wear and tear, etc. A good tenant would be a business person in the area, who went home at weekends. Or a teacher or students, who went home for the holidays. Having another adult in the house could be a comfort if anything went wrong. Having a lodger would have to be on a business footing, with a proper agreement and a rent book. If the house is rented or has a mortgage, it may be necessary to get permission to sublet. A landlord is quite capable of putting the rent up if he or she thinks an extra person is moving in. It would also alter the council tax position, if the lodger were not paying full council tax at another address.

OTHER WAYS OF COPING FINANCIALLY

If one is aged 45 or over when one's spouse dies one may be able to get a bereavement allowance. It will depend on one's age and the age of one's spouse when they died and the national insurance contributions paid. If one is 55 or over one will get the full amount of bereavement allowance for a maximum of 52 weeks. It will stop when state retirement pension becomes payable. It is claimed on form BB1 and must be claimed within three months of the date of death.

It is also possible to obtain a widowed parent's allowance if one's spouse dies and there is at least one child or one is expecting a child. This is also claimed on form BB1 and must be claimed within three months of the death of the spouse.

If one is too old or unable to work, local authorities can arrange services that help people to stay in their own homes after bereavement. They may provide home help with household tasks or home care to help with bathing and dressing. They may be able to arrange 'meals on wheels' for those who are unable to cook, or invite one to join lunch clubs and social clubs or day care centres for company.

Income support or council tax benefit may be available if less money is coming in than before.

SEXUAL DEPRIVATION AND REMARRIAGE

This may be a very real problem for some, particularly in the early stages of a marriage. It is not only the sex but also the hugs, kisses and caresses that are now missing. 'To have and to hold 'til death do us part'. For the Christian it is not the answer to have casual affairs. But everyone needs some tender loving care. Remarriage may be the answer for some and is usually much easier for widowers than widows. People often remarry within five years and sometimes in only two. A great deal of adapting and tolerance is called for. It will not be the same as before. One must have realistic expectations. And having stepchildren second time around can be really difficult for both the man and the woman. But there is no need to feel disloyal to the first marriage. If there are stepchildren on both sides, then it is a good idea to discuss beforehand what disciplines will be enforced, which must be the same for the children of both partners, what pocket money will be given to all, etc. It is also a good idea for all to move into neutral territory, rather than to have to share with others what one considered as one's own space.

OTHER HELP FOR THE BEREAVED

It may be comforting to know that help is available for those who appear to be inconsolable and unable to cope. There are a lot of organisations able to help those who have been bereaved (a list of relevant addresses is found in Appendix V).

CRUSE, the National Organisation for Widows and their Children, arrange counsellors to call, or arrange for people to meet others, who have been bereaved in a similar way, to share their problems, in a relaxing venue. Many areas have drop-in centres. This has proved to be very therapeutic for many people. All the counsellors are volunteers and training is supervised and is given to a professional standard. The counselling is free but a donation would be welcome, if possible.

Cruse is reactive, not proactive. They support for as long as it takes. e.g. official mourning for Sikhs should only last for 15 days, which is too short if someone is responsible for a death and cannot get over it. I heard of one Sikh man who killed a child accidentally by hitting him with a golf club. He needed a lot of help (from Cruse in this case) in order to get through this particular death, which took a long time.

ROADPEACE exists for people bereaved by road accidents.

WINSTON'S WISH was started by clinical psychologist Julie Stokes, to support bereaved children and young people up to the age of 18 and their parents or carers. They help children to understand death and what it means for them, to understand their feelings, to meet with other families with similar experiences, to find ways of remembering the person who has died, and in encouraging families to talk openly together. There is a residential camp for children aged 4 – 18 years with social activities, and simultaneous weekends for parents and carers.

They produce a range of publications and resources, including a very special idea: 'a memory box' where children collect photographs, letters, etc., as a memory store of the person who has died.

Recently they are offering specialist group work for those bereaved by suicide, murder or manslaughter.

THE CHILD'S BEREAVEMENT TRUST also caters for children who have lost a loved one. And there is a CHILD DEATH HELPLINE at Great Ormond St Hospital.

VICTIM SUPPORT may be the people to turn to if a death has been caused by violent behaviour of any kind, possibly more frequent in today's society.

The SAMARITANS, set up originally to help people tempted by suicide, will give a listening ear to anyone suffering from grief of any kind.

MIND The National Association for Mental Health may be able to help.

RAINBOWS set up by the Catholic Church, started off as an informal organisation for child bereavement and then included adults.

SANDS The Stillbirth and Neonatal Death Society exists to comfort parents who have lost babies at or before birth.

The Society of COMPASSIONATE FRIENDS gives help to bereaved parents and others after the death of a child or children. They arrange local group meetings, one-to-one visiting, and a range of publications.

Not all counties have a joint collection of bereavement societies which get together to offer mutual support but Bedfordshire does have a BEREAVEMENT FORUM, which includes a Council of Faith (all religions), A Child Bereavement Service, Compassionate friends, Cruse, the hospices in the county, Road Victims Trust, SANDS, Victim Support and the local hospitals.

Some funeral directors have a bereavement service and the church can act as a kind of godparent and perform a caring role comforting the bereaved.

Some churches have a visitor who will follow up a funeral by visiting the bereaved person or family, where there is felt to be a need. There is a visitor who calls on the widows of clergymen in each diocese in the Church of England.

Hospital chaplains of all denominations comfort the bereaved, often at the bedside or by taking them to the hospital chapel or café or elsewhere to talk.

HELPING THE BEREAVED ON A PERSONAL BASIS

'The true way to mourn the dead is to take care of the living
who belong to them.' *Edmund Burke*

If one knows someone who has suffered bereavement, this is the time to befriend him or her. Most bereaved people are stunned for a while and welcome visits, cards or flowers as a gesture to show that they are cared about and that someone is thinking of them.

Letters of condolence, mentioning some of the special memories that thinking of the deceased brings to mind, can bring a great deal of comfort to the person left behind. They will read them over and over during the healing process. Photographs will also be very much appreciated, recalling happier times.

One should not stay away because one doesn't know what to say. Resist the temptation to give advice. Just sitting listening can be of great value, as is being encouraging on the progress made. One might enquire whether the person has any huge worries at this time (e.g. like being short of cash).

Practical help is often a great service to offer. Making food dishes or a cake, (don't leave it on the doorstep – at the least hand it in), taking the children off their hands for an afternoon, taking the dog for a walk or to the vet, offering to go shopping for them, do the washing or the washing up, the ironing, filling up the car with petrol, offering to baby sit, mowing the lawn – or whatever else needs doing – will be greatly appreciated by the majority of people. Any handy person can offer to do those little jobs about the house that invariably need doing.

One can invite the bereaved for a home cooked meal. They may refuse at first, not trusting themselves not to break down in company but they need to get out of the house eventually, so be persistent.

There are many poems and readings in *Appendix II*, which may be a great comfort to the bereaved in varying circumstances. I often find myself copying out a particular poem and sending it to someone when they are faced with one of the hardest things we are asked to bear – that of losing a loved one.

Be assured that there will be a future for each of us when bereaved. It is not the end of the world just a change of direction. Happiness can and usually will still follow.

Chapter 11

PREPARING FOR DEATH

Death surprises us in the midst of our hopes.
Thomas Fuller 1608 – 1661

It matters not how a man dies but how he lives. The act of dying
is not of importance, it lasts so short a time. *Samuel Johnson 1709 – 1784*

WHAT IS DEATH?

Medically death is a natural process. For many years the body renews all its cells daily but at some time whether from old age, disease, or injury, the body is unable to continue to repair itself and ceases to function. This is called death.

Death is the common lot appointed to man, animals, plants, etc. Everything that has life will one day die. Death is inevitable but most of us do not know whether we shall live to be 100 or die next week. Perhaps it is good that we do not know but it is always good to be prepared. It could be later than you think! 640,000 people die each year in the UK alone; 50 million a year die globally.

There are preparations we can make in advance to make our dying less traumatic for those who are left behind.

MAKING A WILL

The only way to ensure that one's family and other dependants are properly catered for is to make a Will. If there is a marriage, divorce, a beneficiary dies, a new child is born, or new tax legislation is introduced a codicil can be added or an entirely new Will made. This need not be expensive, if one has it on computer (see below).

A man working with old people says:

'I suddenly understood that you really, truly can't take it with you. I don't think I ordinarily grasped the full implications of that. Just look at all the possessions a dead person leaves behind: every last one, even the most treasured. No luggage is permitted, no carry-on items, not a purse, not a pair of glasses. You spend seven or eight decades acquiring your objects arranging them, dusting them, insuring them, then you walk out with nothing at all, as bare as the day you arrived.'
From *A Patchwork Planet* by Anne Tyler (1998)

My favourite sketch of the *Two Ronnies* (Ronnie Barker and Ronnie Corbett) was when, as two tramps, they were discussing a friend who had died. One said, 'How much did he leave'? The other replied, 'All of it. You have to'!

In Scotland, one is not allowed to cut the family completely out of one's will. The wife or husband and any children have a right to one third of the estate, other than that comprising buildings or land.

A surviving spouse or any other dependant person cannot be left entirely out of a Will.

A common-law wife could formerly inherit as though she were a wife, providing the couple had lived together for a number of years. This has recently been revoked, so that couples should either marry to regularize an association or definitely make a Will in favour of the person with whom they live. The same is true for cohabiting homosexual couples, or friends or relatives sharing the same dwelling.

Verbal promises may not be honoured without going to a court of law.

One sometimes hears of some of the survivors contesting the Will, and it taking years to sort out, with the solicitors being the only beneficiaries in the end. This could be guarded against largely by making sure that everyone does make a Will, whatever age they are, and that one is very specific about what one wants to happen to one's possessions after death.

Intestacy (i.e. not making a Will)

If one does not make a Will, one cannot be sure that one's loved ones are protected. Indeed the money may not go to the person one wishes to benefit after one's death.

Therefore it is surprising that 90% of people still do not make a Will. They probably think that there is plenty of time, but it may be 'later than one thinks'. One could live only another two months or twenty or more years. It is wise to make sensible provision.

Princess Diana made a Will even though she was so young.

My second husband did not make a Will; although aged 72 he thought there was plenty of time, and it took seven years for the solicitors to sort it all out! Do not let this happen to one of your family.

THE SOLICITOR

It is necessary to see a solicitor the first time a Will is made, unless the estate is so small and there is only one beneficiary, then a simple form, which can be purchased at any stationers, may suffice. Many people feel that they have nothing to leave, but the house market has risen so much in recent years that it is likely, when everything is added up, that the estate will be larger than one thinks.

It is advisable to telephone one or more solicitors to find out how much they will charge for making a Will. Some advertise a flat fee for any Will. Others will charge according to the time it takes, depending on how complicated the Will is.

Before going to the solicitor, it is best to write down on a sheet of paper, one's own name, address, telephone numbers, e-mail address, etc.; find birth certificates, marriage and divorce certificates, and write down any previous names, etc. One should also list one's bank, mortgage provider, financial adviser if any, pension provider(s), any death-in-service benefits, and all one's assets and liabilities, because without these the solicitor cannot word your Will correctly. Before visiting the solicitor it is also advisable to list everyone to whom one might like to leave something, together with his or her full names, addresses and telephone numbers. These are the beneficiaries of the Will. If the solicitor is also going to be made an executor, his task will be made much easier if he has all this information in advance.

Assets are one's home, any other property, car(s), furnishings (carpets, curtains, antiques, and pictures), silver, jewellery, and any other items of value. Also any financial interests, such as bank accounts, building society deposits, stocks and shares, pension benefits, National Savings certificates, premium bonds, property jointly owned, and insurance policies giving a death benefit.

Liabilities are any mortgage(s), loans, hire purchase agreements, credit card debts, any other money owed, bank overdraft, any tax due (inheritance, income and council) and any other debts (household accounts, telephone, electricity, gas water) etc. The cost of one's funeral and any other expenses will also be a liability, which will come out of the estate.

The estate – Taking the liabilities from the assets gives a fair idea of what the value of the estate will be on death, and will be the amount that will be free to be distributed, as specified in the Will, to one's family, friends.

One may also want one's death to be announced in various specific newspapers or trade journals. These details can go into a letter to one's executors, rather than into the Will itself, to make things easier for the person arranging the funeral.

Usually with a couple, each will leave everything to the other, with the exception of personal bequests.

One may want to put aside something for children's or grandchildren's education, or to leave something particular to each child, grandchild or friend, such as a piece of jewellery, silver, painting, property etc.

Special provision should be made in case a couple dies together in a road, rail or air accident. This will ensure that the children's upbringing and school fees are provided. Guardians should also be stipulated. It is a good idea to ask friends or other members of the family in advance, whether they would be prepared to look after the children in such a circumstance. It should be someone the children like and trust.

One may wish to provide for an elderly parent or other dependant.

Executors are usually chosen whilst making the Will, and should be those who can be trusted to act efficiently and honestly. Anyone can be an executor (sometimes a female may be referred to as an executrix) and they must be mentioned in the Will as such. It is advisable to choose executors younger than oneself and likely to survive one. Sometimes it is members of the family and sometimes it may be one's solicitor, accountant, bank manager, financial adviser, or trusted friend, etc. It is advisable to have two, in case one dies. They can be beneficiaries of the Will (whereas the people witnessing the Will cannot). They need to be people who can handle a complicated issue, if there is for instance a business to sell, or several properties to dispose of. If the solicitor is chosen to be an executor, this will relieve others of the responsibility but often takes much longer before any of the money or effects can be distributed.

Trustees – If money is left 'in trust' for someone, it is usually because the recipient is thought to be too young to inherit a large sum of money or a property. Trustees should have been appointed in the Will. But if this is not the case then trustees, will have to be found, who will be responsible for seeing that the principal (capital amount) ideally increases rather than decreases, until the recipient is old enough to inherit.

It may be stipulated that the beneficiary should only receive the income, not the capital, from the estate or part of it, during his or her lifetime. Trustees will manage the estate meanwhile, until the person receiving the income has died. The capital would then go to the person stated in the Will.

If the trustee(s) is/are a professional body, it is able to charge a fee for this service. Non-professionals, such as family members, are not allowed to profit from such a service.

The Will, if professionally drawn up, will also state what is to happen to any person's share of the estate, if that person predeceases or does not survive the deceased by 28 days.

Codicils are legal alterations to a Will, made subsequent to its being signed and witnessed. It saves the cost of remaking a Will if some small item needs to be added or altered. It is important not to alter any original document oneself, which could invalidate the whole Will. If a solicitor was used to prepare the original Will, it is better to let him or her prepare the codicil. Codicils also have to be dated, signed and witnessed.

Distribution of the estate – Some people, thinking that their estate is substantial will list several legacies of several thousand pounds each… 'and the residue to…'. When it comes to it, and times and circumstances have changed, it may be that there is no residue. The estate may have dwindled considerably over the years, or the person may die at a time when share prices and property values had fallen disastrously, as in 2002. For this reason, it may be better to divide the estate into several portions, and then if all the bequests have to be scaled down, everyone gets the same proportion of the will (see example below). However, it is best to state an exact amount that it is intended to leave to a charity, to avoid legal disputes about the percentages of the Will.

Types of legacies – One can leave a specified amount of money or a percentage of the estate – this is a pecuniary legacy; a particular piece of property, jewellery or a picture – which is a specific legacy; if the residue after all bequests, taxes, debts and expenses have been paid is left to someone, this is known as a residuary legacy. A reversionary legacy is one where the capital is held in trust for someone but in the meantime a partner, friend or family member has the use of it for life or the income from it for a specific time. In this case there may be a fee for someone to manage the trust.

DONATING ONE'S ORGANS AFTER DEATH

This is not usually practical unless the person dies in hospital, because no organs can be removed until the body is declared clinically dead, the death certificate has been signed, and the family have given their permission; and if the coroner is involved this can delay matters further.

Normally arrangements have to be made before death, the relevant people have to be told, and the arrangement recorded in the Will, which the surgeon will want to see. If one is serious about leaving one's organs, one can put oneself on the NHS Organ Donor Register and carry a donor card.

An application for a driving licence carries an opportunity to fill in a form giving voluntary permission for organs to be removed after one's death. One can also register on line (see addresses *Appendix V*).

The British Medical Association would like it to become law that there is 'presumed consent' to use someone's organs on death, unless they have 'opted out' by registering their objection to donation whilst still alive.

In the eighteenth century, corpses were regularly cut open by a surgeon at death, and various organs removed in the interest of medical research.

LEAVING ONE'S BODY TO MEDICAL RESEARCH

For which bodies are accepted for medical research see *Chapter 1.*

If it is desired to leave one's body to medical research, it is necessary to get the forms from HM Inspector of Anatomy. (See address *Appendix V*). There are two forms – one pink to be retained by the London Anatomy Office and a yellow one for the Medical School to which the body is sent. Both will ask the person to agree to the body being used for anatomical examination and retention of parts of the body after the examination is concluded. The medical college accepting the body will want to see the death certificate and a copy of the consent form, which should be kept with the Will. There will be a charge for transporting the body to whichever teaching college agrees to have it.

DISPOSAL OF THE BODY

At the end of a Will, it is usual to state whether the person wishes to be buried or cremated. If a burial, where the coffin is to be interred or if a cremation, what is to happen to the ashes.

INHERITANCE TAX

I am told that most people die with an estate not in the inheritance tax band, despite the fact that house prices have gone up. If there were no inheritance tax to pay, people mentioned in the Will, would get the full amount, or percentage, due to them.

For the tax year 2005/6 inheritance tax at 40% must be paid on an estate over £275,000 (£300,000 from 2007). The amount can vary with each successive budget from the Chancellor of the Exchequer. A good solicitor should be able to advise on ways to minimize inheritance tax but it is difficult to divest oneself of all assets prior to death, for two reasons. One – at what age will one die? Two – as one gets older there may be a greater need to pay for hospitalization and home care, which is becoming more expensive.

In the case of a man and wife, if one dies the assets pass to the survivor and no inheritance tax has to be paid until the survivor dies. The couple is treated as one until both die, so that the surviving spouse is not turned out of the marital home in order to pay the tax. This widow's exemption however cannot be passed on to the children.

In order to avoid excessive tax when the second one of the couple dies, up to £275,000 (£300,000 from 2007) can be given away on the death of the first, and will not count as part of the survivor's estate, even if the wife or husband does not survive for seven years, thus claiming the threshold free of inheritance tax on both lives. On a large estate even more can be disposed of if given to charity or a political party.

Another advantage can be gained by a couple considering equalizing their estates, including their house, (all assets owned half each), before a death occurs and the one who dies first leaves the bulk of their estate to the children.

Each person can give £3,000 to a son or daughter or grandchild getting married. One can also give £250 away to as many people as one wants every year. For larger amounts any tapering rule to the seven years survival does not apply until the nil tax band has already been given away.

Forming a family trust may be the best way to go for some people. Oliver Wendell Holmes famously said 'Put not your trust in money... rather put your money in trust'.

Capital gains can be mitigated on second homes or business assets too, if thought of in advance but everyone's needs are different, so it is best to seek professional advice.

Any arrangements made however need to be flexible i.e. able to be changed if not found to be suitable, and realistic bearing in mind that one must still leave enough to live on. One also needs to make sure that one understands the full implications of any plan offered before signing it.

Further information on inheritance tax may be obtained from the Capital Taxes Office (see addresses *Appendix V)* or from a solicitor or a financial planner.

GIFTS TO REGISTERED CHARITIES

Most charities rely heavily on legacies for their income and the advantage is that this money is currently free from inheritance tax (2005). This is money that might otherwise go to the government, on death, if the total estate were over the inheritance tax limit.

Some charities such as Age Concern have a book of dedication as a tribute to the loyal supporters who have left them a legacy. A dedication card is sent to the person who has indicated that they will leave a legacy to their charity. One can add a message or just sign one's name, and these are put into a book, which is available for everyone to see at the charity's offices.

A form for donating to a charity could be something like this:

> I wish to give the following charitable legacies and I declare that the receipt of the Treasurer or other Proper officer for the time being of the legatees shall be good and sufficient discharge to my executors:

To the charity (name)..... Registered No. ... of (address) the sum of £.....

SUMMARY TO MAKING A WILL

The solicitor will see that the wording used in a Will is not ambiguous (having more than one possible meaning) and that the Will is legal in every respect, dated, witnessed and signed.

If one is computer literate, it is still advisable to consult a solicitor in the first instance but after that if the Will is put on a disc it can be changed as circumstances change without further charge, but beware of introducing illegal terms. Any new Will must be re-dated, run off, signed and witnessed each time, and the old Will destroyed.

Having made a Will, it is important to leave it with the solicitor and an executor or to leave it in an obvious place, with the caption, 'to be opened only in the event of my death'. Sealed copies of the Will can be given to trusted family members if desired.

It is also a good idea to leave a list of persons to be informed at one's death. This can be updated regularly as the Will is updated, because people die, move house and change names (e.g. on marriage) etc. Any Will should be updated regularly, at least every five years.

Sometimes it is expedient that no one knows what is in one's Will.

One person left a request that someone should take her cat when she died, making sure it had all the love and care and companionship that she had given it during her lifetime. It was not to be put down. Many friends, family and neighbours were asked to take it in but they all refused. Finally a lonely widow was found who agreed to take the cat. It was love at first sight for both of them and they settled down into a cosy future. After a month of domestic bliss, the solicitor called to make sure all was well and that the cat had settled in. When he was quite sure that everything was acceptable, he told the widow that £20,000 had been left to the person who had made a home for the cat!

Another person left '30 pieces of silver' to an unfaithful former wife, which took the form of 30 x 50p pieces or £15 (fifteen pounds).

OTHER PREPARATIONS ONE CAN MAKE

It is a good idea for couples living together to learn each other's tasks, so that if left alone, the survivor can still function without too much upheaval. Both should learn how to cook, to change a fuse, to cope with bills, some house, garden and car maintenance, etc.

It is also a good idea to have separate bank accounts or at least a joint bank account or savings, so that the one who is left can still draw money out for various sundries, until the estate is settled.

One woman was desolated at her husband's death and because he had dealt with all the financial side of the marriage, she found that she hadn't even enough money to provide a funeral tea for the relatives who were coming from far away.

If one partner feels that they may be incapable of handling their financial affairs in the near future, it is a good idea to give the other partner, or someone else whom one knows to be trustworthy, **an enduring power of attorney**. A solicitor can handle this. It means filling in a couple of forms, whilst the person who is relinquishing power is of a sound mind and agrees with the process.

Some people make a cassette recording to the family, or even make a video before they die, so that future generations can know what their grandparents or great grand parents looked and sounded like. They may also store images on a computer.

LIVING WILLS

A living Will is a document giving instructions about how one would like to be treated when not able to communicate at any time in the future, such as being unconscious, in a coma.

It is usual to state that one does not wish to be resuscitated or that one does wish to be kept alive at all costs, and force fed or etc.

PLANNING ONE'S OWN FUNERAL

Queen Victoria planned her own funeral and had her effigy made at the same time as her husband Prince Albert's, so that they could always be together. A previous Archbishop of Canterbury, Dr Robert Runcie, planned his own funeral and the practice is becoming more popular.

It is necessary to give these details to a person one can trust, in case it is not discovered until after the funeral has taken place. One can decide in advance where the service is to take place, who is to officiate, and where the wake is to be held. Hymns and readings can be chosen, and who is to do the readings and give the eulogy; whether to have flowers or donations, etc. Or one can simply say 'I do not want any kind of service, I just want to be buried in a woodland site.'

Some people produce a service sheet, which can be completed and sent to the printer on their death when all the other information and the date of death are known. Deciding on the form that one would like one's funeral to take could be helpful to those left behind.

PAY NOW – DIE LATER – PRE-NEED (PREPAYMENT) FUNERALS

It is not necessary to pay for any funeral in advance, although this is becoming a popular thing to do. In either case the funeral expenses are taken out of the estate before inheritance tax is calculated.

Prepayment funerals have become fashionable. They were introduced into the UK in 1985 by SCI (US), and by the year 2001, 300,000 people had prepaid their funeral costs. Now many firms can offer prepaid funeral schemes. Help the Aged have a scheme, which also agrees a benefit to the Woodland Trust, who will plant a tree for each person prepaying for a funeral.

The price one pays is exactly the same as if the funeral were today and no extra charges will be imposed for the service one has paid for, however long it is before the funeral takes place. This is because the money is put into a trust fund, run by a bank or insurance company, or other reputable company, who manage the money until it is required. The interest gained will cover the rate of inflation, for however long before death occurs. One of the largest trust funds is run by the Royal Exchange, with J P Morgan as investment managers and Price Waterhouse Coopers as auditors. Help the Aged use Lloyds TSB and Baillie Gifford. One can also pay by instalments over five years.

No funeral director is paid for carrying out a prepaid funeral until the funeral has taken place. They are usually paid within 21 days of the trust receiving an invoice.

The average cost of a funeral in the UK (in 2004) is £1,200 according to the location (compare this with 1970 when it was £95.17s.6d and a century ago when it was £1) but there are various levels of funerals offered and a choice can be made. The costs will vary as to whether it is a burial or a cremation and the kind of coffin or casket ordered, how many cars are required, and flowers, music, etc., can be specified.

When the person dies, the funeral director stipulated in the funeral plan (or chosen by the person arranging the funeral), will carry out the funeral as it has been booked and paid for. There is nothing more to pay, unless some additional item or items are requested.

If one wishes to cancel the arrangements there may be no charge if using Help the Aged. SCI, after 28 days, would retain the set-up fee. It is advisable to note the conditions on the application form in question.

If the person or company with which one has taken out a prepayment funeral goes into liquidation, then another funeral director will take over the agreement.

If the person who has taken out the prepayment plan moves to another area, the plan can be transferred to another funeral director in the new neighbourhood.

Plans usually cover the cost of transporting the body from anywhere in the UK, so there is no worry if one dies away from home.

If a funeral has been prepaid, a copy of the agreement should be attached to the Will or given to a trustworthy person.

There is a National Association of Prepaid Funeral Plans, who has a code of practice (see address in *Appendix V*).

PROS AND CONS OF PREPAYMENT

Some of the selling points are that there is an inflation-proof guarantee, so that the funeral will not cost more than it did when you paid for it, unless somebody adds more details that were not stipulated at the beginning; that it takes pressure off the family to make any decisions when the time comes, because the deceased has already agreed the kind of funeral he (or she) would like to have.

However, if one particularly wanted a certain firm to do the funeral and the owner died, the funeral could be given to another firm that one would perhaps not have wanted. Also the money invested now in a prepayment funeral plan comes out of the capital that could generate income whilst one is still alive.

All these things need to be considered before making a final decision. Certainly it would be wise to shop around before signing with any particular scheme (see useful addresses *Appendix V*).

The alternative could be to put aside the cost of one's funeral into a special bank account placed in trust for a survivor. On death the survivor can withdraw the money on proof of death and identity. In the US this is known as a Totten Trust. One can also take out a policy with an insurance company, so that money is available on death for a survivor.

HELP FOR THE DYING: HOSPICES AND PALLIATIVE CARE CENTRES

Hospices have a valuable role comforting patients during their last days and in comforting the bereaved families thereafter.

It is good practice not to move a family member or visitor away from the deceased too quickly after death but to allow them to sit with the person they have lost for a while to make their last goodbyes.

In 2005 there were more than 300 palliative care teams in Great Britain with over 2,800 beds, about 40,000 people being treated during the year. 96.4% of people treated were white, most living in the London area, the age ranges were 6% under 24, 46% 24–65 (mostly females), 48% 65–84 and 6% over 84.

Out of the 27,000 patients who died in palliative care, 94.7% had cancer.

The areas with the most units for palliative care (i.e. giving temporary relief or lessening pain) in England are the North West and South East.

World wide there are over 7,000 palliative care initiatives either operational or under development in more than 100 countries (2003). All have dedicated hospice and palliative care staff, who are knowledgeable, caring and sympathetic. Their reward is not in the amount they are paid but in satisfaction with a job well done. Rather than being just a home for the dying, people can go for a week or two at a time, to give their carers a rest and time to recuperate.

The following is a poem written by Phyllis McCormack. She was in a hospice; she couldn't speak but was occasionally seen writing. After her death, this was found in her locker and is a plea for nurses to appreciate patients as the people they really are or were, not as they now appear, a shadow perhaps of their former selves:

What do you see when you see me?
Are you thinking when you are looking at me
a crabbit old woman, not very wise,
uncertain of habit, with faraway eyes,
with bathing and feeding, the long days to fill?
Is that what you're thinking, is that what you see?
Then open your eyes; you're not looking at me!
I'll tell you who I am as I sit here so still,
as I do at your bidding, as I eat at your will,
I'm a small child of ten, with a father and mother,
brother and sister, who love one another;
a young girl of sixteen with wings on her feet,
dreaming that now soon a lover she'll meet.
A bride soon at twenty – my heart gives a leap,
remembering the vows that I promised to keep.
At twenty-five now, I have young of my own,
who need me to build a secure happy home;
a woman of thirty, my young now grown fast,
bound to each other with ties that should last.
At forty, my young sons now grown and all gone,
but my man stays beside me to see I don't mourn.
At fifty once more babies play round my knee:
again we know children, my loved one and me.
Dark days are upon me, my husband is dead;
I look at the future, I shudder with dread,
for my young are all busy rearing young of their own
and I think of the years and the love that I've known.
I'm an old woman now and Nature is cruel,
tis her jest to make old age look like a fool.
The body it crumbles, grace and vigour depart,
but inside this old carcass a young girl still dwells
and now and again my battered heart swells.
I remember the joys, I remember the pain,
and I'm loving and living all over again.
I think of the years all too few – gone too fast,
and accept the stark fact that nothing can last.
So open your eyes, open and see
not a crabbit old woman
look closer – See me!

Hospitals Most hospitals have one or more hospital chaplains, ministers from one or more denominations and faiths to comfort the ill and dying. Some patients are given the 'last rites' and are anointed with oil (especially Catholics). At Bedford, a medium sized east Midlands town, there is a Catholic, an Anglican, a Free Church minister, and a Muslim Imam on hand at the hospital. All use the hospital chapel for services at differing times.

Churches Regular churchgoers are often visited by their minister, pastor or priest during an illness. Or sometimes there is a team within a lively church who will take it upon themselves to visit the sick on a regular basis. Many churches also have prayer groups to pray for the sick in their church or parish.

Samaritans The Samaritan organization, originally formed to help suicides, will give a listening ear to anyone in distress about dying or grief in bereavement.

The Terrance Higgins trust deals with people with AIDS or are HIV positive or for people who have lost a loved one through aids.

Cancerbacup gives advice for those who have someone suffering from cancer.

The Natural Death Centre was launched in 1991. It aims to support those dying at home and their carers, and to help people arrange inexpensive do it yourself and green funerals. It is also interested in helping to improve the 'quality of dying'.

NEAR DEATH EXPERIENCES

Many books have been written by or about people who although pronounced clinically dead, have returned to life, some with extraordinary visions or experiences to report. Some have felt that they have risen above their bodies and looked down upon themselves lying dead. Some have entered dark tunnels with bright lights shining at the end calling them on, or a lovely sunny valley beautiful beyond description.

Many who believe that they have had such experiences say that these have changed their lives forever. Now they are not afraid to die but assume that they have been returned to life, because there is something more for them to do.

Others appear to have seen some terrible vision of people suffering. This has made them change their lives around, so that this is not a fate awaiting them.

Still others feel that the people did not really die, that this was merely their active conscience working. The good saw a future full of light. The bad anticipated a hell to come.

Or it may only be a physiological phenomenon, where the brain is deprived of oxygen for a certain time, producing visions. No one has yet conclusively found the answer to this experience.

DEATH A FRIEND OR FOE?

Death may be considered a foe, if it comes too early, or a friend, if one has reached a mature age or is in pain from some illness or misfortune. When King George VI died, Sir Winston Churchill remarked that 'death came as a friend', because the king was very ill with lung cancer.

SHOULD ONE BE AFRAID OF DEATH?

Should one be afraid of death? Death is the only place to go after birth for everyone.

> 'What is death at most? It is a journey for a season, a sleep longer than usual. If thou fearest death, thou shouldest also fear sleep.' St John Chrysotom c. 347–407 AD

> 'How strange this fear of death is, yet we are never frightened at a sunset,' said *George MacDonald*; 'and what is death to the Christian, but a glorious sunset and the dawning of a more blessed day in a summer-land where eyes are never wet with the tears of separation.' *Herbert Lockyer*

> I'm not afraid of dying; I just don't want to be there when it happens! *Woody Allen* (1935), often attributed to Spike Milligan.

SUMMARY OF WHAT MAY HAPPEN AFTER DEATH.

It is interesting to speculate about what happens after death, although not especially relevant to the purpose of this book. These are the main thoughts expressed by various religions and none.

1) For some there is no God; oblivion of the personality as well as the disintegration of the body therefore follows death.

2) Some think that procreation is an attempt to defeat death. People will only live on in their children and in their children's children.

3) Some believe it will be the constant cycle of death and rebirth – reincarnation into another human, animal or plant.

4) For others, a spirit only world awaits, without a body.

5) For yet others, they are sure that there will be a resurrection day, followed by judgement, then everlasting life in its fullness (either on a renewed earth or in heaven) for some, or in a hell for others, which will provide either everlasting torment, annihilation, or a corrective procedure of some sort.

6) Some think, before reaching the final goal of heaven or hell, there will be a period of refining of some sort to fit the person for the place to which they are ultimately going.

FOREKNOWLEDGE OF DEATH?

When I was due to have a hip replacement I looked up in my *Daily Bible* the reading for the date of the operation. It said 'Today you will be with me in paradise!' For a moment I was stunned and shocked, then I realized that death could not happen to everyone that read this verse on 19 February. Maybe I would survive after all – and I did.

It reminded me of the would be Bible reader who was looking for guidance, so he stuck a pin in and came up with, 'and Judas went out and hanged himself'. This not being very acceptable he tried again and came up with, 'Go and do thou likewise!' He could not have done as instructed or he would not have been alive to tell the tale.

Some people may be tempted to try to bargain with God. 'If you let me survive this operation, I promise I will go to mass every Sunday from now on,' said one lapsed Catholic man. He did survive and kept his part of the bargain. He went to mass religiously for the next 15 years. This doesn't always work of course. One cannot override God's prerogative.

A friend was going to see her sister in hospital and all the way there she had a vision of her sister sitting up in bed and the clock over the bed saying 5 pm. The sister was usually never sitting up because she was so ill. However when my friend arrived at the hospital her sister was sitting up, and she died at 5 pm that very day.

Three men were asked what they would do if a doctor told them they had only six months to live. One of them said 'I would retire to the country and live out my days in peace and tranquility.' The second man said, 'I should sell all my possessions and go on a binge, spending it all on wine, women and song! The third man wisely said 'I should get a second opinion'.

During a war, mothers have sometimes announced, 'John is dead,' and looked at the clock. Sometime later a telegram has come stating the time that John had died, which was the very same moment.

A friend who was dying of cancer, woke up one day and announced, 'This is my last day on earth!' He died later that day.

> I hear a voice you cannot hear, that says I must not stay
> I see a hand you cannot see, that beckons me away.

> Hope is a strange invention, a patent of the heart
> In unremitting action, yet never wearing out.
> *Emily Dickinson 1830 – 1886*

However, most people have no idea when they will die, nor that their end is nigh. This may be a great blessing. But let us all try to be prepared for death, if only for the sake of those dear ones we will leave behind. Let us make it easier for them. Let us comfort them in the only way we now can.

The
Bereavement
Register

What is The Bereavement Register?

The Bereavement Register is a service with one simple aim: To reduce the amount of direct mail sent to those who have died and consequently make the passage of bereavement that little bit easier.

Our names and addresses appear on many databases and mailing files which means, unfortunately, that we are often bombarded with mail we just don't want. Imagine if that mail is sent to someone whose family member or friend has recently died. The distress and upset that can cause is immeasurable.

From our own personal experiences, we understood there was a need to provide a solution to this ever increasing problem. So, in 2000 The Bereavement Register was launched as a service specifically designed to remove from databases and mailing files, the names and addresses of people who have died. At this difficult time, the bereaved will want to remember the good times with fondness and not be bombarded or bothered by direct mail sent to a loved one who has recently passed away.

Mail of this kind serves no purpose so let us help put an end to these sad reminders.

If you would like more information on The Bereavement Register, please contact us by calling 01732 460000;

writing to The Bereavement Register, FREEPOST, Sevenoaks, Kent TN13 1YR;

or visit our website at www.the-bereavement-register.org.uk

Tel: 01732 460000 www.the-bereavement-register.org.uk

A REaD Group Service

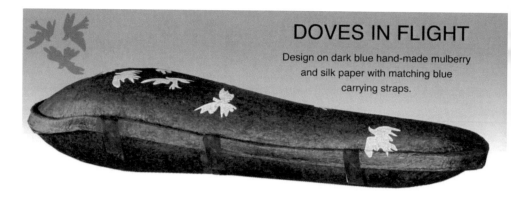

DOVES IN FLIGHT

Design on dark blue hand-made mulberry and silk paper with matching blue carrying straps.

An ecopod with dove decoration, lined with silk or feathers.

Acorn ecopod for the storage of ashes, from Arka.

A dove, in memory of a loved one, can be released at a funeral.
The White Dove Co.

1. Womb shaped coffin made for someone who came into this world in the foetal position and wished to go out in the same way.

2. Skip Coffin designed and made for Mr John Gratton Fisher, who has been in the skip business as Grove Haulage for six years. It cost £550.00 in 2001, but barring accidents, John will not be needing his specialised coffin for many years.

3. A Narrow boat coffin made for a man who had lived all his life on a narrow boat.

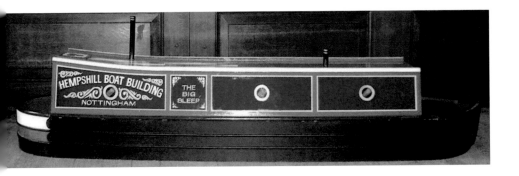

A spring garden, with memorial kerb stones along the edge of bed, where ashes have been scattered. Bedford Crematorium Complex.

Coastal cemetery at Great Orme, North Wales

Columbarium for the burial of ashes above ground with marble plaques and vases for flowers. Norse Road Crematorium Bedford.

Beehive type granite containers to take two urns containing ashes. Norse Road, Crematorium, Bedford.

Woodland funeral site chapel at Colney, Norwich. Note the pulpit is a branch of a tree, and mourners sit overlooking a mature wood.

Vintage lorrry hearse by David Hall in the SW, who can make a great display with raked boards to take the flowers. Ideal for lorry drivers, showmen and travellers' funerals.

Chapel, showing catafalque at The Garden of England Crematorium,
built August 2003 near Sittingbourne, Kent

The cremator at The Garden of England Crematorium

The only cemetery in England for American Servicemen near Cambridge. The last funeral to take place there with full honours was in 2003 for a 23 year old. His remains were found 57 years after he died.

A typical British parish church.

A typical coffin and hearse with four bearers.

Horse drawn hearse, purchased 1880s from Marsden, the Rolls Royce of coach builders at that time. Still in weekly use today by J.J. Burgess & Sons of Hatfield.

A four horse shillabeer - coffin and mourners can travel together in the same carriage.

A white horse drawn carriage, with glass sides and pretty ornate top. Suitable for a child's funeral. Available from T. Cribb & Sons, East London.

A Rolls Royce combined child hearse and limousine from A.W. Lymn, The Family Funeral Service, Nottingham.

A hand held bier which carries a coffin, saving the bearers much heavy work.

The hand held bier at the funeral of the Chief Fire Officer of Hatfield, William Toms, 1920. The bearer party includes 3 generations of Burgesses, who still own the firm today.

Vintage Car hearse, a 1933 Austin, with appropriate number plate!
Available from T Cribb & Sons (1881) of Beckton, E. London.

A trike and hearse available from Bill Tanner and Tony Crathern of the
Essex Chapter of the Harley Davidson Owners' Group

Motorcycle and sidecar hearse and funeral in process.

This picture shows the cardboard coffin developed by Robert Morphet and Joan Hay Morphet of Bradford. It is made in 'Toughwall' double thickness corrugated board and costs £50.00 (2003). Bradford, Yorks. Photo by Guzelian.

The Coffin Cover is used to transport the cardboard coffin to the crematorium, or the burial site, the cardboard coffin is then discreetly slipped out. Patents are pending for this revolutionary idea. Photo by R.J. Morphet.

This modern Crematorium Complex in Norse Road, Bedford was awarded the Hanson Brick award for the best brick built building of the decade 1990 - 2000.
The building cost two million pounds. Photo by Michael Day.
The architects were Bedford Borough architects:
Sherry Hooper, Jim Burnett, Neil Marshall & Connie McGrath.

A modern mausoleum at Norse Road Crematorium Complex.

Appendix I
PRAYERS

Suitable to be read at funerals
(alternative words in brackets, as appropriate)

If the prayers are printed on the service sheet, people who wish to remember the special words spoken at the funeral can take them away with them. The minister will advise in advance which prayers he will be using.

CHRISTIAN: BIBLICAL

Initial sentences

(The following, up to the Lord's Prayer, were spoken or sung at the Queen Mother's Funeral 2002.)

I am the Resurrection and the Life, saith the Lord: he that believeth in me, though he were dead, yet shall he live: and whosoever liveth and believeth in me shall never die *John 11:25,26.*

In the midst of life, we are in death. *Anglican funeral service. The Book of Common Prayer 1549.*

I know that my redeemer lives, and at last he will stand on the earth; and after my skin has been thus destroyed, then from my flesh I shall see God. *Job 19:25-26.*

We brought nothing in to this world, and it is certain we shall carry nothing out *1Tim 6:7.* The Lord gave and the Lord hath taken away, blessed be the name of the Lord *Job 1:21.* Or this may be sung to music by *William Croft (1678-1727) organist of Westminster Abbey (1708–1727).*

I heard a voice from heaven saying, 'Write this, blessed are the dead who die in the Lord henceforth'. 'Blessed indeed', says the Spirit, 'that they may rest from their labours, for their deeds follow them'. *Rev. 14:13.*

The hour is coming, and now is, when the dead will hear the voice of the Son of God, and those who hear will live. Because I live, you will live also. *Methodist Service Book.*

Thou knowest Lord the secrets of our hearts; shut not thy merciful ears unto our prayer; but spare us Lord most holy, O God most mighty, O holy and most merciful Saviour, thou most worthy judge eternal. Suffer us not, at our last hour, for any pains of death, to fall from thee, Amen. Or this may be sung to music by *Henry Purcell (1659-95) Organist* of Westminster Abbey *(1679–95)* Words from *The Book of Common Prayer.*

As our Father has taught us so we pray *The Lord's Prayer*
Our Father which art in heaven, hallowed be thy name. Thy kingdom come, Thy will be done, on earth as it is in heaven. Give us this day our daily bread. And forgive us our trespasses as we forgive those who trespass against us. And lead us not into temptation; but deliver us from evil: for thine is the Kingdom, the power, and the glory, for ever and ever, Amen. *Matt. 6:9–13.*

Or one may prefer a modern version of *The Lord's Prayer*
Our Father in heaven, hallowed be your name, your kingdom come, your will be done, on earth as it is in heaven. Give us today our daily bread. Forgive us our sins, as we forgive those who sin against us. Lead us not into temptation but deliver us from evil. For the kingdom, the power, and the glory are yours, now and forever. Amen.

The Lord bless you and keep you, the Lord make his face to shine upon you: The Lord lift up the light of his countenance upon you, and give you peace. *Num. 6:24–26.*

The Apostles Creed
I believe in God, the Father almighty
Creator of heaven and earth.
I believe in Jesus Christ, his only Son, our Lord.
He was conceived by the power of the Holy Spirit
and born of the Virgin Mary.
He suffered under Pontius Pilate,
was crucified, died and was buried.
He descended to the dead.
On the third day he rose again.
He ascended into heaven,
and is seated at the right hand of the Father.
He will come again to judge the living and the dead.
I believe in the Holy Spirit,
the holy Catholic Church,
the communion of saints,
the forgiveness of sins,
the resurrection of the body,
and the life everlasting. Amen

Other Christian prayers

O Lord, support us all the day long of this troublous life, until the shadows lengthen and the evening comes, and the busy world is hushed, the fever of life over, and our work done. Then, O Lord, in your mercy grant to us and to those we love safe lodging, holy rest and peace at the last, through our Lord Jesus Christ. Amen. *John Henry Newman, Moravian Funeral Service and Church of England Alternative Service Book (ASB).*

God of mercy who brought us to birth, by whose grace we live, and in whose love we are held at last: contain and comfort us; in our sadness and confusion give us assurance and hope, and embrace us in the love of the one who gave his life for us all, your Son, Jesus Christ, Amen.

Grant us, Lord, the wisdom and the grace to use aright the time that is left to us here on earth. Lead us to repent of our sins, the evil we have done and the good we have not done; and strengthen us to follow the steps of your Son, in the way that leads to the fullness of eternal life; through Jesus Christ our Lord. Amen. *ASB Funeral service.* p.314.

Eternal God, our heavenly father, you love us with an everlasting love and can turn the shadow of death into the light of morning. Help us now to wait upon you with reverent and submissive hearts. In the silence of this hour, speak to us of eternal things, that with patience and the comfort of your holy Word we may embrace and hold fast the blessed hope of eternal life that you have given us in your Son, our Lord Jesus Christ. Amen. *Moravian prayer.*

Most holy and merciful God, the refuge and strength of those who trust you, we thank you for the multitude no man can number whom you have received into your eternal joy; we praise you that you have forgiven them all their sins and that they dwell with you, beyond evil and sorrow for ever. We thank you also for all to whom amid the trials of this mortal life you give the faith that overcomes the world; who have peace in you and rejoice in hope of your glory; through Jesus our Lord. Amen. *The Moravian Church, Alternative Orders of Worship.*

Eternal God, the Lord of life, the conqueror of death, our help in every time of trouble, comfort us who mourn and give us grace, in the presence of death, to worship you, that we may have sure hope of eternal life and be enabled to put our whole trust in your goodness and mercy, through Jesus Christ our Lord. *Methodist Service Book, 1975.*

Dear Lord, may we look backwards with gratitude, forwards with courage, and upwards with confidence.

Almighty God, our refuge and strength, you have given us a High Priest who understands our human weakness. Help us to trust in him and come with confidence to the throne of grace, that we may receive mercy and find grace in time of need, through Jesus Christ our Lord. *Methodist Service Book.*

Lord, we remember with gratitude all those people whom we have loved – and those who have loved us. May that love be a link between this world and the next, and may their souls rest in peace. *Marjorie Bereza.*

We look not to the things that are seen but to the things that are unseen; for the things that are seen are transient but the things that are unseen are eternal. *2 Cor. 4:18.*

Today we come together to remember before God our (brother/sister – *NAME)* to give thanks for (his/her) life and to comfort one another in our grief.

Father in heaven, we thank thee because thou hast made us in thine own image and given us gifts in body, mind and spirit.

We thank thee now for *NAME* and what (he/she) meant to each of us. As we honour (his/her) memory, make us more aware that thou art the one from whom cometh every perfect gift, including the gift of eternal life through Jesus Christ our Lord. Amen.

Lord, make me a channel of Thy peace; where there is hatred may I bring love; where there is injury, pardon; where there is doubt, faith; where there is despair, hope; where there is darkness, light; and where there is sadness, joy. O Divine Lover, grant that we may not so much seek to be consoled as to console; to be understood, as to understand; to be loved as to love; for it is in giving that we receive, it is in pardoning that we are pardoned, and it is in dying that we are born to eternal life. *St Francis of Assisi.*

O God, give me the serenity to accept the things I cannot change, the courage to change the things I can, and the wisdom to know the difference. *Reinhold Niebuhr.*

Lord, we pray for the bereaved, asking that their heartbreak may be healed by the balm of God's comfort, and that beyond the dreadful silence of death, they may hear the songs of the angels, bringing the hope of heaven. Through Jesus Christ our Lord. *New Evening Morning, pub BBC.*

Forgiving God, in the face of death we discover how many things are still undone, how much might have been done otherwise. Redeem our failure. Bind up the wounds of past mistakes. Transform our guilt to active love, and by your forgiveness make us whole. Lord in your mercy, hear our prayer. *Scottish Episcopal Funeral Rite.*

God our Redeemer, you love all that you have made, you are merciful beyond our deserving. Pardon your servant's sins, acknowledged or unperceived. Help us also to forgive as we pray to be forgiven, through him who on the cross asked forgiveness for those who wounded him. Lord in your mercy, hear our prayer. *Scottish Episcopal Funeral Rite.*

O Lord, the first and the last, the beginning and the end: You who were with us at our birth be with us through our life; You who are with us through our life, be with us at our death; and because your mercy will not leave us then, grant that we die not, but rise to the life everlasting. *Pauline Webb.*

Lord, I know you will not send any trouble to day that you and I together cannot handle. *African prayer.*

O God the maker and redeemer of all mankind; grant us, with our loved one and all the faithful departed, the sure benefits of your Son's saving passion and glorious resurrection, that in the last day, when you gather up all things in Christ, we may with them enjoy the fullness of your promise, through Jesus Christ our Lord. Amen. *ASB Funeral service.*

Heavenly Father, in your Son Jesus Christ you have given us a true faith and a sure hope. Strengthen this faith and hope in us all our days, that we may live as those who believe in the communion of saints, the forgiveness of sins and the resurrection to eternal life, through your Son Jesus Christ our Lord. Amen.

Teach us, good Lord, to serve Thee as thou deservest: to give and not to count the cost: to fight and not to heed the wounds: to toil and not to seek for rest: to labour and not to ask for any rewards, save that of knowing that we do Thy will: through Jesus Christ our Lord. Amen.

Bring us, O Lord God, at our last awakening into the house and gate of heaven, to enter into that gate and dwell in that house where shall be no darkness nor dazzling, but one equal light; no noise nor silence, but one equal music; no fears nor hopes, but one equal possession; no ends nor beginnings, but one equal eternity; in the habitations of thy glory and dominion, world without end. Amen. *John Donne c.1572–1631.*

Almighty God, Father of all mercies and giver of all comfort: deal graciously, we pray, with those who mourn, that casting all their care on you, they may know the consolation of your love; through Jesus Christ our Lord. Amen. *ASB p335.*

May God in his infinite love and mercy bring the whole church, living and departed in the Lord Jesus, to a joyful resurrection and the fulfilment of his eternal kingdom. Amen.

Father of spirits, we have joy at this time in all who have faithfully lived and in all who have peacefully died. We thank Thee for all fair memories and all lively hopes; for the sacred ties that bind us to the unseen world; for the dear and holy dead who compass us as a cloud of witnesses and make the distant heaven a home to our hearts. May we be followers of those who now inherit the promises, through Jesus Christ our Lord. *Methodist Book of Offices.*

Eternal God, whose love is stronger than death, we rejoice that the dead as well as the living are held in your love and care. As we remember with thanksgiving those we have loved who have gone before us, we pray that we may look forward with confidence to the day when we shall be reunited in the joy and peace of your everlasting kingdom. *Pauline Webb.*

We remember, Lord, the slenderness of the thread, which separates life from death, and the suddenness with which it can be broken. Help us to remember that on both sides of that division we are surrounded by your love. Persuade our hearts that when our dear ones die neither they nor we are parted from you. In you may we find our peace and in you be united with them in the glorious body of Christ, who has burst the bonds of death and is alive for evermore, our Saviour and theirs forever. *Dick Williams.*

May he give us all the courage that we need to go the way he shepherds us. That when he calls we may go unfrightened. If he bids us come to him across the waters, that unfrightened we may go. And if he bids us climb a hill, may we not notice that it is a hill, mindful only of the happiness of his company. He made us for himself, that we should travel with him and see him at the last in his unveiled beauty in the abiding city where he is light and happiness and endless home. *Father Bede Jarrett OM.*

God be in my head, and in my understanding. God be in mine eyes, and in my looking; God be in my mouth, and in my speaking; God be in my heart, and in my thinking; God be at mine end, and at my departing. *Sarum prayer.*

We leave this service knowing that Love is eternal, whether we be on this earth in the confines of time and space, or on an entirely different plane: that God will be with us, wherever we are, and will take care of us for all eternity, in the company of those who have gone before, and of those who are to follow, one body in Christ in fellowship with him and with each other. Amen. *Dorothy Richards.*

God of all grace, who didst send thy Son our Saviour Jesus Christ to bring life and immortality to light: most humbly and heartily we give thee thanks that by his death he destroyed the power of death, and by his glorious resurrection opened the kingdom of heaven to all believers. Grant us assuredly to know that because he lives we shall live also, and that neither death nor life, nor things present nor things to come, shall be able to separate us from thy love, which is in Christ Jesus our Lord. Amen. *Book of Common Order of the Church of Scotland.*

Almighty God, Father of all mercies and giver of all comfort: deal graciously we pray, with those who mourn, that casting all their care on thee, they may know the consolation of thy love; through Jesus Christ our Lord. Amen.

Of old thou hast created me from nothing and honoured me with thy divine image. But when I disobeyed thy commandment, thou hast returned me to the earth whence I was taken. Lead me back again to thy likeness. Refashioning my ancient beauty. *Orthodox Funeral Service.*

Give rest, O Lord, to the souls of thy servants, where there is no pain, no sorrow, no sighing, but life without end. *Orthodox Funeral Service.*

Before the Bible reading

We are met in this solemn moment to commend NAME into the hands of Almighty God, our heavenly Father. In the presence of death, Christians have sure ground for hope and confidence and even for joy, because the Lord Jesus Christ, who shared our human life and death, was raised again triumphant and lives for ever more. In him his people find eternal life. Let us then in humble heart hear the words of Holy Scripture. *Methodist Service Book.*

Prayers for the committal

Forasmuch as it has pleased almighty God of his great mercy to take unto himself the soul of our dear (brother/ sister) here departed, we therefore commit (his/ her) body to be consumed to the earth, ashes to ashes, dust to dust, in sure and certain hope of the resurrection to eternal life of the body, through our Lord Jesus Christ, who shall change our vile body, that it may be like unto His glorious body, according to the mighty working, whereby he is able to subdue all things to himself, before whom we all shall stand and give an account of the things that we have done in the body. *Book of Common Prayer.1662.*

Let us commend our (brother /sister) to the mercy of God our Maker and Redeemer.

Heavenly Father, by your mighty power you gave us life, and in your love you have given us new life in Christ Jesus. We entrust NAME to your merciful keeping: in the faith of Jesus Christ your Son our Lord, who died and rose again to save us, and is now alive and reigns with you and the Holy Spirit in glory for ever. Amen.

Almighty God, always ready to forgive, no prayer is offered to you in vain. Speak to us your word of consolation and in our sorrow draw us closer to yourself, so that in doing your will we may know your righteousness and mercy. Amen.

Father of all, we pray for those whom we love, but see no longer. Grant them your peace; let light perpetual shine upon them; and in your loving wisdom and almighty power work in them the good purpose of your perfect will; through Jesus Christ our Lord. *Methodist Service Book.*

Committal for a child

Almighty God, giver of every good and perfect gift, we thank you for the happiness and love this child has brought and for the assurance we have that (he/she) is in your care. Strengthen us to commit ourselves to your gracious providence, so that we may live our lives here in the peace and joy of faith, until at last we are united with all the children of God in the brightness of your glory, through Jesus Christ our Lord. Amen. *Methodist Service Book.*

For a baby

Heavenly Father, all life comes from you and you are the source of all love. We thank you for a very special child. We thank you for the happiness (he /she) gave to others and for all the love and care that (he/ she) received. We believe that you have received (his/ her) soul and that (he/ she) is now in your care. We believe that as Jesus blessed children here on earth, so he must surely be caring for them in heaven. So we give (him/ her) back to you; we entrust (him/ her) to your safekeeping and we pray that the blessing of Jesus may rest upon (him/ her) now and always. Amen.

For a young person's funeral

Lord God, source and destiny of our lives
in your loving providence you gave us *NAME*
to grow in wisdom, age, and grace.
Now you have called (him /her) to yourself.

As we grieve the loss of one so young,
we seek to understand your purpose.

Draw (him/ her) to yourself
and give (him/ her) full stature in Christ.
May (he/ she) stand with all the angels and saints
who know your love and praise your saving will.
We ask this through Christ our Lord. Amen.
Roman Catholic Order of Christian Funerals No. 28, p.416

A prayer for parents

Dear God, help me as I try to explain death and resurrection to (this child / these children). Reassure me about the ability of children to understand and their capacity to believe, and make my faith equal to theirs. Then grant me the right words at the right time to satisfy the mind and comfort the spirit of (this your child / these your children). Amen. From *Water Bugs and Dragonflies* by Doris Stickney. Mowbray's.

A prayer for those bereaved through suicide

Father of all, have mercy on those who have taken their own lives. We do not know what tensions or what deprivations led them to this act. Help us to become more understanding and more loving to the lonely, the hurt and unlovely of this world so they will not take the same way out. Wrap those who have killed themselves in your love so that they will live anew with you in your kingdom and come to glorify you, world without end. Amen. *Florence Roe*

A prayer for parents or close friends who have died together

Father of all, who never changes, who is always with us in joy and sorrow, in life and in death, help us to remember what we have learned from those who have gone before us, their love and concern for us throughout our lives, the way they led us to you, and nourished our spirits, our bodies and our minds. May they now rest in peace, life's work completed in true and faithful service. We ask this in Jesus's precious name. Amen. *Dorothy Richards*

Faith

Lord Jesus Christ, we thank you for our faith. We thank you that you have taught us not to be afraid of you, but to trust in your love. Give us a vision of heaven that will strengthen us in the days and years ahead. May we offer you thanksgiving and praise, and give help and support to others in the time of their troubles. Bind us to yourself by your Holy Spirit and enable us to live for your glory and for your kingdom on earth. This prayer we offer in your name. Amen.

Holy Father we ask you to comfort all who mourn the death of *NAME.*
May they be made strong in faith and hope and love, through Jesus Christ who died on the cross for us, but whom God raised from the dead that we might believe in him. To you be all glory and power and thanksgiving and praise, both now and for all eternity. Amen.

The blessing

Give back to no-one evil for evil. Strengthen the faint hearted. Support the weak. Help the afflicted. Honour all people. Love and serve the Lord – rejoicing in the power of the Holy Spirit. And the blessing of Almighty God, the Father, the Son and the Holy Spirit be upon you and remain with you, now and always. Amen.

JEWISH PRAYERS

Support us, Lord, when we are silent through grief. Comfort us when we are bent down with sorrow. Help us as we bear the weight of our loss. Lord our rock and our redeemer, give us strength. *Jewish Funeral Service.*

In the presence of death, let us not fear. We share it with all who have ever lived and with all who will ever be. For it is only the dust which returns to dust as it was, but the spirit returns to God who gave it, and in His hand is the care of every soul. The world we inhabit is a corridor to the world beyond. We prepare ourselves in the corridor to enter His presence. He is our employer who knows our sorrows and our labour. Faithful is he to give us the reward of our good deeds. He redeems us from destruction and leads us in the way of everlasting life. *Jewish Funeral Service.*

Have mercy upon him, pardon all his transgressions, for there is not a just man upon earth who does good and does not sin. *Jewish prayer.*

Lord, we turn to you in our grief and our bewilderment, for a mystery surrounds the birth and death of man. Your will summons us into the world and then calls us to depart, but Your plan is so vast and Your purposes so deep that our understanding fails, and our reason cannot follow. Yet You have taught us that time and space are not the measure of all things. Beyond them is the life of eternity. We do not die into the grave but into the love of God. It has been Your will to receive the soul of *NAME* to bring him/her to life everlasting, and (he/she) is beyond the tragedies of this world. We find our comfort in Your teaching. Beyond the grave we shall meet together in the life that has no end. *Jewish Funeral Service.*

BAHA'I PRAYER FOR THE DEAD

(Essential to be read at every funeral for a *Baha'i over 15 years of age. One person reads it whilst the people stand.)*

O my God! This is Thy (servant/handmaiden) and the (son/handmaiden) of Thy (servant/ handmaiden) who hath believed in Thee and in Thy signs, and set his/her face towards Thee, wholly detached from all except Thee. Thou art verily, of those who show mercy the Most Merciful.

Deal with (him/her), O Thou who forgivest the sins of men and concealest their faults, as beseemeth the heaven of Thy bounty and the ocean of Thy grace. Grant (him/her) admission within the precincts of Thy Transcendent mercy that was before the foundation of earth and heaven. There is no God but Thee, the Ever Forgiving, the Most Generous.

This is followed by repeating six times the greeting: 'Allahu Abha'

Then nineteen times:
We all, verily, worship God.
We all, verily, bow down before God.
We all, verily, are devoted unto God.
We all, verily, give praise unto God.
We all, verily, yield thanks unto God.
We all, verily, are patient in God.

Compilations, Baha'i Prayers, p.39

CHRISTIAN SCIENCE INTERPRETATION OF THE LORD'S PRAYER

Our Father which art in heaven	*Our Father-Mother God all harmonious,*
Hallowed be Thy name	*Adorable One.*
Thy kingdom come	*Thy kingdom is come; Thou art ever present*
Thy will be done, as it is in heaven.	*Enable us to know, 'as in heaven so on earth,' God is omnipotent, supreme.*
Give us this day our daily bread	*Give us grace for today; feed the famished affections;*
and forgive us our debts,	
as we forgive our debtors;	*And Love is reflected in love;*
and lead us not into temptation,	*And God leadeth us not into temptation, but delivereth us*
but deliver us from evil;	*from sin, disease and death.*

for Thine is the kingdom, and the power, and the glory, forever. Amen.

For God is infinite, all power, all Life, Truth, Love, over all, and All.

(From Matthew 6:9–13 *and pp* 16–17 *Science and Health with Key to the* Scriptures *by* Mary Baker Eddy*)*

Appendix II
READINGS

**Suitable to be read at funerals or meditated on at
home, or for when one is facing death**

These readings are arranged in alphabetical first lines for easy reference. They
are not arranged into various religions – people can tell what is appropriate to
their own circumstances. If printed on the service sheet, mourners can take
them away and reread them in the days to come.

A late lark twitters from the quiet skies,
and from the west,
where the sun, his day's work ended,
lingers as in content,
there falls on the old, grey city
an influence luminous and serene
a shining peace.
The smoke ascends
in a rosy-and-golden haze. The spires
shine and are changed. In the valley
shadows rise; the lark sings on. The sun,
closing his benediction
sinks, and the darkening air
thrills with a sense of the triumphing night ;
Night with her train of stars
and her great gift of sleep.

So be my passing!
My task accomplished and the long day done,
my wages taken, and in my heart
some late lark singing.
Let me be gathered to the quiet west,
the sundown splendid and serene,
Death.
William Ernest Henley 1849 – 1903

All the heavy days are over;
leave the body's coloured pride
underneath the grass and clover,
with the feet laid side by side.

One with her are mirth and duty;
bear the gold embroidered dress,

for she needs not her sad beauty,
to the scented oaken press;

Hers the kiss of Mother Mary,
the long hair is on her face;
still she goes with footsteps wary,
full of earth's old timid grace.

With white feet of angels seven
her white feet go glimmering;
and above the deep of heaven,
flame on flame, and wing on wing.
The Countess Catherine in Paradise - W B Yeats (Irish) *1865 – 1939*

All you who sleep tonight
far from the ones you love,
no hands to left or right,
and emptiness above -
know that you're not alone.
The whole world shares your tears,
some for two nights or one
and some for all their years.
Vikram Seth 1952–

Always remember, our loved ones just go
beyond the sight of our vision,
and the touch of our hands.
They are waiting for us on 'the other side'
where time is not counted by years
and there are no separations.

And if I go while you're still here…
know that I live on,
vibrating to a different message
behind a thin veil you cannot see through.

You will not see me,
so you must have faith.

I wait for the time when we can soar together again
both aware of each other.

Until then, live your life to its fullest,
and when you need me,
just whisper my name in your heart,
…I will be there.

An individual existence should be like a river – small at first, narrowly contained within its banks, rushing passionately past boulders and over waterfalls. Gradually the river grows wider, the banks recede, the waters flow more quietly as at the end without any visible break, they become merged with the sea and perilously lose their individual being. The man or woman, who in old

age can see his or her life in this way, will not suffer from the fear of death, since the things they care for will continue.
Bertrand Russell (Atheist) 1872 – 1970

As a child she watched me grow,
nursed me through illness, tales of woe,
always there with sympathy,
my Mum was my whole world to me.

A wife and mother I became,
with home and children, just the same,
a chat, advice, a cup of tea,
my Mum was always there for me.

When pain and fear struck on that day,
when serious illness took her away,
she left this life too quickly,
heartache, a hole where Mum should be.

But I remember happy times,
with friends and family that make me smile,
so many good times that we shared,
my heart is warmed, I know she cared.

The memories mean so much, you see,
I'll always have my Mum with me.
To my Mum

A second is spent remembering,
a tear is wiped away;
sadness and sorrow flood the good times
leaving only grief;

but in a second spent remembering
I turn and look at the rich green grass,
the shady pleasant trees
and the laughing water;

and in a second spent remembering
I recall the good times
and the warm summer sun
and can celebrate life again.
Kelly Jessop 2002

As rainbows are formed from both sunshine and rain,
so our lives are a mixture of joy and some pain.
If we bear with the darkness and learn from it too
the rain clouds will part and the sun will break through.
Doris Stickney

A ship sails and I stand
watching till she fades on the horizon
and someone at my side says,

'She is gone,' gone where?
gone from my sight, that is all;
she is just as when I saw her.
The diminished size,
and total loss of sight is in me,
not in her,
and just at the moment
when someone at my side says
'She is gone,'
There are others who are watching her coming,
and other voices take up a glad shout,
'There she comes!' – and that is dying.
Bishop Brent (after Victor Hugo see 'I am standing on that foreshore)'

As the months pass and the seasons change
something of tranquility descends, and
although the well remembered footsteps
will not sound again, nor the voice call
from the room beyond,
there seems to be about one, in the air,
an atmosphere of love, a living presence.

A smile costs nothing, but gives much;
it enriches those who receive, without making poorer those who give.
It takes but a moment, but the memory of it sometimes lasts forever.
None is so rich or mighty that he can get along without it,
and none is so poor but that he can be made rich by it.
A smile creates happiness in the home, fosters good will in business,
and is the countersign of friendship.
It brings rest to the weary, cheer to the discouraged, sunshine to the sad
and it is nature's best antidote for trouble.
It cannot be bought, begged, borrowed or stolen,
for it is of no value to anyone until it is given away.
Some people are too tired to give you a smile. Give them one of yours,
as no one needs a smile as one who has no more to give.
Jim Bailey – War Flying 1944

A team of swans was flying down the valley
the hunter fired, one fell with broken wing
and as she fell she knew that she was dying
and calling to her friends, aspired to sing.

They, from the frozen winds replied:
never shall we forget you, loved playmate,
never in the meadow or on the fjord
forget you, never… their departing wing beats sighed.
Jim Bailey – War Flying 1944

Before the Romans came to Rye or out to Severn strode,
the rolling English drunkard made the rolling English road;
a reeling road, a rolling road, that rambles round the shire,
and after him the parson ran, the sexton and the squire;
a merry road, a mazy road, and such as we did tread
the night we went to Birmingham by way of Beachy Head.

I knew no harm of Bonaparte and plenty of the Squire,
and for to fight the Frenchman I did not much desire;
but I did bash their bayonets because they came a'raged
to straighten out the crooked road an English drunkard made
where you and I went down the lane with ale mugs in our hands,
the night we went to Glastonbury by way of Goodwin sands.

His sins they were forgiven him; or why do flowers run
behind him; and the hedges all strengthening in the sun?
The wild thing went from left to right and knew not which was which
but the wild rose was above him when they found him in the ditch.
God pardon us, nor harden us: we did not see so clear
the night we went to Bannockburn by way of Brighton pier.

My friends we will not go again or ape an ancient rage,
or stretch the folly of our youth to be the shame of age,
but walk with clearer eyes this path that wandereth
and see undrugged in evening light the decent inn of death;
for there is good news yet to hear and fine things to be seen,
before we go to Paradise by way of Kensal Green.
G K Chesterton – The Rolling English Road
(this poem was read by Peter O'Toole at the cremation of Geoffrey Bernard at
Kensal Green)

Call me Death!
and that tall, brighter angel cried in a voice
that broke like a clap of thunder:
'Call Death! – call Death!'
and the echo sounded down the streets of heaven
till it reached away back to that shadowy place,
where Death waits with his pale, white horses.

And Death heard the summons,
and he leaped on his fastest horse,
pale as a sheet in the moonlight.
Up the golden street Death galloped,
and the hoofs of his horse struck fire from the gold,
but they didn't make no sound.
Up Death rode to the Great White Throne,
and waited for God's command.
And God said 'Go down Death, go down,
go down to Savannah, Georgia,
down to Yamacraw,
and find Sister Caroline.

She's borne the burden and heat of the day,
she's laboured long in the vineyard,
and she's tired and
she's weary –
go down, Death, and bring her to me.

And Death didn't say a word,
but he loosed the reins on his pale, white horse,
and he clamped the spurs to his bloodless sides,
and out and down he rode,
through heaven's pearly gates,
past suns and moons and stars;
on Death rode,
and the foam from his horse was like a comet in the sky;
on Death rode,
leaving the lightning's flash behind;
straight down he came.

While we were watching round her bed,
she turned her eyes and looked away,
she saw what we couldn't see;
she saw Old Death. She saw Old Death,
coming like a fallen star.
But death didn't frighten Sister Caroline;
he looked to her like a welcome friend.
And she whispered to us: I'm going home',
and she smiled and closed her eyes.

And Death took her up like a baby,
and she lay in his icy arms,
but she didn't feel no chill.
And Death began to ride again
up beyond the evening star,
out beyond the morning star,
into the glittering light of Glory,
on to the Great White Throne.
And there he laid Sister Caroline
on the loving breast of Jesus.

And Jesus took his own hand
and wiped away her tears,
and he smoothed the furrows from her face,
and the angels sang a little song,
and Jesus rocked her in His arms,
and kept-a-saying: take your rest,
take your rest, take your rest.

Weep not, weep not,
she is not dead;
she's resting in the bosom of Jesus.
Negro spiritual from the southern US states

Christ is the morning star,
who when the night of this world is past
brings to his saints the promise of the Light of Life
and opens everlasting day.
Venerable Bede. c. 673 – 735

Come not to mourn for me with solemn tread
clad in dull weeds of sad and sable hue,
nor weep because my tale of life's told through,
casting light dust on my untroubled head.
Nor linger near me while the Sexton fills
my grave with earth – but go gay garlanded,
and in your halls a shining banquet spread
and gild your chambers o'er with daffodils.
Fill your goblets with white wine and red,
and sing brave songs of gallant love and true,
wearing soft robes of emerald and blue,
and dance, as I your dances oft have led,
and laugh, as I have often laughed with you -
and be most merry – after I am dead.
No mourning by request – Winifred Holtby 1898 – 1935

Come to me in my dreams, and then
by day I shall be well again!
For then the night will more than pay
the hopeless longing of the day.

Come as thou com'st a thousand times
a messenger from radiant climes
and smile on thy new world, and be
as kind to others as to me.

Or, as thou cam'st in sooth
come now, and let me dream it truth
and part my hair and kiss my brow
and say: My love! Why sufferest thou?

Come to me in dreams, and then
by day I shall be well again!
For then the night will more than pay
The hopeless longing of the day.

At the loss of a young person:
Dear Master, all the flowers are Thine,
and false the whisper, 'ours' and 'mine'.
We lift our hearts to Thee and say,
'Lord it was Thine to take way'.

And yet, though we would have it so,
Lord, it is very good to know

125

that Thou art feeling all our pain,
and we shall have our flowers again.

So help us now to be content
to take the sorrow Thou has sent.
Dear Lord, how fair Thy house must be
with all the flowers we've lent to Thee.
Amy Carmichael

Death, be not proud, though some have called thee
mighty and dreadful, for thou art not so;
for those whom thou think'st thou dost overthrow
die not, poor death, nor yet cans't thou kill me.

From rest and sleep, which but thy pictures be,
much pleasure – then, from thee much more must flow;
and soonest our best men with thee do go,
rest of their bones and soul's delivery.

Thou'rt slave to fate, chance, kings and desperate men,
and dost with poison, war and sickness dwell;
and poppy or charms can make us sleep as well,
and better than thy stroke. Why swell'st thou then?
one short sleep past, we wake eternally,
and death shall be no more. Death thou shalt die.

Death is only the beginning;
the bluebells quiver in the soft dusty earth;
the trees waver as if in greeting;
the thick lush grass is covered in morning dew.

An icy grip looms in the distance
circling everyone, not just me.
One day those fingers will close
and darkness will seem to surround us all:

but on that day, do not cry for me
for I am at one with the earth
and everything around you.
I am among the beautiful things
the birds, the trees, the flowers:
so, yes, I may have passed away;
but in nature, and in your hearts,
I will live on.
Katy Bulmer 2002

Death hides but it cannot divide
thou art but on Christ's other side
thou with Christ and Christ with me
and so together still are we.

Death is nothing at all.
I have only slipped away into the next room.
I am I, and you are you.
Whatever we were to each other, that we still are.

Call me by my old familiar name,
speak to me in the easy way which you always used.
Put no difference in your tone,
wear no forced air of solemnity or sorrow.

Laugh as we always laughed at the little jokes we enjoyed together.
Play, smile, think of me, pray for me.
Let my name be ever the household word that it always was,
let it be spoken without effort, without the trace of a shadow on it.

Life means all that it ever meant.
It is the same as it ever was:
there is absolutely unbroken continuity.

Why should I be out of mind because I am out of sight.
I am waiting for you, for an interval,
somewhere very near, just around the corner.
All is well.
Henry Scott Holland 1847 – 1918 (Canon of St Paul's Cathedral).

Death stand above me, whispering low
I know not what into my ear;
of his strange language all I know
I-is, there is not a word of fear.
Walter Savage Landor 1775 – 1864

Death will be gentle with me
like an old friend dropping in to see me
and asking me to come along
for a stroll towards the sun.

I will not hesitate to entrust myself into his company.
I will not pause in my steps to look back.

Or perhaps it will come while I am sitting in my soft chair,
wrapped in a blanket.
I will not sigh, so that others can go on with their
business thinking me to be asleep.

I will know then what I always suspected,
that death is not a mystery but a guide to birth.
When death comes – Chief Dan George, American Native Indian. Died 1981.

Deep peace of the running waves to you.
Deep peace of the flowing air to you.
Deep peace of the quiet earth to you.
Deep peace of the shining stars to you.

Deep peace of the gentle night to you.
Moon and stars pour their healing light on you.
Deep peace of Christ the Light of the World to you.
Deep peace of Christ to you.

Do not stand at my grave and weep.
I am not there, I do not sleep.
I am a thousand winds that blow.
I am the diamond glints in snow.
I am the sunlight on ripened grain.
I am the gentle autumn rain.

When you awaken in the morning's hush
I am the swift uplifting rush
of quiet birds in circled flight.
I am the soft stars that shine at night.

Do not stand at my grave and cry.
I am not there; I did not die.
So heed, hear, when you awaken, what I say.
I live with you and guard your way.
Native North American Prayer

Father before this sparrow's earthly flight
ends in the darkness of a winter's night;
Father, without whose word no sparrow falls,
hear this, thy weary sparrow, when he calls.

Mercy, not justice, is his contrite prayer,
cancel his guilt, and drive away despair;
speak but the word, and make his spirit whole,
cleanse the dark places of his heart and soul.

Speak but the word, and set his spirit free;
mercy, not justice, still his constant plea.
So shall thy sparrow, crumpled wings restored,
soar like the lark, and glorify his Lord.
The Sparrow's prayer – Lord Hailsham 1907 – 2001
(could also be adapted as a woman speaking)

Fear no more the heat o' the sun
nor the furious winter's rages;
thou thy worldly task has done,
home art gone and ta'en thy wages:
golden lads and girls all must,
as chimney sweepers, come to dust.

Fear no more the frown o' the great;
thou art past the tyrant's stroke;
care no more to clothe and eat;
to thee the reed is as the oak:
the sceptre, learning, physic, must

all follow this and come to dust.

Fear no more the lightening flash,
nor the all dreaded thunder-stone;
fear not slander, censure rash;
thou hast finish'd joy and moan:
all lovers young, all lovers must
consign to thee and come to dust.
William. Shakespeare 1564 – 1616

Firmly I believe and truly
God is Three, and God is One;
and I next acknowledge duly
manhood taken by the Son.
And I trust and hope most fully
in that manhood crucified;
and each thought and deed unruly
do to death, as He has died.
Simply to His grace and wholly
light and life and strength belong,
and I love supremely, solely,
Him the holy, Him the strong.

And I hold in veneration,
for the love of Him alone,
Holy church, as His creation,
and her teachings, as His own.
And I take with joy whatever
now besets me, pain or fear,
and with a strong will I sever
all the ties which bind me here.
Adoration aye be given,
with and through the angelic host,
to the God of earth and heaven,
Father, Son, and Holy Ghost.
From The Dream of Gerontius – Cardinal John Henry Newman 1801 – 1890

For every year of life we light
a candle for your cake
to make the simple sort of progress
anyone can make.

And then, to test your nerve or give
a proper view of death,
you're asked to blow each light, each year,
out with your own breath.
James Simmons

Full fathom five thy father lies:
of his bones are coral made;
those are pearls that were his eyes:

129

nothing of him that doth fade,
but doth suffer a sea change
into something rich and strange.
Sea nymphs hourly ring his knell:
Hark! now I hear them
Ding, dong, bell.
A Sea Dirge – William Shakespeare 1564 – 1616

Grieve for me, for I would grieve for you.
Then brush away the sorrow and the tears
life is not over, but begins anew,
with courage you must greet the coming years.
To live forever in the past is wrong:
can only cause you misery and pain.
Dwell not on memories overlong;
with others you must share and care again.
Reach out and comfort those who comfort you;
recall the years, but only for a while.
Nurse not your loneliness, but live again.
Forget not, but remember with a smile.
A Navajo prayer

On the death of a child or a serviceman:
He/she shall grow not old as we that are left grow old.
Age shall not weary him/her nor the years condemn.
At the going down of the sun and in the morning
we shall remember him/her.
For the Fallen by Laurence Binyon 1869 – 1943 (September 1914)

Her laughter was better than birds in the morning,
her smile turned the edge of the wind,
her memory disarms death
and charms the surly grave.
Early she went to bed,
too early we saw her light put out;
yet we could not grieve
more than a little while.
For she lives in the earth around us,
laughs from the sky.
Cecil Day Lewis (Irish) 1904 – 1972

Holy spirit of my soul I adore thee;
enlighten, guide, strengthen and console me;
tell me what I ought to do and command me to do it,
I promise to be submissive in everything that Thou shalt ask of me
and to accept all that Thou permittest to happen to me,
only show me what is Thy will.

I am standing upon that foreshore
a ship at my side, spreads her white sails to the
morning breeze and starts for the blue ocean.
She is an object of beauty and strength and I shall stand
and watch her, until at length she hangs like a
speck of white cloud just where the sea and sky
come down to mingle with each other.
Then someone at my side says, 'There! she's gone!'
Gone where? Gone from my sight that is all.
She is just as large in mast and spar and hull
as ever she was when she left my side;
just as able to bear her load of living freight
to the place of her destination.
Her diminished size is in me, not in her.
And just at that moment, when someone at my side says:
'There!, she's gone!' there are other eyes watching her coming
and other voices ready to take up the glad shout,
'Here she comes!'
From Toilers of the Sea – Victor Hugo 1802 – 1885

I don't believe in death,
who mocks in silent stealth;
he robs us only of a breath,
not of a lifetime's wealth.

I don't believe the tomb
imprisons us in earth;
it's but another loving womb
preparing our new birth.

I do believe in Life
empowered from above;
'Til, freed from stress and worldly strife,
We soar through realms above.

I do believe that then,
in joy that never ends,
we'll meet all those we've loved, again,
and celebrate our friends.
Pauline Webb

I fall asleep in the full and certain hope
that my slumber shall not be broken;
and that though I be all forgetting,
yet shall I not be all-forgotten,
but continue that life in the thoughts and deeds
of those I loved.

For a suicide funeral:
If I can choose between a death of torture
and one that is simple and easy,
why should I not select the latter?
As I choose the ship in which I sail
and the house which I inhabit,
so will I choose the death by which I leave life.
Seneca c. 55 BC – 40 AD

If I could save time in a bottle,
the first thing that I'd like to do
is to save every day 'til eternity passes away
just to spend them with you.

If I could make days last forever,
if words could make wishes come true
I'd save every day like a treasure
then again, I would spend them with you.

If I had a box for wishes
and dreams that had never come true;
the box would be empty, except
for the memory of how they were answered by you.

If I should die and leave you here awhile,
be not like others sore undone, who keep
long vigils by the silent dust, and weep.
For my sake – turn again to life and smile,
nerving thy heart and trembling hand to do,
something to comfort other hearts than thine.
Complete those dear unfinished tasks of mine,
and I, perchance may therein comfort you.
Hugh Price Hughes (Welsh) 1847 – 1902

On the death of an Englishman/woman dying and being buried abroad:
If I should die, think only this of me:
that there's some corner of a foreign field
that is forever England. There shall be
in that rich earth a richer dust concealed;
a dust whom England bore, shaped, made aware,
gave, once, her flowers to love, her ways to roam,
a body of England's, breathing English air,
washed by the rivers, blest by suns of home.

And think, this heart, all evil shed away,
a pulse in the eternal mind, no less
gives somewhere back the thoughts by England given;
her sighs and sounds; dreams happy as her day;
and laughter, learnt of friends; and gentleness,
in hearts at peace, under an English heaven.
Rupert Brooke 1887 – 1915

If I should go before the rest of you
break not a flower, nor inscribe a stone,
nor when I'm gone speak in a Sunday voice
but be the usual selves that I have known.
Weep if you must, parting is hell,
But life goes on, so sing as well!
Joyce Grenfell 1910 – 1979, from Joyce By Herself and Friends published by
Macmillan

If tears could build a stairway
and memories a lane
we'd walk right up to heaven
and bring you back again.

If we will but be still and listen, I think we shall hear these sad trials talking to us saying 'Your tent has been pitched in pleasant places among those of dear relations and tried friends, and now they are disappearing from around you. The stakes are loosened one by one, and the canvas is torn away, with no vestige left behind, and you want something that will not be taken away. You want something large enough to fill your heart, and imperishable enough to make it immortal like itself. That something is God.
From Letter to a bereaved friend. – Samuel Palmer 1805 – 1881

I had thought that your death
was a waste and a destruction;
a pain of grief hardly to be endured.

I am only beginning to learn
that your life was a gift and a growing
and a loving left with me.

That desperation of death
destroyed the existence of love,
but the fact of death
cannot destroy what has been given.

I am learning to look at your life again
instead of your death and your departing.
From The Existence of Love – Marjorie Pizer

I have no fear of death – but I shall welcome
a helping hand to see me through
for it is said that just as everyone has a guardian angel,
so to each one comes somebody to help us over the stile.

Once I am over, I know a door will open on a new loveliness
and freshness of colour, form and light which is far more beautiful
than anything I have ever seen or imagined.
From The Wind in the Oak – Oliver Hall

I have seen death too often to believe in death.
It is not an ending, but a withdrawal.
As one who finishes a long journey,
stills the motor, turns off the lights,
steps from the car, and walks up the path -
to the home that awaits him.
Anon

God speaking – on the death of a child:
'I'll lend you for a little time a child of Mine,' He said.
'For you to love the while he lives, and mourn for when he's dead.
It may be six or seven years or twenty two or three,
but will you, till I call him back, take care of him for me?

He'll bring his charms to gladden you, and should his stay be brief,
you'll have his lovely memories as solace for your grief.
I cannot promise he will stay, since all from earth return,
but there are lessons taught down there I want this child to learn.

I've looked this wide world over in my search for teachers true
and from the throngs that crowd life's lanes, I have selected you.
Now will you give him all your love, nor think the labour vain,
nor hate me when I come to call and take him back again?'

I fancied that I heard them say, 'Dear Lord Thy will be done
for all the joy the child shall bring; for the risk of grief we'll run.
We'll shelter him with tenderness, we''ll love him while we may
and for the happiness we've known forever grateful stay.

But should the angels call for him much sooner than we planned
we'll brave the bitter grief that comes and try to understand.'
Anon

I said to the man who stood at the Gate of the Year,
'Give me a light that I may tread safely into the unknown'.
And he replied, 'Go out into the darkness and put your hand into the hand of
God. That shall be to you better than light and safer than a known way!'
The Gate of the Year – Minnie Louise Haskins 1875 – 1957

I see myself now at the end of my journey, my toilsome days are ended. I am
going now to see that head that was crowned with thorns, and that face that was
spit upon for me.

I have formerly lived by hearsay and faith but now I go where I shall live by sight,
and shall be with Him in whose company I delight myself.

I have loved to hear my Lord spoken of; and wherever I have seen the print of
his shoe in the earth, there I have coveted to set my foot too.

His name to me has been as a civet box; sweeter than all perfume. His voice to
me has been most sweet; and his countenance I have more desired than they
that have most desired the light of the sun.

His word I did use to gather for my food, and for antidotes against my faintings. 'He has held me, and hath kept me from mine iniquities; yea my steps hath he strengthened in his way.'

Glorious it was to see how the open region was filled with horses and chariots, with trumpeters and pipers, with singers and players on stringed instruments, to welcome the pilgrims as they went up, and followed one another in at the beautiful gate of the city.
From Pilgrim's Progress – John Bunyan 1628 – 1688

Ben gave the following poem to his mother before he died of a brain tumour that he had battled with for four years, in December,1997.
I see the countless Christmas trees around the world below
with tiny lights, like Heaven's stars reflecting on the snow.
The sight is so spectacular, please wipe away the tear,
for I am spending Christmas, with Jesus Christ this year.

I hear the many Christmas songs that people hold so dear,
but the sounds of music can't compare, with the Christmas choir up here.
I have no words to tell you, the joy their voices bring,
for it is beyond description, to hear the angels sing.
I know how much you miss me; I see the pain inside your heart,
but I am not so far away, we really aren't apart.
So be happy for me dear ones, you know I hold you dear,
and be glad I'm spending Christmas with Jesus Christ this year.

I sent you each a special gift, from my heavenly home above,
I sent you each a memory of my undying love.
After all love is a gift, more precious than pure gold,
it was always most important, in the stories Jesus told.

Please love and keep each other, as my Father said to do,
for I can't count the blessings or the love he has for each of you.
So have a Merry Christmas and wipe away the tear,
remember, I am spending Christmas with Jesus Christ this year.
My First Christmas in Heaven – Ben, 13 years old.

I strove with none, for none was worth my strife;
nature I loved and next to nature art,
I warmed both hands before the fire of life;
it sinks; and I am ready to depart.
Walter Savage Landor 1775 – 1864

I thank thee God that I have lived
in this great world and known its many joys;
the song of birds, the strong, sweet scent of hay;
and cooling breezes in the secret dusk;
the flaming sunsets at the close of day;
hills and the lovely, heather covered moors;
music at night, and moonlight on the sea;
the beat of waves upon the rocky shore;
and wild, white spray flung wide in ecstasy.

The faithful eyes of dogs, and treasured books;
the love of kin and fellowship of friends,
and all that makes life dear and beautiful.

I thank thee too, that there has come to me
a little sorrow, and sometimes defeat,
a little heartache and the loneliness
that comes with parting and the word 'Goodbye';

Dawn breaking after dreary hours of pain,
when I discovered that night's gloom must yield
and morning light break through to me again.

Because of these and other blessings poured
unasked upon my wondering head,
because I know that there is yet to come
an even richer and more glorious life,
and most of all, because thine only Son
once sacrificed life's loveliness for me –
I thank thee God, that I have lived.
Anon

It is not growing like a tree,
in bulk doth make a man better be:
or standing long an oak, three hundred year,
to fall a log at last, dry, bald and sere.
A lily of a day is fairer far in May
although it fall and die that night
it was the plant and flower of light.
In small proportions, we just beauties see
and in short measures, life may perfect be.
Ben Johnson 1570 – 1638

It matters not when I am dead
where this dull clay shall lie,
nor what the dogmas, creeds and rites
decree to us who die.
I only know that I shall tread
the paths my dead have trod,
and where the hearts I love have gone,
there shall I find my God.
Kendall Banning

It seems such waste, such stupid waste; his great thoughts, his fine body,
that love of life, all the friendship, the aspiration, the love… all thrown away,
gone, wasted for ever.

Who says that it is wasted? It is his body that has served its turn and is cast
away. His great thoughts, the friendship, the aspiration, the love; can we say that
these die? Nay, rather, these shall not die; these shall live in the courts of the
Lord, for ever.
E. Nesbit 1858 – 1924

To a Hindu mother from her baby:
It is time for me to go mother, I am going.
When in the paling darkness of the lonely dawn
you stretch out your arms for your baby in the bed,
I shall say 'baby is not there' – mother, I am going.

I shall become a delicate draught of air and caress you;
and shall be ripples in the water when you bathe
and kiss you and kiss you again.

In the dusky night when the rain patters the leaves
you will hear my whisper in your bed,
and my laughter will flash with the lightening
through the open window of your room.

If you lie awake thinking of your baby till late at night,
I shall sing to you from the stars 'Sleep, mother, sleep'.
On the straying moonbeams I shall steal over your bed,
and lie upon your bosom while you sleep.

I shall become a dream, and through the opening of your eyelids,
I shall slip into the depths of your sleep,
and when you wake up and look around startled,
like a twinkling firefly I shall flit out into the darkness.
When on the great festival of Puja,
the neighbours' children come and play around the house,
I shall melt into the music of the flute
and throb in your heart all day.

Dear auntie will come with Puja presents and will ask
'Where is our baby sister?' Mother you will tell her softly
'she is in the pupils of your eyes,
she is in my body and in my soul.'

It's wondrous what a hug can do
a hug can cheer you when you're blue;
a hug can say 'I love you so'
Or 'I hate to see you go'.
A hug is 'Welcome back again!'
and 'Great to see you!' or
'Where've you been?'
A hug can soothe a small child's pain
and bring a rainbow after rain.
The hug! There's just no doubt about it,
we scarcely could survive without it.
A hug delights and warms and charms,
it must be why God gave us arms.
Hugs are great for fathers and mothers,
sweet for sisters, even for brothers,
and chances are some favourite aunts
love them more than potted plants.
Kittens crave them, puppies love them;

heads of state are not above them.
A hug can break the language barrier
and make the dullest day seem merrier.
No need to fret about the store of 'em
the more you give
the more there are of 'em.
So stretch those arms without delay
and give someone a hug today.
I like hugs!

Just think! Some night the stars will gleam
upon a cold, grey stone, and trace a name
with silver beam, and lo! twill be your own.

That night is speeding on to greet your epitaphic rhyme;
your life is but a little beat, within the heart of time.

A little gain, a little pain, a laugh, lest you may moan!
A little blame, a little fame, a star-gleam on a stone.

Jesu, Maria – I am near to death,
and Thou art calling me; I know it now.
Not by the token of this faltering breath,
this chill at heart, this dampness on my brow,
Jesu have mercy! Mary, pray for me!
'tis this new feeling, never felt before,
Be with me Lord in my extremity!
that I am going, that I am no more.
'Tis this strange innermost abandonment
Lover of souls! Great God I look to Thee,
this emptying out of each constituent
and natural force, by which I come to be.
Pray for me, O my friends; a visitant
is knocking his dire summons at my door,
the like of whom, to scare me and to daunt,
has never, never come to me before;
…O loving friends, your prayers!
From *The Dream of Gerontius – The very Reverend The Provost Cardinal John Henry Newman 1801 – 1890*

Let me die
as the leaves die,
gladly.

Clad in the golds and reds of triumph
they make the mountains a miracle
and the valleys a fairyland of wonder.

Yet these leaves are dying.
They are about to flutter from the trees
down to the waiting earth where in death
they will become soft mulch, brown mold,

and indistinguishable earth,
and then new leaves again.

So they die,
refusing to remember with anguish
other days long ago,
when they were fresh little tendrils
breaking from the buds in the fresh warmth of Spring,
or the summer days when they were green luxurious foliage
swept by the threat of sudden storm.

Instead, they deck themselves in joy,
because after the mulch and the mold and the earth
they will become new leaves again.
This must be the meaning of their reds and golds.
They are happy as they die.

Let me die
as the leaves die,
gladly.
D C Clausen

Let none fear death, for the death of the Saviour has set us free.
He has destroyed death by undergoing death...
Christ is risen, and life reigns in freedom.
Christ is risen, and there is none left in the tomb.
The Mystical Theology of the Eastern Church – St John Chrysotom

Let us be content with what has happened
and be thankful for all that we have been spared.
Let us accept the natural order of things in which we move.
Let us reconcile ourselves to the mysterious rhythm of our destinies,
such as they may be in this world of space and time.
Let us treasure our joys but not bewail our sorrows.
The glory of light cannot exist without its shadows.
Life is a whole, and good and ill must be accepted together.
The journey has been enjoyable and well worth making – once.
Winston Spencer Churchill 1874 – 1965

Lord, the trouble with life just now
is that I seem to have all things
which don't matter, and to have
lost all the things, which do matter.

I have life;
I have enough money to live on:
I have plenty to occupy me:
but I am alone,
and sometimes I feel that
nothing can make up for that.

Lord compel me to see
the meaning of my faith.
Make me to realise
that I have a hope
as well as a memory, and
the unseen cloud of witnesses
is around me;
that you meant it when you said
that you would always be with me;
and make me to realise that
as long as you leave me here
there is something that
I am meant to do;

And in doing it, help me
to find the comfort and the
courage that I need to go on.
Published by Tim Tiley Ltd. S130

Love doesn't end with dying
or leave with the last breath.
For someone you've loved deeply,
love doesn't end with death.
John Addey

Loveliest of lovely things are they on earth
that soonest pass away.
The rose that lives in its little hour is prized
beyond the sculptured flower.

On the death of a child
Man proposes, God in his time disposes,
and so I wandered up to where you lay,
a little rose among the little roses,
and no more dead than they.

It seemed your childish feet were tired of straying,
you did not greet me from your flower strewn bed,
yet still I know that you were only playing -
playing at being dead.

I might have thought that you were really sleeping,
so quiet lay your eyelids to the sky,
so still your hair, but surely you were peeping;
and so I did not cry.

God knows, and in His proper time disposes,
and so I smiled and gently called your name,
added my rose to your sweet heap of roses,
and left you to your game.
Richard Middleton

Man was not made to come to nought,
but to be made perfect.
This wonderful being … capable of so much,
aspiring to do much,
with such capacities for delight and happiness,
was not born for death but Immortality;
he was not sent here for defeat,
and incompleteness, and disappointment,
but to grow from 'grace to grace',
into the likeness of the Son of God.

We talk of life cut short,
of great hopes extinguished,
of vast usefulness arrested,
of high powers given only to be taken away;
but indeed there is nothing lost,
nothing has been in vain -
the incompleteness and the failure
are only relative to us,
and while we are here in the darkness.
Early death – R W Church

May the road rise up to greet you
may the wind be always at your back
may the sun shine warm upon your face
may the rain fall soft upon your field
and until we meet again
may God hold you in the palm of his hand.
Gaelic Blessing

Memories are like rain showers
sprinkling down upon you
catching you unaware.
And then they are gone,
leaving you warm and refreshed.

Sometimes,
memories are like thunderstorms
beating down upon you,
relentless in their downpour.
And then they will cease,
leaving you tired and bruised.

Sometimes,
memories are like shadows
sneaking up behind you,
following you around.
Then they disappear,
leaving you sad and confused.

Sometimes,
memories are like comforters

surrounding you with warmth,
luxuriously abundant.
And sometimes they stay,
wrapping you in contentment.

Mist that hangs like silk
soaking in the rain;
trees that rise like ghosts
bearing people's names;
and a sea that takes me
where I do not know
but I gladly go.
Shrouded in the sweetest grass
I've ever known
this is my earthly bed
my beloved home
but the voice that calls me
to the far away
I can only trust every word you say

And here I am
out on the edge of the world
with you, with you;
shall I leave the print of my knees
upon the sand.
This is my final prayer
in my native land;
shall I turn my face
towards the shining sea;
taste the salt of my tears
for those I have to leave.
Edge of the World

Music when soft voices die,
Vibrates in the memory;
odours when sweet violets sicken,
live within the sense they quicken.
Rose leaves when the rose is dead
are heaped for the beloved's bed.
And so thy thoughts, when thou art gone,
love itself shall slumber on.
Percy Bysshe Shelley 1792 – 1822

My Lord God, I have no idea where I am going.
I do not see the road ahead of me.
I cannot know for certain where it will end.

Nor do I really know myself,
and the fact that I think I am following your will
does not mean that I am actually doing so.

But I believe that the desire to please you does in fact please you,
and I hope that I have that desire in all that I am doing.
I hope that I never do anything apart from that desire.

And I know that if I do this
you will lead me by the right road
though I may know nothing about it.

Therefore I will trust you always,
though I may seem to be lost and in the shadow of death
I will not fear, for you are ever with me
and you will never leave me to face my peril alone.
Thomas Merton 1915 – 1968

My love came back to me
under the November tree
sheltered and dim.

He put his hand upon my shoulder
he did not think me strange or older
nor I him.
All Souls Night – Frances Cornford 1886

No longer mourn me when I am dead
than you shall hear the surly sullen bell
give warning to the world, that I am fled
from this vile world, with vilest worms to dwell;
nay as you read this line, remember not
the hand that writ it; for I love you so,
that I in your sweet thoughts would be forgot
if thinking on me then should make you woe.
O if, I say, you look upon this verse
when I perhaps compounded are with clay,
do not so much as my poor name rehearse,
but let your love even with my life decay;
lest the wise world should look into your moan,
and mock you with me after I am gone.
William Shakespeare 1564 – 1616

No man is an island entire of itself;
every man is a piece of the continent
a part of the main.

If a clod be washed away by the sea,
Europe is the less,
as well as if a promontory were.

Any man's death diminishes me,
because I am involved with mankind;

and therefore never send to know
for whom the bell tolls;
it tolls for thee.
From Meditation XVII – John Donne 1572 – 1631

Not, how did he die, but how did he live?
Not, what did he gain, but what did he give?
These are the units to measure the worth
Of a man or a woman, regardless of birth.

Not, what is his church, nor what was his creed?
But, did he befriend those really in need?
Was he ever ready, with a word of good cheer
To bring back a smile, to banish a tear?

Not, what did the sketch in the newspaper say
But, how many were sorry when he passed away?

No pain beyond, no tears, no fear.
No thought of death – for I'm still near.
No hugs I know, nor sweet caress,
but I'm still close to love and bless.

No quiet word, nor gentle touch
but don't despair – I love you much.
No gesture, kind, to show I care;
the veil's drawn but I'm still there.

Grieve not too long – but look around
in earthly things I shall be found.
A falling leaf, a growing tree,
in every breeze you will feel me.

I walk in life; death holds no pain.
Be reassured, we'll meet again.
Remember me

Not till the loom is silent
and the shuttles cease to fly
shall God unroll the canvas
and explain the reason why
the dark threads are as needful
in the weaver's skilful hand
as the threads of gold and silver
in the patterns he has planned.
Then shall I know – Corrie ten Boom (Dutch) 1892 – 1983

Of all the money that e'er I spent
I spent it in good company.
And all the harm that e'er I done
alas it was to none but me.

For all I've done for want of wit
to memory now I can't recall;
so fill to me a parting glass
goodnight and joy be with you all.

O Christ you wept when grief was raw,
and felt for those who mourned their friend;
come close to where we would not be
and hold us, numbed by this life's end.
The well loved voice is silent now
and we have much we meant to say;
collect our lost and wandering words
and keep them 'til the endless day.

We try to hold what is not here
and fear for what we do not know;
O, take our hands in yours, good Lord,
And free us to let our friend go.

In all our loneliness and doubt
through what we cannot realise
address us from your empty tomb
and tell us that life never dies.
From the Iona Community

One night a man had a dream;
he dreamed he was walking along a beach with the Lord
across the sky flashed scenes from his life.
For each scene, he noticed two sets of footprints in the sand;
one belonged to him, and the other to the Lord.
When the last scene of his life flashed before him,
he looked back at the footprints in the sand;
he noticed that many times along the path of his life
there was only one set of footprints,
he also noticed that it happened at the very lowest
and saddest times in his life.

This really bothered him and he questioned the Lord about it,
'Lord, you said that once I decided to follow you,
you'd walk with me all the way;
but I have noticed that during the most troublesome times in my life,
there is only one set of footprints.
I don't understand why when I needed you most you would leave me.'

The Lord replied, 'My precious, precious child,
I love you and I would never leave you;
during your times of trial and suffering,
when you see only one set of footprints,
it was then that I carried you.'
Footprints – Anon

On the road that all must travel
you have travelled on ahead,
out into the morning light,
out of reach and out of sight,
but not so very far away
for every night and every day

on the wings of memory
something brings you back to me.
Some simple and familiar thing
will start my heart remembering
the times we had, the good, the bad,
the days, the years, sweet things and sad,
a tune, a joke, a cup of tea,
something brings you back to me.

O snatched away in beauty's bloom!
On thee shall press no ponderous tomb;
but on thy turf shall roses rear
their leaves the earliest of the year,
and he wild cypress wave in tender gloom:

and oft by yon blue gushing stream
shall sorrow lean her dropping head,
and feed deep thought with many a dream,
and lingering pause and lightly tread;
fond wretch! as if her step disturb'd the dead.

Away! we know that tears are vain,
that death nor heeds nor hears distress:
will this unteach us to complain?
or make one mourner weep the less?
and thou, who tellst me to forget,
thy looks are wan, thine eyes are wet.
Elegy – Lord Byron

Our belief is that Jesus was raised from the dead
for our benefit, through the love and power of God.
Through his death he identified with us in our pain,
our suffering, our ignorance, and our despair.
Did he not cry, 'My God, my God, why have you forsaken me?'
Does he not know that there are situations where belief
in the goodness of God becomes impossible and unacceptable?
This is my answer to those who rage against him
and think they have defeated any claims to faith.

Likewise, I put my trust, while I am of sound mind,
in the goodness, the compassion and the love of God.
By his grace he has made us what we are.
And whilst our weaknesses cause us to stumble
yet his providence is always over us.
He cares, he accepts, he forgives and requires
that we shall be like that to others.
I hand my spirit over to him when I die.
This is what he did when he died, and it worked!

God will not fail us. He did not create us for nothing;
we are his pride and joy. We are his best beloved:
with Jesus we inherit a place in a home of many rooms.

He calls us to share in his resurrection;
he has prepared a place for us. What more could we ask?
In the meantime, show pity and humility to others;
work and pray for his kingdom on earth;
that our children and our children's children
may know a world of justice and peace
where all people are valued for their likeness
to the one who created them.
My Resurrection and Yours – Reverend Canon John A Tibbs.

Our revels now are ended
these our actors,
as I foretold you,
were all spirits and are melted into air,
into thin air;
and like the baseless fabric of this vision,
the cloud capped towers, the gorgeous palaces,
the solemn temples, the great globe itself,
yea all which it inherit, shall dissolve
and like this insubstantial pageant faded,
leave not a rack behind.
We are such stuff as dreams are made of,
And our little life is rounded in a sleep.
From The Tempest – William Shakespeare 1564 – 1616

Out of the night that covers me
black as the pit from pole to pole
I thank whatever gods may be
for my unconquerable soul.

In the fell clutch of circumstance
I have not winced nor cried aloud:
under the bludgeonings of chance
my head is bloody and unbowed.

Beyond this place of wrath and tears
looms but the horror of the shade
and yet the menace of the years
finds and shall find me unafraid.
It matters not how straight the gate,
how charged with punishments the scroll,
I am the master of my fate:
I am the captain of my soul.
Atheist's prayer: – William Ernest Henley 1849 – 1903

Pause at death's brink
and notice through the haze
the disappearing pain and need
and shedding of ephemera,
the platitudes and trivia.

Detach, let fall pretence, the mask,
and face the inner self, the core,
despite surrounding love, alone,
in solitude recalling past,
the good, the less than good,
both much regretted now,
the leaving or the doing.

Reach out ahead, to those who went before
and trust, for one who trod that path
is here to take your loneliness, remorse,
in battered, perfect hands
and lift you to himself.
At the brink of death – Brenda Marshal

Perhaps, if we could see
the splendour of the land
to which our loved are
called from you and me;
we'd understand.

Perhaps, if we could hear
the welcome they receive,
from old familiar voices
all so dear;
we would not grieve.

Perhaps, if we could know
the reason why they went,
we'd smile, and wipe away
the tears that flow;
we'd wait content.

Regret not me, beneath the sunny tree
I lie uncaring, slumbering peacefully.
Yet gaily sing until the pewter ring
those songs we sang when we went gypsying

And lightly dance in some triple timed romance
in coupled figures and forget mischance;

and mourn not me beneath the yellowing tree;
for I shall mind not, slumbering peacefully.
Regret Not Me – Thomas Hardy 1840 – 1928

Remember the fun, the gaiety, the sunshine,
remember the jokes, the laughter, the music
remember the beautiful babies coming;
think how lucky a family is to love each other.
Remember all the love given and received;
let this be my legacy.
My Legacy

Remember me when I am gone away,
gone far away into the silent land;
when you can no more hold me by the hand,
nor I half turn to go, yet turning stay.
Remember me when no more day by day
you tell me of our future that you planned:
Only remember me; you understand
it will be late to counsel then or pray.
Yet if you should forget me for a while
and afterwards remember, do not grieve:
for if the darkness and corruption leave
a vestige of the thoughts that once I had,
better by far you should forget and smile
than that you should remember and be sad.
Christina Georgina Rossetti 1830 – 1894

A prayer from a husband who is left:
September has come, it is hers
whose vitality leaps in the autumn,
whose nature prefers trees without leaves
and a fire in the fireplace.

So I give her this month and the next
though the whole of my year should be hers
who has rendered already so many of its days intolerable
or perplexed but so many more happy.

Who has left a scent on my life, and left my walls
dancing over and over with her shadow.
Whose hair is twined in all my waterfalls
and all of London is littered with remembered kisses.

Sleep to the noise of running water
tomorrow will be crossed, however deep
there is no river of the dead or Lethe.
Tonight we sleep on the banks of the Rubicon –
the die is cast.
There will be time to audit the accounts later
There will be sunlight later
And the equation will come out at last.
Louis MacNeice 1907 – 1963

Some people come into our lives and quickly go.
Some people move our souls to dance.
They awaken us to new understanding with the
passing whisper of their wisdom.

Some people make the sky more beautiful to gaze upon.
They stay in our lives for a while,
leave footprints on our hearts,
and we are never, ever, the same.
Flavia Weedn

A Prayer from a partner who is left:
Stop all the clocks, cut off the telephone,
prevent the dog from barking with a juicy bone,
silence the pianos and with muffled drum
bring out the coffin, let the mourners come.

Let aeroplanes circle moaning overhead
scribbling on the sky the message 'he is Dead',
put crepe bows round the white necks of the public doves,
let the traffic policemen wear black cotton gloves.
He was my north, my south, my east and west,
my working week and my Sunday rest,
my noon, my midnight, my talk, my song;
I thought that love would last for ever:
I was wrong.

The stars are not wanted now; put out every one,
pack up the moon and dismantle the sun,
pour away the ocean and sweep up the wood;
for nothing now can ever come to any good.
Funeral Blues – W H Auden 1907 – 1973

For a sailor or lifeboat man:
Sunset and evening star,
and one clear call for me!
and may there be no moaning of the bar,
when I put out to sea.

But such a tide as moving seems asleep,
too full for sound and foam,
when that which drew out from the boundless deep
turns again home.

Twilight and evening bell,
and after that the dark!
And may there be no sadness of farewell,
when I embark;

For though from out our bourne of Time and Place
the flood may bear me far,
I hope to see my Pilot face to face
when I have crossed the bar.
Crossing the Bar – Alfred, Lord Tennyson 1809 – 1892

Thanks to the human heart by which we live,
thanks to its tenderness, its joys, and fears.

To me the meanest flower that blows can give
thoughts that do often lie too deep for tears.
William Wordsworth 1770 – 1850

The brave red-faced little children laugh
dressed in orange-yellow caps
facing an uncertain world;
many sorely handicapped
they miss the smell of green grass
and the blue skies above;
they sense death is drawing close
they fill the world with love.

Faces streaked with indigo
play Indian squaws and braves
till death reaches out to them
Violet drapes on small graves.

Children have left or maybe
they're still shining in the sky
little rainbows of colour
for small children never die.

When you look up in wonder
at the beauty of rainbows
it is not Mother Nature
it's small children giving shows.
Little Rainbows – Granville Cooke (1997)

The curtain has fallen upon
and apparently shut out from view
our dear departed;
but they are not always hidden.

They come to us in our dreams,
they seem to whisper together in our memory;
so many times in the day
they stir up our thoughts towards them;

again and again we feel their gentle touch
in sympathetic pressure on our souls;
across the great abyss they join hands with us
in our worship; and that is no parting.

The door of death is made of gold,
that mortal eyes cannot behold:

but when the mortal eyes are closed,
and cold and pale the limbs reposed,

the soul awakes, and, wondering, sees
in her mild hand the golden keys.

The grave is Heaven's golden gate,
and rich and poor around it wait.
William Blake 1757 – 1862

The garden grieves,
the cool rain sinks into the flowers.
The summer shudders
and silently meets its end.

Leaf upon leaf drops golden
from the tall acacia tree.
Wondering, faintly, summer smiles
in the dying garden's dream.

Long by the roses,
she lingers, yearning for peace.
Slowly she closes her wide
wearied eyes.

For a seaman:
The Lord is my pilot, I shall not drift:
He lighteth me across the dark waters,
He steereth me in deep channels
He keepeth my log.
He guideth me by the star of holiness
for his name's sake.
Yea, though I sail mid the thunders
and tempests of life,
I will dread no danger,
for Thou art near me
Thy love and Thy care,
they shelter me.
Thou preparest a harbour before me
in the homeland of eternity.
Thou annointest the waves with oil
my ship rideth calmly.
Surely sunlight and starlight shall favour me
on the voyage I take,
and I will rest in the port of God forever.

For the death of an Australian:
The love of field and coppice
of green and shaded lanes,
of ordered woods and gardens
is running in your veins.

Strong love of grey-blue distance,
brown streams and soft, dim skies?
I know, but cannot share it,
my love is otherwise.

I love a sun-burnt country
a land of sweeping plains,
of rugged mountain ranges,
of droughts and flooding rains.

I love her far horizons,
I love her jewel sea,
her beauty and her terror,
the wide brown land for me.

The stark white ring-barked forests,
all tragic to the moon,
the sapphire misted mountains,
the hot gold hush of noon.

Green tangle of the brushes
where lithe lianas coil,
the orchids deck the treetops,
and ferns the warm dark soil.

Core of my heart, my country!
her pitiless blue sky,
when, sick at heart, around us
we see the cattle die?

But then the grey clouds gather
and we can bless again
the drumming of an army,
the steady, soaking rain.

Core of my heart, my country!
land of the rainbow gold,
for flood and fire and famine
she pays us back threefold.

Over the thirsty paddocks,
watch, after many days,
the filmy veil of greenness
that thickens as we gaze.

An opal hearted country,
a wilful lavish land.
All you who have not loved her,
you will not understand.

Though earth holds many splendours,
wherever I may die,
I know to what brown country,
my homing thoughts will fly.
My Country – Dorothea Mackellar (Australian)1885-1968

For a child who dies before 15 or before birth:
The master says 'There is a garden of God. Human beings are trees growing therein. The Gardener is our Father. When he sees a little tree in a place too small for her development, He prepares a suitable and more beautiful place, where she may grow and bear fruit. Then he transplants that little tree.'

The other trees marvel, saying 'This is a lovely little tree. For what reason does the gardener uproot it?

'The Divine Gardener, alone, knows the reason. You are weeping, Rivaniyyih, but if you could see the beauty of the place where she is, you would no longer be sad. Your child is now free, and, like a bird, is chanting divine joyous melodies. If you could see that sacred Garden, you would be content to remain here on earth. Yet this is where your duty lies now.'
Death the Messenger of Joy – The Garden of God (Baha'i Faith)

The rich and poor listen to the voice of death
the learned and the unlearned listen;
the proud and the humble listen;
the honest and deceitful listen,
the old and the young listen;
but when death speaks to us,
what does it say?

Death does not speak about itself.
it does not say 'Fear me'
it does not say 'Wonder at me'.
it does not say 'Understand me'.
but it says to us, 'Think of life;
think of the privilege of life;
think how great a thing life may be made'.
Anon

A prayer on the death of a parent:
There is no greater gift in life
than the gift our parents give
it's a wonderful example
of the way that we should live.

Thoughts on Bereavement
There is so much that we have lost,
apart from the sheer physical presence;
our joy in the delight of the child;
our faith, not perhaps in God entirely,
but in God's all enveloping power to protect.
Our faith in prayer that cannot restore

'What used to be' and make it 'what is'.
Our own youth and innocence, the zest has gone;
enthusiasm demands a conscious effort.
The fairy story ending where everyone lives
'Happily ever after' and stands out clearly
as the myth we can no longer accept.
In our mind's eye,
we have become losers, always on the defensive,
wondering where the next blow will fall;
our fears are different now
more distinctive.
The ultimate fear of death is nullified,
for beyond that far horizon
we may see again the beloved face;
fear lies in mental anguish rather than pain.
Like Jesus we have spent time in the wilderness,
and must question our capacity to withstand
a fresh assault on our reason.
One lesson we learn – to count our blessings;
the 'completeness' that we were unaware of
has gone forever, so, like a physical cripple
our remaining senses become sharper
in compensation.
As a child I wondered at the link between
'Sadder and Wiser', but now I see
the essential truth;
We gain compassion and understanding,
we gain wisdom beyond our years, whatever our age,
we who are left with empty arms and a heart full of love.
Alison Hopper

They are not long, the weeping and the laughter,
love and desire and hate:
I think they have no portion in us after
we pass the gate.

They are not long, the days of wine and roses:
out of a misty dream our path emerges for awhile,
then closes within a dream.
Ernest Dowson 1867 – 1900

On the death of a Down's syndrome child:
They said on his first day on earth,
better by far if he'd died at birth;
how could they know,
how could they tell the joy he'd bring;
he taught our heart the way to sing,
we loved him so.
We learned together through the years
to show the joy, but hide the tears

they must not see.
They'd never learn the hurt they caused
through thoughtless stares that on him paused
so carelessly.

And as he grew, we never grieved
to see how little he achieved,
no praise he'd lose.
His progress made in life's tough school
we measured with a shorter rule
than scholars use.

I can't believe he owed his day
to some genetic disarray
wrongly conceived.
He came into this world, and there
he lived to teach us how to care;
this he achieved.
Anon

They that love beyond the world
cannot be separated by it.
Death cannot kill what never dies.
Nor can spirits ever be divided
that love and live in the same divine principle:
the root and record of their friendship.
If absence be not death, neither is theirs.
Death is but crossing the world,
as friends do the sea;
They live for one another still.
This is the comfort of friends:
that though they may be said to die,
yet their friendship and society are
in the best sense immortal,
because they are ever present.
Fruits of Solitude – William Penn 1644 – 1718

This day I will bury my friend
the one I laughed with, lived for,
dreamt with, loved.

Though I am dead, grieve not for me with tears;
think not of death with sorrowing and fears,
I am so near that every tear you shed
touches and tortures me, though you think me dead.

But when you laugh and sing in glad delight,
my soul is lifted upwards to the light:
laugh and be glad for all that life is giving,
and, I though dead, will share your joy of living.
From Funerals – Bentley Best & Hunt

Time is too slow for those who wait
too swift for those who fear
too long for those who grieve
too short for those who rejoice
but for those who love time is eternity.

A letter from heaven
To my dearest family, some things I'd like to say,
but first of all to let you know, that I arrived okay.
I'm writing this from heaven – here I dwell with God above;
here, there's no more tears of sadness – here is just eternal love.
Please do not be unhappy just because I'm out of sight;
remember that I'm with you every morning, noon and night.
The day I had to leave you when my life on earth was through
God picked me up and hugged me and he said 'I welcome you.
it's good to have you back again, you were missed while you were gone.
as for your dearest family – they'll be here later on.
I need you here so badly, you are part of my plan;
there is so much that we can do to help our mortal man'.
God gave me a list of things, that he wished for me to do;
and foremost on the list was to watch and care for you.
And when you lie in bed at night, the day's chores put to flight
God and I are closest to you … in the middle of the night.
When you think of my life on earth, and all those loving years,
because you are only human, they are bound to bring you tears.
But do not be afraid to cry, it does relieve the pain;
remember there would be no flowers, unless there were some rain.
I wish that I could tell you all that God has planned
but if I were to tell you, you wouldn't understand.
But one thing is for certain, though my life on earth is o'er,
I'm closer to you now, than I ever was before.
There are rocky roads ahead of you and many hills to climb;
but together we can do it, taking one day at a time.
It was always my philosophy and I'd like it for you too,
that as you give unto the world, the world will give to you.
If you can help somebody, who is in sorrow and pain,
then you can say to God at night, 'My day was not in vain'.
And now I am contented, that my life, it was worthwhile,
knowing as I passed along, I made somebody smile.
So if you meet somebody who is sad and feeling low,
just lend a hand to pick them up, as on your way you go.
When you're walking down the street and you've got me on your mind,
I'm walking in your footsteps, only half a step behind.
And when it's time for you to go – from that body to be free,
remember you're not going, you're coming here to me!

For a couple who die together:
To those whom death again did wed
this grave's their second marriage bed;

for though the hand of fate could force
twixt soul and body a divorce;
it could not sunder man and wife
because they both lived but one life;
peace the lovers are asleep.
They, sweet turtles, folded lie
in the last knot that love could tie.
Richard Crashaw 1613 – 1649

Tread lightly, she is near
under the snow,
speak gently, she can hear
the daisies grow.

All her bright golden hair
tarnished with rust,
she that was young and fair
fallen to dust.

Lily like, white as snow,
she hardly knew
she was a woman, so
sweetly she grew.

Coffin board, heavy stone,
lie on her breast,
I vex my heart alone,
she is at rest.

Peace, peace, she cannot hear
lyre or sonnet,
all my life's buried here,
heap earth upon it.
Oscar Wilde (Irish) 1854 – 1900

Under the wide and starry sky,
dig the grave and let me lie
gladly did I live and gladly die,
and I laid me down with a will

This be the verse you grave for me:
'Here he lies where he longed to be;
home is the sailor, home from sea
and the hunter home from the hill'.
Requiem – R L Stevenson 1850-1894

We seem to give them back to Thee, O God,
who gavest them to us.
Yet as Thou didst not lose them in giving,
so we do not lose them by their return.
Not as the world givest,
givest Thou, O lover of souls.

What Thou givest Thou takest not away,
for what is thine is ours also if we are Thine.
And life is eternal and love is immortal,
and death is only an horizon,
and an horizon is nothing,
save the limit of our sight.

Lift us up strong Son of God that we may see farther;
cleanse our eyes that we may see more clearly;
draw us closer to Thyself that we may know ourselves
to be near to our loved ones, who are with Thee.

And while Thou dost prepare a place for us,
prepare us also for that happy place,
that where Thou art,
we may be also for evermore.
William Penn 1644 – 1718

We watched her breathing through the night,
her breathing soft and low,
as in her breast the wave of life
kept heaving to and fro.

But when the morn came dim and sad
and chill with early showers,
her quiet eyelids closed – she had
another morn than ours.
The Death Bed – Thomas Hood 1799 – 1845

We who are left, how shall we look again
happily on the sun or feel the rain
without remembering how they who went
ungrudgingly, and spent
their all for us, loved too the sun and rain?

A bird among the rain-wet lilac sings –
but we, how shall we turn to little things,
and listen to the birds and winds and streams
made holy by their dreams,
nor feel the heartbreak in the heart of things?
Lament by Wilfrid Wilson Gibson 1878 – 1962

What is love? …it's a kind of sharing
that holds two hearts together,
in loyalty, caring and respect.
It is an understanding
that one finds only too seldom,
a meeting of the minds.
It is a gift of God.
A blessing from above
that fills the earth with fragrance…
that is love.

What is this life if full of care,
we have no time to stand and stare;
no time to stand beneath the boughs
and stare as long as sheep and cows.

No time to see, when woods we pass,
where squirrels hide their nuts in grass.
No time to see, in broad daylight,
streams full of stars, like skies at night.

No time to wait till her mouth can
enrich that smile her eyes began.
A poor life this, if full of care,
we have no time to stand and stare.
W H Davies (Welsh) 1871 – 1940

What is our life? A play of passion,
our mirth the music of division.
Our mothers' wombs the tiring houses be,
where we are dressed for this short comedy.
Heaven the judicious sharp spectator is,
that sits and marks still who doth act amiss;
our graves that hide us from the searching sun
are like drawn curtains when the play is done.
Thus march we, playing, to our latest rest;
only we die in earnest, that's no jest.
All the World's a Stage – William Shakespeare 1564 – 1616

On the death of those fallen in battle
What passing bells for these who die as cattle?
only the monstrous anger of the guns.
Only the stuttering rifles' rapid rattle
can patter out their hasty orisons.

No mockeries for them; no prayers nor bells,
nor any voice of mourning save the choirs,
the shrill demented choirs of wailing shells;
and bugles calling for them from sad shires.

What candles may be held to speed them all?
not in the hands of boys, but in their eyes
shall shine the holy glimmer of goodbyes.

The pallor of girl's brows shall be their pall;
their flowers the tenderness of patient minds,
and each slow dusk a drawing down of blinds.
Anthem for Doomed Youth – Wilfred Owen 1893 – 1918

What though the radiance which was once so bright
be now forever taken from my sight,
though nothing can bring back the hour
of splendour in the grass, of glory in the flower;

we will grieve not, rather find
strength in what remains behind.
Intimations of Immortality – William Wordsworth 1770 – 1850

When death walks by with quiet tread
to touch a loved one who's then led
away from sleep, away from pain,
to wake in joy, to live again.

You'll hear her on a whispered breeze,
a calling bird, in swaying trees.
Do not weep long, but lift your eyes,
you'll see her glory in God's skies.

She'll be there in a swallow's flight
her eyes in stars on a velvet night:
her courage strong in every tree;
her name carved well, for eternity.

Hide not your love within your heart,
for she will always be a part
of you and all you do;
for death is nought, when love is true.
Everlasting Life

When I am dead, cry for me a little.
think of me sometimes, but not too much.
think of me now and again as I was in life,
at some moment it is pleasant to recall but not for long.
Leave me in peace, and I shall leave you in peace;
but while you live, let your thoughts be with the living.

When I am dead, my dearest
sing no sad songs for me;
plant thou no roses at my head,
nor shady cypress tree:
be the green grass above me
with showers and dewdrops wet;
and if thou wilt, remember,
and if thou wilt, forget.

I shall not see the shadows,
I shall not feel the rain;
I shall not hear the nightingale
sing on, as if in pain;
and roaming through the twilight
that doth not rise or set,
haply I may remember,
and haply may forget.
Christina Georgina Rossetti 1830 – 1894

When I am gone, release me, let me go.
I have so many things to see and do.
You musn't tie yourself to me in tears;
be happy that we had so many years.

I gave to you my love, you can only guess
how much you gave to me in happiness.
I thank you for the love you each have given,
but now it's time I travelled to my 'heaven'.

So, grieve a while for me if grieve you must,
then let your grief be comforted by trust.
It's only for a while that we must part,
so bless the memories within your heart.

I won't be far away, for life goes on
so if you need me, call and I will come.
Though you cannot see or touch me, I will be near
and if you listen with your heart you'll hear
all my love around you, soft and clear.

And when this journey becomes your own,
I'll greet you with a smile and 'Welcome home!'

When I come to the end of the road,
and the sun has set for me,
I want no rites in a gloom filled room;
why cry for a soul set free?

Miss me a little – but not too long
and not with your head bowed low.
Remember the love that once we shared,
Miss me – but let me go.

For this is a journey we all must take
and each must go alone.
It's all part of the Master's plan;
a step on the road to home.

When you are lonely and heavy of heart
go to the folks we know,
and free your sorrows on doing good deeds.
Miss me – but let me go.

When I have fears, as Keats had fears,
of the moment I cease to be
I console myself with vanished years
remembered laughter, remembered tears,
and the peace of the changing sea.

When I feel sad, as Keats felt sad,
that my life is so nearly done
It gives me comfort to dwell upon
remembered friends who are dead and gone

and the jokes we had and the fun.
How happy they are I cannot know
but happy am I who loved them so.
Noël Coward 1899 – 1973

When I have fears that I may cease to be
before my brain has glean'd my teeming brain,
before high piled books, in charact'ry
hold like rich garners the full ripened grain;
when I behold, upon the night's starr'd face,
huge cloudy symbols of high romance,
and think that I may never live to trace
their shadows, with the magic hand of chance;
and when I feel, fair Creature of an hour
that I shall never look upon thee more,
never have relish in the fairy power
of unreflecting love – then on the shore
of the wide world I stand alone, and think
till Love and Fame to nothingness do sink.
John Keats 1795 – 1821

When I lie where shades of darkness
shall no more assail mine eyes,
nor the rain make lamentation
when the wind sighs;
how will fare the world whose wonder
was the very proof of me?
Memory fades, must the remembered
perishing be?

O when this my dust surrenders
hand, foot, lip, to dust again,
may these loved and loving faces
please other men!

May the rusting harvest hedgerow
still the Traveller's Joy entwine,
and as happy children gather
posies once mine.

Look thy last on all things lovely,
every hour. Let no night
seal thy sense in deathly slumber
till to delight

thou hast paid thy utmost blessing;
since that all things thou wouldst praise
beauty took from those who loved them
in other days.
Walter de la Mare 1873 – 1956

When I must leave you for awhile,
please do not grieve and shed wild tears,
and hug your sorrow to you through the years,
but start out bravely with a gallant smile;
and for my sake and in my name,
live on and do all things the same.
Feed not your loneliness on empty days,
but fill each waking hour in useful ways;
reach out your hand in comfort and hold me dear,
and I in turn will comfort you and hold you near,
and never, never be afraid to die,
for I am waiting for you in the sky.
Anon

When I need someone to listen,
when I need someone to care,
when I need someone to lean on
I know that you are there.

Thank you for the times you've listened,
thank you for showing you care,
thank you for being strong for me
thank you for being there.

When the end of earth life comes, let us not
think that we have reached the twilight,
or that for the last time
the golden sky is fading in the west.

Let us not think that night has come,
but that a grander sunrise awaits us beyond the grave.
We must meet death as we meet sleep,
knowing that the morning follows night.
Thus shall we enter the dawn called death.
Death is but the name given to the
door through which we enter,
to reach another phase of our existence.

What appears a dream between the shores
of birth and death is a great reality, and though
we seem to stand upon the verge of crumbling time,
to love, to hope, and disappear,
yet it is the greatest of life's many certainties
that each individual life will never die,
because each one of us is part of the Divine Mind.
J A Findlay

When the present has latched its postern
behind my tremulous stay,
and the May month flaps its glad green leaves like wings,
delicate-filmed as new-spun silk, will the neighbours say,

'He was a man who used to notice such things'?

If it be in the dusk when, like an eyelid's soundless blink,
the dew-fall hawk comes crossing the shades to alight
upon the wind-warped upland thorn, a gazer may think,
'To him this must have been a familiar sight'.

If I pass during some nocturnal blackness, mothy and warm,
when the hedgehog travels furtively over the lawn,
one may say, 'He strove that such innocent creatures should come to no harm,
but he could do little for them; and now he's gone'.

If, when hearing that I have been stilled at last, they stand at the door,
watching the full starred heavens that winter sees,
will this thought rise on those who will meet my face no more,
'He was one who had an eye for such mysteries'.

And will any say when my bell of quittance is heard in the gloom,
and a crossing breeze cuts pause in its out-rollings,
till they rise again, as they were a new bell's boom,
'He hears it not now, but used to notice such things'?
Thomas Hardy 1840 – 1928

When tomorrow starts without me, and I'm not there to see;
If the sun should rise and find your eyes all filled with tears for me;
I wish so much you wouldn't cry the way you did today,
While thinking of the many things we didn't get to say.

I know how much you love me, as much as I love you,
And each time you think of me I know you'll miss me too;
But when tomorrow starts without me, please try to understand,
That an angel came and called my name and took me by the hand,
And said my place was ready, in heaven far above and that I'd have
to leave behind, all those I dearly love.
But as I turned to walk away, a tear fell from my eye,
For all my life, I'd always thought I didn't want to die.
I had so much to live for and so much yet to do,
It seemed almost impossible that I was leaving you.
I thought of all the yesterdays, the good ones and the bad,
I thought of all the love we shared and all the fun we had.

If I could relive yesterday I thought, just for a while,
I'd say goodbye and kiss you and maybe see you smile,
But then I fully realised that this could never be,
For emptiness and memories would take the place of me.
And when I thought of worldly things that I'd miss come tomorrow
I thought of you, and when I did, my heart was filled with sorrow.

But when I walked through heaven's gate, I felt so much at home,
When God looked down and smiled at me from His great golden throne,
He said 'This is eternity and all I promised you'
Today for life, for what is past but here it starts anew.
I promise no tomorrow, but today will always last,

And since each day's the same day there's no longing for the past.

But you have been so faithful, so trusting, so true,
Though there were times you did some things you knew you shouldn't do.
But you have been forgiven and now at last you're free.
So won't you take my hand and share my life with me?
So when tomorrow starts without me, don't think we're far apart,
For every time you think of me, I'm right here in your heart.
When Life Starts without Me – Riki Visani

When to the sessions of sweet silent thought
I sum up remembrance of things past,
I sigh the lack of many a thing I sought,
and with old woes new wail my dear time's waste.

Then can I drown an eye, unused to flow,
for precious friends hid in death's dateless night,
and weep afresh love's long since cancelled woe,
and moan the expense of many a vanished sight.

Then can I grieve at grievances foregone
and heavily from woe to woe tell o'er
the sad account of fore bemoaned moan,
which I new-pay as if not paid before.

But if the while I think on thee, dear friend,
all losses are restored and sorrows end.
Remembrance of things past – William Shakespeare 1552 – 1618

When you have tidied all things for the night,
and while your thoughts are fading to their sleep,
you'll pause a moment in the late firelight,
too sorrowful to weep.
The large and gentle furniture has stood
in sympathetic silence all the day
with that old kindness of domestic wood:
nevertheless the haunted room will say:
'Someone must be away.'

The little dog rolls over half awake,
stretches his paws, yawns, looking up at you,
wags his tail very slightly for your sake,
that you may feel he is unhappy too.

A distant engine whistles, or the floor
creaks, or the wandering night wind bangs a door;
silence is scattered like a broken glass;
the minutes prick their ears and run about,

then one by one subside again and pass
sedately in, monotonously out.
You bend your head and wipe away a tear.
Solitude walks one heavy step more near.
Solitude – Harold Monro 1879 – 1932

You can shed tears that she is gone
or you can smile because she has lived.
You can close your eyes and pray that she will come back,
or you can open your eyes and see all she's left.
Your heart can be empty because you can't see her
or you can be full of the love you shared.
You can turn your back on tomorrow and live yesterday
or you can be happy for tomorrow because of yesterday.
You can remember her and only that she's gone
or you can cherish her memory and let it live on.
You can cry and close your mind, be empty and turn your back,
or you can do what she'd want: smile, open your eyes,
love and go on.
Anon. (can also be changed to refer to a male)

You did not ask a lot from life,
you just wanted someone to share
all the treasures that this life can give,
to know no restrictions, quite simply to live.
People just didn't realise all your true worth;
so now on this day, as you return to earth,
I'll be remembering you and the good times we had;
and I'll look to the future and try not to be sad.
To May – Lesley Gray

For a mother who has died:
You gave me all that a mother could give;
You gave me your love and a reason to live.
You've been my best friend for so many years;
We've shared happy times and also our tears.
There's no-one that means as much as you do
after all you've done for me, and all we've been through;
so we'll never be parted – it just cannot be;
for you know I love you, and I know you love me.
For my Mum – Lesley Gray

Prayer for a loved one departed:
You shared your life with us
God give eternal life to you

You gave your love to us
God give his deep love to you

You gave your time to us
God give his eternity to you

You gave your light to us
God give everlasting light to you
Go upon your journey dear soul
to love, light, and life eternal.
David Adam

You touched my life
and turned my heart around.
It seems when I found you
it was really me I found.

You opened my eyes
and now my soul can see
our moments may be over
of just you here with me.

Love lives on beyond Goodbye
the truth of us will never die.
Our Spirits will shine
long after we've gone,
and so our love lives on.

There was so much
I didn't understand
when you brought me here
far from where we all began.

The changes you made
to my life will never end.
I'll look across the distance
and know I have a friend.

Love lives on beyond Goodbye
the truth of us will never die.
our spirits will shine
long after we've gone,
and so our love lives on.
Anon

BIBLICAL READINGS:

In order of their appearance in the Bible: either from the revised standard version or from a more modern translation, where shown.

'The Bible never grows out of date, because the subjects with which it deals are those subjects which retain their relevance from one century to another'.
F F Bruce.

Old Testament

Gen. 3:19 By the sweat of your brow you will eat your food until you return to the ground, since from it you were taken; for dust you are and to dust you will return'.

Deut. 33:27 The eternal God is your refuge, and underneath are the everlasting arms.

Job 1:21 The Lord gave, and the Lord has taken away, blessed be the name of the Lord.

Job 19:25 I know that my Redeemer liveth and that He shall stand at the latter day on the earth.

Job 34:15–16 If it were his intention and he withdrew his spirit and breath, all mankind would perish together and man would return to the dust.

Ps. 16

> Preserve me O God, for in thee I take refuge.
> I say to the Lord, 'Thou art my my Lord;
> I have no good apart from thee…
> The Lord is my chosen portion and my cup; thou holdest my lot.
> The lines have fallen for me in pleasant places;
> yea I have a goodly heritage.
> I bless the Lord who gives me counsel;
> in the night also my heart instructs me.
> I keep the Lord always before me,
> because he is at my right hand, I shall not be moved.
> Therefore my heart is glad, and my soul rejoices;
> my body also dwells secure.
> For thou dost not give me up to Sheol,
> or let thy godly one see the Pit.
> Thou dost show me the path of life;
> in thy presence there is fullness of joy;
> in thy right hand there are pleasures evermore.

Ps. 23

> The Lord is my shepherd, I shall not want;
> he makes me lie down in green pastures.
> He leads me beside still waters; he restores my soul.
> He leads me in paths of righteousness for his name's sake.
> Even though I walk through the valley of the shadow of death,
> I fear no evil; for thou art with me; thy rod and thy staff, they comfort me.
> Thou preparest a table before me in the presence of my enemies;
> thou anointest my head with oil, my cup overflows.
> Surely goodness and mercy shall follow me all the days of my life;
> and I shall dwell in the house of the Lord for ever.

Ps. 46

> God is our refuge and strength, a very present help in trouble.
> Therefore we will not fear though the earth should change,
> though the mountains shake in the heart of the sea;
> though the waters roar and foam, though the mountains tremble with its tumult…
> 'Be still and know that I am God, I am exalted among the nations, I am exalted in the earth!'
> The Lord of hosts is with us; the God of Jacob is our refuge.

Ps. 89:48

> What man can live and not see death, or save himself from the power of the grave?

Ps. 103

Bless the Lord O my soul; and all that is within me, bless his holy name!
Bless the Lord O my soul, and forget not all his benefits,
who forgives all your iniquity, who heals all your diseases,
who redeems your life from the Pit,
who crowns you with steadfast love and mercy,
who satisfies you with good as long as you live
so that your youth is renewed like the eagle's...
He does not deal with us according to our sins,
nor requite us according to our iniquities.
For as the heavens are high above the earth,
so great is his steadfast love toward those who fear him;
as far as the east is from the west, so far does he remove our
transgressions from us.
As a father pities his children, so the Lord pities those who fear him.
For he knows our frame; he remembers that we are dust.
As for man, his days are like grass; he flourishes like a flower of the
field;
for the wind passes over it and it is gone, and its place knows it no more.
But the steadfast love of the Lord is from everlasting to everlasting,
upon those who fear him, and his righteousness to children's children,
to those who keep his covenant and remember to do his
commandments.

Ps. 121

I will lift mine eyes to the hills, from whence does my help come?
My help comes from the Lord, who made heaven and earth.
He will not let your foot be moved, he who keeps you will not slumber.
Behold, he who keeps Israel will neither slumber nor sleep.
The Lord is your keeper, the Lord is your shade on your right hand.
The sun shall not smite you by day, nor the moon by night.
The Lord will keep you from all evil; he will keep your life.
The Lord will keep your going out and your coming in
from this time forth and forever more. *(Queen Mother's Funeral 2002)*

Ps. 150

Praise the Lord! Praise God in his sanctuary.
praise him in his mighty firmament!
Praise him for his mighty deeds;
praise him according to his exceeding greatness.
Praise him with trumpet sound;
praise him with lute and harp!
praise him with timbrel and dance;
praise him with sounding cymbals;
praise him with loud crashing cymbals!
Let everything that has breath, praise the Lord! Praise the Lord!

Eccles. 3: 1–14, 19–20

For everything there is a season. and a time for every matter under heaven:
a time to be born and a time to die;
a time to plant and a time to pluck up that which is planted;
a time to kill, and a time to heal;
a time to break down, and a time to build up;
a time to weep, and a time to laugh;
a time to mourn, and a time to dance;
a time to cast away stones, and a time to gather stones together;
a time to embrace, and a time to refrain from embracing;
a time to seek, and a time to lose;
a time to keep, and a time to cast away;
a time to rend, and a time to sew;
a time to keep silence, and a time to speak;
a time to love, and a time to hate;
a time for war, and a time for peace...
What gain has the worker from his toil?
I have seen the business that God has given to the sons of men to be busy with.
He has made everything beautiful in its time;
also he has put eternity into man's mind,
yet so that he cannot find out what God has done from the beginning to the end.
I know that there is nothing better for them than to be happy
and enjoy themselves as long as they live;
also that it is God's gift to man that everyone should eat and drink
and take pleasure in his toil.
For the fate of the sons of men and the fate of beasts is the same;
as one dies, so dies the other. They all have the same breath,
and man has no advantage over the beasts; for all is vanity.
All go to one place; all are from the dust, and all turn to dust again.

Eccles. 9:5 For the living know that they will die, but the dead know nothing.

Eccles. 12:1–7 Remember now thy Creator in the days of thy youth, before the evil days come, and the years draw nigh, when you will say, 'I have no pleasure in them' ; before the sun and the light and the moon and the stars are darkened and the clouds return after the rain ... the almond tree blossoms, the grasshopper drags itself along and desire fails; because man goes to his eternal home, and the mourners go about the streets; before the silver cord is snapped, or the golden bowl is broken, or the pitcher is broken at the fountain, or the wheel broken at the cistern, and the dust returns to the earth as it was; and the spirit return to God who gave it. *(Read at Queen Mother's Funeral 2002)*

New Testament

Matt. 5:4 Jesus said 'Blessed are those who mourn, for they shall be comforted'.

Matt. 7: 12–14 So whatever you wish that men should do to you, do so to them; for this is the law and the prophets. 'Enter by the narrow gate; for the gate is wide and the way is easy, that leads to destruction, and those who enter it are many. For the gate is narrow and the way is hard, that leads to life, and those who find it are few'.

Matt. 25:31–40 (or 46) When the Son of Man comes in his glory, and all the angels with him, then he will sit on his glorious throne. Before him will be gathered all the nations, and he will separate them one from another as a shepherd separates the sheep from the goats, and he will place the sheep at his right hand, but the goats at the left.

Then the King will say to those at his right hand, 'Come, O blessed of my Father, inherit the kingdom prepared for you from the foundation of the world; for I was hungry and you gave me food, I was thirsty and you gave me drink, I was a stranger and you welcomed me, I was naked and you clothed me, I was sick and you visited me, I was in prison and you came to me. Then the righteous will answer him 'Lord when did we see thee hungry and feed thee, or thirsty and give thee drink? And when did we see thee a stranger and welcome thee, or naked and clothe thee? And when did we see thee sick or in prison and visit thee? And the King will answer them 'Truly I say to you, as you did it to one of the least of these my brethren, you did it to me.

Mark 10:14a1–6 (especially suitable for a child's funeral) Let the children come to me, do not hinder them; for to such belongs the kingdom of God. Truly I say to you, whoever does not receive the kingdom of God like a child shall not enter it. And he took them in his arms and blessed them laying his hands upon them.

John 5:28 'The hour is coming when all who are in the tombs will hear his voice and come forth, those who have done good, to the resurrection of eternal life, and those who have done evil, to the resurrection of judgement.'

John 6: 35–40 Jesus said to them 'I am the bread of life; he who comes to me shall not hunger, and he who believes in me shall never thirst. But I said to you that you have seen me and yet do not believe. All that the Father gives me will come to me; and him who comes to me I will not cast out. For I have come down from heaven, not to do my own will, but the will of him who sent me; and this is the will of him who sent me, that I should lose nothing of all that he has given me, but raise it up at the last day. For this is the will of my Father, that everyone who sees the Son and believes in him should have eternal life; and I will raise him up at the last day'.

John 8:12 Again Jesus spoke to them 'I am the light of the world; he who follows me will not walk in darkness, but will have the light of life'.

John 11:25–26 'I am the resurrection and the life – he who believes in me, though he die, yet shall he live, and whoever lives and believes in me shall never die'.

John 14: 1–6 'Let not your hearts be troubled; believe in God, believe also in me. In my Father's house are many rooms; if it were not so, would I have told you that I go to prepare a place for you? And when I go and prepare a place for you, I will come again and will take you to myself, that where I am you may be also' ... 'I am the way, the truth and the life; no one comes to the Father but by me'.

Rom. 8: 31 to end. What then shall we say to this? If God be for us, who is against us? He who did not spare his own son but gave him up for us all, will he not also give us all things with him? Who shall bring any charge against God's elect? It is God who justifies; who is to condemn? Is it Christ Jesus who died, yes, who was raised from the dead, who is at the right hand of God, who indeed intercedes for us? Who shall separate us from the love of Christ? Shall tribulation, or distress, or persecution, or famine, or nakedness, or peril, or sword? As it is written 'For thy sake we are being killed all the day long; we are regarded as sheep to be slaughtered.' No, in all these things we are more than conquerors through him who loved us. For I am sure that neither death, nor life, nor angels, nor principalities, nor things present, nor things to come, nor powers, nor height, nor depth, nor anything else in all creation, will be able to separate us from the love of God in Christ Jesus our Lord.

Rom. 14:7- 9 None of us lives to himself, and none of us dies to himself. If we live, we live to the Lord, and if we die, we die to the Lord; so then, whether we live or die, we are the Lord's. For to this end Christ died and lived again, that he might be Lord both of the dead and of the living.

1 Cor. 13 If I speak with the tongues of men and of angels, but have not love, I am a noisy gong or a clanging cymbal. And if I have prophetic powers, and understand all mysteries and all knowledge, and if I have all faith, so as to remove mountains, but have not love, I am nothing. If I give away all that I have, and if I deliver my body to be burned, but have not love, I gain nothing. Love is patient and kind; love is not jealous or boastful; it is not arrogant or rude. Love does not insist on its own way; it is not irritable or resentful; it does not rejoice at wrong, but rejoices in the right. Love bears all things, believes all things, hopes all things, endures all things. Love never ends; as for prophesies, they will pass away; as for tongues, they will cease; as for knowledge, it will pass away. For our knowledge is imperfect and our prophecy is imperfect; but when the perfect comes, the imperfect will pass away. When I was a child, I spoke as a child, I thought like a child, I reasoned as a child; when I became a man, I gave up childish ways. For now we see in a mirror dimly, but then face to face. Now I know in part; then shall I understand fully, even as I have been fully understood. So faith, hope, love abide, these three; but the greatest of these is love.

1 Cor. 15:21–22 For as by a man came death, by a man has come also the resurrection of the dead,. For as in Adam all die, so in Christ shall all be made alive. But each in his own order: Christ the first fruits; then, at his coming, those who belong to Christ. Then comes the end, when he delivers the kingdom to God the Father after destroying every rule and every authority and power, for he must reign until he has put all his enemies under his feet.

2 Cor. 1:5 For we know that if the earthly tent we live in is destroyed…

Phil. 4: 4–9 Rejoice in the Lord always; again I will say rejoice. Let all men know your forbearance. The Lord is at hand, have no anxiety about anything, but in everything by prayer and supplication with thanksgiving let your requests be made known to God. And the peace of God, which passes all understanding will keep your hearts and minds in Christ Jesus. Finally brethren whatever is true, whatever is honourable, whatever is just, whatever is pure, whatever is lovely, whatever is gracious, if there is any excellence, if there is anything worthy of praise, think about these things.

1 Thess. 4:13–18 But we would not have you ignorant, brethren, concerning those who are asleep, that you may not grieve, as others do who have no hope. For since we believe that Jesus died and rose again, even so, through Jesus, God will bring with him those who have fallen asleep. For this we declare to you by the word of the Lord, that we who are alive, who are left until the coming of the Lord, shall not precede those who have fallen asleep. For the Lord himself will descend from heaven with a cry of command, with the archangel's call, and with the sound of the trumpet of God. And the dead in Christ will rise first; then we who are alive, who are left, shall be caught up together with them in the clouds to meet the Lord in the air; and so we shall always be with the Lord. Therefore comfort one another with these words.

Rev. 7:9–17 And after this I saw a great multitude which no man could number, from every nation, from all tribes and peoples and tongues, standing before the throne and before the Lamb, clothed in white robes, with palm branches in their hands, and crying out with a loud voice, 'Salvation belongs to our God who sits upon the throne, and to the Lamb!' And all the angels stood round the throne and round the elders and the four living creatures, and they fell on their faces before the throne saying 'Amen! Blessing and glory and wisdom and thanksgiving and honour and power and might be to our God for ever and ever! Amen.'

Then one of the elders addressed me, saying, 'Who are these clothed in white robes, and whence have they come?' I said to him, 'Sir, you know.' And he said to me, 'These are they who have come out of the great tribulation; they have washed their robes and made them white in the blood of the Lamb. Therefore are they before the throne of God, and serve him day and night within his temple; and he who sits upon the throne will shelter them with his presence. They shall hunger no more, neither thirst any more; the sun shall not strike them, nor any scorching heat. For the Lamb in the midst of the throne will be their shepherd, and he will guide them to springs of living water; and God will wipe away every tear from their eyes.' *(Read at the Queen Mother's funeral 2002)*

Rev. 21:1–7 Then I saw a new heaven and a new earth; for the first heaven and the first earth had passed away, and the sea was no more. And I saw the holy city, new Jerusalem, coming down out of heaven from God, prepared as a bride adorned for her husband; and I heard a loud voice from the throne saying, 'Behold, the dwelling of God is with men. He will dwell with them, and they shall be his people, and God himself will be with them; he will wipe away every tear from their eyes, and death shall be no more, neither shall there be mourning nor crying nor pain any more, for the former things have passed away.'

Appendix III
MUSIC

Music at a funeral is a very individual matter. Everything from classical to pop to jazz has been played at funerals. Anything meaningful to the life of the person, or the family, and the minister, is appropriate.

And although one would like to choose the music for any event, in the end one may be restricted to what the organist can play with confidence, or for which recorded music is available.

Quiet and reflective music at the beginning of the service, without being sentimental, would be suitable. After the service something noble, enriching and positive could be chosen.

SPECIAL OCCASIONS

State funerals usually have the sombre Chopin's *Funeral March* played by one of the forces bands, perhaps during a procession along the streets, if a large crowd is expected. Other suitable processional music may be Elgar's *Nimrod, No 9* from the *Enigma Variations; Elegy* by Thalben-Ball (if there is an organ); Handel's *Dead March from Saul* or *I know that my Redeemer liveth;* Purcell's *Dido's lament,* from *Dido and Aneas;* Ravel's *Pavane for a Dead Princess;* or Gounod's *Ave Maria;*

At the Queen Mother's Funeral (2002) the following music was played: *Fantasia and Fugue in G minor; Piece d'Orgue; Passacaglia in C minor; Liebster Jesu, wir sind hier;* all by J S Bach, 1685–1750 and *Solemn Melody* by Henry Walford Davies,1869–1941. At the end of the service *Prelude and Fugue in E flat* by Bach.

OTHER CLASSICAL PIECES MAY INCLUDE

Faure's *Pie Jesu;* Bach's voluntaries *Bist du bei mir, Komm, susser Tod, God's time is the best,* and *Jesu joy of man's desiring, Sheep may safely graze,* and various preludes, fantasias and fugues; Gluck's *Marcia religiosa* from *'Alceste';* Couperin's *Chaconne in G minor;* Kieff Melody *Russian contakion of the departed* (see *New English Hymnal 526, Common Praise 350);* Peeters *Aria;* Mendelssohn's *Slow movement in A flat from Organ Sonata No 1,* the slow movement (Andante) in D from Organ Sonata No. 6, Allegretto from Sonata No 4, Andante tranquillo from Sonata No 3; Handel's *Largo (from Xerxes),* the *Aria in E flat,* or the *Minuet from Berenice;* Beethoven's *Ode to Joy;* Chopin's *Nocturne in F minor;* Vaughan Williams's *Rhosymedre;* Wright's *Prelude on 'Brother James's Air'.* Dunhill's *Cantilena Romantica;* Guilmant's *Cantilene Pastorale;* Howells's *Master Tallis's Testament;* Widor's *Symphony No. 6: Movements II & IV;* Dupré's *Choral 'Salve Regina' opus 57 No 1,* or *Souvenir from September Pieces opus 27;* Boellmann's *3rd movement from the Gothic Suite.*

Committal Music is usually more solemn. Something suitable would be Chopin's *Prelude in C minor,* or a part of Mozart's *Andantino in E flat.*

I once went to a funeral at Golder's Green, where there were no music or readings; the deceased was a Christian but the surviving partner was not! It did not feel right at all.

FAVOURITES CHOSEN

Prokofiev's *Winter Bonfire* was chosen by Jane Spottiswoode for her husband Nigel's funeral, a non religious 'Do it yourself' affair.

Paul Gambacini would like to die to Grieg's *Piano Concerto in A minor.*

Dame Gillian Weir, a New Zealand born organist, would like to have Berlioz's *Te Deum* and some plain song (Gregorian chant). *(Night and Day, 3 Dec. 2000)*

Colin Dexter, the author of Inspector Morse, would like a choir at his funeral to sing *'In Paradisum' from* Faure's *Requiem. (Mail on Sunday 23 July 200)*

At Bernard Levin's funeral October 2004 the Duke quartet played *Mozart's Adagio in C minor and Schubert's string quartet in A minor.* The choir also sang from *Psalm 90.*

A bandleader at his funeral had *Red Sails in the Sunset* played, because it was his own signature tune. The minister also chose the reading about sailing over the horizon as being the most appropriate one to accompany this tune (see *A Ship sails and I stand* in readings *Appendix II*).

We'll meet again, where the Sun is shining (Ann Ridler's poem sung to music by *Richard Strauss*), was very popular during and after the Second World War.

A family called Rainbow, had the song *Somewhere Over the Rainbow* sung at the Mother's Funeral, as did the family of a young girl, who had been abused and could not get over it, but turned instead to drink and drugs.

At Princess Diana's funeral Elton John sang and played a specially adapted rendering of *Candle in the Wind,* which he originally wrote for Marilyn Monroe.

A piper played *Samantha's Lullaby* at Holly Wells and Jessica Chapman's memorial service in Ely Cathedral in August 2002 (two girls of ten, who were abducted and murdered from Soham in Cambridgeshire).

Other modern funerals have incorporated: *Wind beneath my wings* (Bette Midler), *My Heart will go on* (Celine Dion), *I will always love you* (Whitney Houston), *Simply the Best* (Tina Turner), *Angels* (Robbie Williams), *You'll never walk alone* (Gerry & the Pacemakers); *Candle in the Wind* (Elton John); *Unchained melody* (Righteous Brothers); *Bridge over Troubled Water* (Simon and Garfunkel); *Time to say Goodbye* (Sarah Brightman); *Unforgettable* (Nat King Cole); *Memories* (Barbra Streisand) *I'm going to live forever; My Way* (Frank Sinatra); *Walking in the Air; Imagine; No-one shall sleep; Wish me luck as you wave me Goodbye!; Wonderful world; Smoke gets in your eyes* (for a charcoal maker); *Mood Indigo; the Dambuster's March;* the theme from *Chariots of Fire; Phantom of the Opera, 1987. The Drinking Chorus* or *Have a drink on me* (for a publican); *Those magnificent men in their flying machines* or *Come Fly with me* (a pilot or anyone in the airforce); and even *In the mood;* etc. Some people request the music to their favourite soap.

HYMNS

Suitable for use at funerals

(in alphabetical order of first lines, with suggested music in italics)
* = suitable for a Child's funeral

Abide with me, fast falls the eventide – *to Eventide.*
All creatures of our God and King -to *Lasst uns erfreuen.*
All people that on earth do dwell – *to The old 100th.*
* All things bright and Beautiful – *to All things Bright and Beautiful* – or *Royal Oak*
Amazing Grace – *to a traditional American melody*
* Angel voices ever singing – to *Angel voices.*
* Be still, for the presence of the Lord, the holy one is here.
Blest are the pure in heart, for they shall see our God – *to Franconia*
   Breathe on me breath of God, fill me with life anew – *to Carlisle.*
* Christ, who once among us – *to Pastor bonus*
Dear Lord & Father of mankind, forgive our foolish ways – *to Repton*
Eternal Father, strong to save – (For those in peril on the sea) – *to Melita*
Father hear the prayer we offer – *to Marchingor to Sussex*
Fight the good fight with all thy might – *to Duke Street*
Fill Thou my life, O Lord my God – *to Richmond*
For all the Saints, who from their labours rest – *to Sine Nomine*
* For the beauty of the earth, for the beauty of the skies – *to Dix or to England's Lane*
Forth in thy name, O Lord, I go -to *Angel's Song*
God be in my head and in my understanding – *by Walford Davies*
Great is Thy Faithfulness, O God my Father – *to Great is Thy Faithfulness*
Guide me O Thou great Redeemer – *to Cwm Rhondda (a Welsh favourite)*
(played at the Queen Mother's 2002 & Princess Diana's funerals)
He who would valiant be (by Percy Dearmer after John Bunyan) – *to Monks Gate*
How shall I sing that majesty – *to Coe Fen*
Immortal Love for ever full, for ever flowing free – *to Bishopthorpe.*
Immortal, Invisible, God only wise – *to St Denio* (Queen Mother's funeral 2002)
In heavenly love abiding – *to Penlan*
I vow to thee my country – *to Thaxted* (Princess Diana's funeral 1997)
* Jesus good above all other – *to Quem pastores*
Jesu lover of my soul, let me to thy bosom fly – *to Aberystwyth or to Hollingside*
Jesus lives, thy terrors now can no more, O death, appal us – *to St Albinus*
* Just as I am without one plea – *to Saffron Walden or Misericordia*
Lead us, heavenly Father lead us – *to Mannheim*
Lord dismiss us with thy blessing – *to Dismissal*
Lord enthroned in heavenly splendour (especially for a Requiem) – *to St Helen or Rhuddlan*
Lord for the Years – to *Lord for the years*
Lord we thank thee for the pleasure – to
Lord of All Hopefulness, Lord of All Joy – *to Slane or to Miniver*
Love divine all loves excelling, joy of heaven, to earth come down – *to Love Divine or to Blaenwern.*

Loving Shepherd of thy sheep – *to Buckland*
* Make me a Channel of your peace (Princess Diana's funeral 1997)
New every morning is the Love – *to Melcombe*
Now thank we all our God – *to Nun danket*
* Now the day is over – *to Eudoxia*
O Christ, you wept when grief was raw (from the Iona Community) – *to Rockingham or Angelus*
O God Our help in ages past, our hope for years to come – *to St Anne*
* O Jesus I have promised – *to Wolvercote*
O Lord my God, when I in awesome wonder – *to How Great Thou Art*
O love that wilt not let me go – *to Colkirk (by Paul C. Edwards 1994) or St. Margaret*
On a hill far away *to The Old Rugged Cross*
Onward Christian soldiers – *to St Gertrude*
O worship the King all glorious above – *to Hanover*
O worship the Lord in the beauty of holiness – *to Was lebet*
O for a thousand tongues to sing my dear Redeemer's praise – *to Richmond or to Selby*
Peace perfect peace – *to Pax tecum*
Praise and thanksgiving, Father we offer – *to Bunessan*
Praise my soul, the King of heaven (Psalm 103) – *to Praise my soul*
Praise to the holiest in the height – *to Gerontius.*
Receive her soul, receive her soul, and present her to God the most high. *(Catholic hymn)*
Rock of ages cleft for me, let me hide myself in Thee – *to Petra*
Saviour again to Thy dear name we raise – *to Ellers*
The day Thou gavest Lord is ended – *to St Clement*
The God of love my Shepherd is, and he that doth me feed – *to University*
The King of Love my Shepherd is – to *Dominus regit me* (Princess Diana's funeral) *or to St. Columba*
The Lord's my Shepherd – (Psalm 23) – *to Crimond*
* There is a green hill far away, without a city wall – *to Horsley*
There is a land of pure delight – *to Beulah*
The strife is o'er the battle done – *to Gelobt sei Gott or Victory*
Thine be the glory, risen conquering Son – *to Maccabaeus*
Through the night of doubt and sorrow – *to Rustington or St. Oswald or to Marching*
* What a friend we have in Jesus – *to Converse.*
When all Thy mercies, O my God – *to Contemplation.*
When I survey the wondrous cross, on which the Prince of Glory died – *to Rockingham.*
Who would true valour see (by John Bunyan) – *to Monks Gate*
Ye holy angels bright, who wait at God's right hand – *to Darwell's 148th*

Modern Hymns:

Give me joy in my heart (sung at Holly Wells and Jessica Chapman's memorial service 2002)
Jesus stand among us at the meeting of our lives
Lord, the love of your light is shining (sung at Holly Wells and Jessica Chapman's funeral 2002)

Morning has broken – *to Bunessan*
There is a Redeemer – *to Melody Green.*

W I Members as it is the official W.I. hymn, often choose: *And did those feet in ancient time* – (by William Blake) – *to Jerusalem.*

Service people's funerals:

I vow to thee my country – (written by Cecil Spring Rice 1859-1918, who died the following day. He was about to go to Canada for his country.) (Also sung at Princess Diana's funeral, because she put her 'duty' as she saw it, before everything.) It has subsequently been put to music by *Ralph Vaughan Williams,* although the usual tune that is played for it is an adapted version of *Gustav Holst's Jupiter from his Planet suite – Thaxted.*
Onward Christian Soldiers – *to St Gertrude*
The strife is o'er the battle done – *to Gelobt sei Gott or Victory*

Rotarians may choose the Rotary Hymn *Eternal God.*

Welsh Funerals often have *Guide me O Thou Great Redeemer* or *Abide With Me.*

Someone connected with the navy, lifeboats or fishing etc. may wish to have *'Eternal Father strong to save'.*

Many people will choose *All Things Bright and Beautiful* because this is the only one they remember from their childhood.

It was also sung appropriately at the memorial service in Ely Cathedral, for Holly Wells and Jessica Chapman (2002).

Appendix IV

PET FUNERALS AND CEMETERIES

Animals are part of the family, especially for children, and they can be devastated by the death of a beloved pet. Having a funeral for a pet and burying it in the garden can help them come to terms with the loss, and prepare them for the death of close relationships thereafter. Most pets in the UK are buried in the gardens where they have lived. All my cats are buried in my own garden.

The royal dogs are buried in the grounds of whichever royal castle the Queen happens to be at the time, and small tombstones mark their graves. Her carpenter makes a small wooden coffin and the animal is interred with a posy of flowers from the estate.

The gardens of other stately homes usually contain a pets' cemetery.

There are currently 60 public pet cemeteries in England (2005). Fourteen counties are listed on the Internet as having one or more pet cemeteries but there are many more. Most handle the burial or cremation of pets in a similar way to those for people, with dignity. It is possible to have an actual funeral service. Headstones are available as well as plots, or the ashes can be scattered in a garden.

There are many more pet cemeteries in the USA. I remember visiting one near Palm Springs, California, where Liberace's dog was buried, along with the pets of other famous people. It is a growing industry both here and abroad.

I have a friend, who buries all her horses in the field where they have spent all their lives. She cannot bring herself to send her 'friends' to the knacker's yard.

There is a however a 'horse only' cemetery near Huddersfield (see useful addresses in *Appendix V*).

There is mass burial or cremation of some animal carcasses and commercial or clinical waste, and the people responsible for this activity also take bodies from veterinarians. These must be licensed by the Environment Agency or Local Authority. European legislation may soon alter the rules and regulations on landfill, so expect some changes in the near future.

For a more personal service there is an *Association of Private Pet Cemeteries,* who put forward a strict code of practice (see addresses in *Appendix V*). *Paws to Rest* in Carlisle caters for small animals.

Peaceful Pets in Norfolk take care of horses as well as smaller animals, in 1,300 acres of beautiful rural countryside. Farmers are being asked to consider a pet cemetery as a viable alternative to farming.

Humans can currently legally be buried in a pet cemetery with their pet(s) but at the moment pets cannot be buried with or without their owners in an Anglican churchyard or most civic cemeteries.

One exception was made at St Mary Redcliffe in Bristol. The church cat, that served the church for 15 years, catching mice and keeping down the pigeons in the churchyard, was given a proper funeral in the church with music. During his lifetime he had processed with the choir, sat next to the blind organist at every service, and often slept on the lap of one of the congregation for the sermon. He attended more services than the clergy but was not allowed in the chancel. His small coffin was carried by the verger and accompanied by the vicar and churchwardens to the churchyard where he is buried, with a commemorative stone, saying 'The Church Cat 1912–1927'. (From a leaflet written by Stephen Richards, grandson of Eli Richards, the verger.)

Another exception was a cat buried in the churchyard at St Mary's, Fairford, Gloucestershire, after 17 years of service. He was a tabby and lived from 1963 to 1980. At the time of the cat's death a stonemason was working in the church, so he carved a cat statue as a headstone for Tiddles and the cat was buried facing the church door. People still leave the odd flower on his grave, although the stone has sadly weathered rather badly. A cat-loving lady in the parish asked for her ashes to be buried next to Tiddles in the churchyard and this was done.

It is doubtful whether a faculty (permission from the diocese) was requested to bury a cat in the churchyard in either case; it is much more likely that it was done regardless!

A dog that sat on his master's grave in Edinburgh for several years was also buried beside him when his own time finally came. This story has been made in to a short tear-jerking film for Television, called *Greyfriars Bobby*.

If an adult loses a beloved pet, this can be as traumatic an experience as losing a member of their family. They may have been sole companions for years together and may grieve excessively for a lost pet. The Blue Cross has a *Pet Bereavement Support Group* at Burford in Oxfordshire. And the BSAVA (British Small Animal Veterinary Association) have a leaflet about pet bereavement.

ANIMALS AND THE HEREAFTER

Some people feel that animals do not have souls and therefore will not appear in heaven (whether this means a renewed earth or somewhere else). Animals are not people; they are different. A dog may be a man's best friend but can he pray with him? But all animals live and die as we do.

The Bible tells us that the wolf will lie down with the lamb, the leopard with the kid, and the calf with the young lion, so they would all have to be there, in the Millennium at least, according to *Isa. 11:6–8,* even if not in the subsequent new heaven and the new earth, referred to in the book of Revelation. There will however be plants, '...on either side of the river, the tree of life with its twelve kinds of fruit, yielding its fruit each month; and the leaves of the tree were for the healing of the nations.' *Rev. 22: 2.*

And some people feel that, wherever it will be, it would not be a heaven anyway without animals!

Appendix V

Useful Addresses

Age Concern	Astral House 1268 London Road Norbury, London SW16 4ER	020 8765 7200 028 9024 5729 Fax 020 8765 7211	www.ageconcern.org.uk
Age Concern - Northern Ireland			
Age Concern - Scotland	113 Rose Street Edinburgh Scotland EH2 3DT	0131 220 3345 Fax 0131 220 2779	
Age Concern - Wales (Cymru)	4th Floor, 1 Cathedral Rd Cardiff CF1 9SD	029 2037 1566 Fax 029 2037 1566	
AIDS bereavement help see FACTS & Lon. Lighthouse			
Alzheimer's Society (The)	Gordon House 10 Greencoat Place London SW1P 1PH	020 7306 0606	
American Military Cemetery	Supt. James A Schoenecker Coton Cambridge CB3 7PH	01954 210 350 Fax 01954 211 130	
Asian Family Counselling Service	Suite 51 Windmill Place 2-4 Windmill Lane Southall Mddsx UB2 4NJ	0208 571 3933	
Asian Funeral Company	158 Melton Road Leicester	0116 261 1171	
Assoc. of Private Pet Cemeteries & Crematoria	Loning Garth, Lambley Bank Scotby Carlisle Cumbria CA4 9JT	01252 844 478	www.dignitypetcrem.co.uk contact@appcc.co.uk
Association of Natural Burial Grounds	c/o Natural Death Centre 6 Blackstock Mews Blackstock Road London N4 2BT	020 7359 8391	
B & P Green Burials Ltd The Sustainability Centre	South Downs Natural Burial Site Droxford Road East Meon Hants	01730 823005	
Bedfordshire Bereavement Forum	Saxon Centre 230 Bedford Road Kempston Bedford MK42 8PP		

Bedfordshire Child Bereavement Services	Macmilllan Office Gt Bramingham Lane Luton Beds LU5 3NT	01582 497812	
Benefits Agency	see business sect phone book		
Bereavement Register (The)	The Clock House Blighs Road Sevenoaks Kent TN13 1DA	01732 460000 Fax 01732 460036	
Body bags (Thorley Smith)	Britannia Mill Clayton Street Wigan WN3 4DG	01942 243331 Fax 01942 821592	
Britannia Shipping Co (burials at sea)	Newton Poppleford Nr Sidmouth Devon EX10 0EF		
British Association of Cancer Patients BACUP	3 Bath Place Rivington Street London EC2A 3JR	020 71613 2121 Freephone 0808 800 1234	www.cancerbacup .org.uk
British Humanist Association	Bradlaugh House 47 Theobalds Road London WC1X 4SP	020 7430 0908	
British Medical Association	BMA House Tavistock Street London WC1H 9JP	020 7387 4499	
British Organ Donor's Society (BODY)	Balsham Cambridge Cambs. CB1 6DL	01223 893 636	body@argonet.co. uk
British Oxygen Co. Hackney Ltd - (ice)	59 Eastway London E9 5NS	020 8985 5544	
British Small Animal Veterinary Association (BSAVA)	Woodrow House, 1 Telford Way Waterwells Business Park Quedgeley Glos. GL2 2AB	01452 726700	
Burial at Sea - Newhaven, E. Sussex	Angus Radford Sovereign Harbour Marina Newhaven E. Sussex	01424 424109 Fax 01424 444642	
Burial at Sea - North Shields	Defra Fish Office, Bell Street Northshields Tyne & Wear NE30 1LT	0191 257 4520 Fax 0191 257 1595	rodney.a.henderso n@defra.gsi.gov. uk
Burial at Sea – Poole, Dorset (see also Britannia)	Alex Mackenzie for burials off the Needles Isle of Wight	01202 677539 Fax 01202 678598	
Cancerlink	11-21 Northdown Street London N1 9BN	0800 132 095 Freephone 0808 808 0000	cancerlink@canlin k.demon.co.uk
Capital Taxes Office	Ferrers House P.O.Box 38 Castle Meadow Road Nottingham NG2 1BB	0845 302 0900	www.inlandrevenu e.gov.uk/cto
Cardboard Coffins - Joseph A Hey & Sons	470 Great Horton Road Bradford Yorkshire BD7 3HR	01274 834602	

Care for the Carers Ltd	Braemar House 28 St Leonard's Road Eastbourne E Sussex BN21 3UT	01323 738 390	
Chartered Institute of Arbitrators	12 Bloomsbury Square London WC1A 2LP	0207 421 7444	www.arbitrators. org
Child Bereavement Trust	Aston House The High Street West Wycombe HP14 3AG	01494 446648	
Child Death Helpline	Bereavement Services Dpt. Gt. Ormond St Hosp. Trust Gt. Ormond St London WC1N 3JH	0800 282 986	
Children's caskets and baby cribs	Wells Caskets, Unit 1B Littledale Workshops Colliers Green Kent TN17 2LS	01580 212040	
Citizens Advice Bureau (CAB)	Yellow Pages/ Telephone book		
City Cruises (scattering ashes in the Thames)	Cherry Garden Pier Cherry Garden Street Rotherhithe London SE16 4TU	020 7740 0400 Fax 0207 740 0495	www. citycruises.com
Co-operative Funeral Care	Trafford Plaza Seymour Grove Old Trafford Manchester M16 OLD	0161 772 6280	
Co-operative Funeral Service	King's Walk Earl Shildon Leicestershire	01455 844400	
Coffin Covers Limited / Joseph A Hey & Sons	470 Great Horton Road Bradford Yorks. BD7 3HR	01274 571021	www.coffincovers. co.uk
Coffins - chipboard oak veneer - quick delivery	E C Hodge (MF) Ltd New Drove Off Weasenham Lane Wisbeach PE13 2RZ	01945 587477 Fax 01945 466063	
Colney Woodland Burial Park	Watton Road Colney Norwich Norfolk NR4 7TY	01603 811556 Fax 01603 811770	

Compakta Coffins	Old White Cottage 2 Newhold Road Desford Leicester	01455 828642	
Compassionate Friends	53 North Street Bristol BS3 1EN	0117 953 0630 Fax: 0117 914 4368	www.tcf.org.uk
Cot Death Helpline	Artillery House 11/19 Artillery Row London SW1A 2HH	0870 787 0554	
Cremation Society of Great Britain	Brecon House (2nd floor) 16-16a Albion Place Maidstone Kent ME14 5DZ	01622 688 292/3	Cremsoc @aol.com
CRUSE – Bereavement Care – Cruse House	126 Sheen Road Richmond Surrey TW9 1UR	020 8940 4818 Brvemt line 0845 758 5565 Fax 020 8940 7638	
DEFRA Marine Consents & Licences	3-8 Whitehall Place (2nd floor) Area D London SW1A 2HH	020 7238 5870 Fax 020 7238 5724	www.mceu.gov.uk
DEFRA Marine Consents (Phil Moore)	Phil Moore Eastbourne Marina	01424 216765	
DEFRA Sea Fisheries Inspectorate	Nick Albright The Fish Market Rock-a-nore Road Hastings E. Sussex TN34 3DW	01424 424109 Fax 01424 44642	
Department of Health	PO Box 777 London SE1 6XH	Fax 01623 724524	
Department of Social Security- Social Services	Yellow Pages / Telephone book		
DVLA - Car Licensing & refunds	Customer Enquiries Group Contact Centre Sandringham Park Swansea SA7 0EE	01792 766269 Fax 10792 766368	http://www.dvla. gov.uk
Eco Friendly Coffins - Ecopods - ARKA	37 Western Road Hove E. Sussex BN3 1AF	01273 746011	
Enduring Power of Attorney Helpline		0845 330 2963	www.publictrust. gov.uk/enduring
Environment Agency	Rio House, Waterside Drive Aztect West Almondsbury Bristol BS32 4UD	08708 506 506 Hot line emergency 0800 807 060	www.environment -agency.gov.uk

Equine Crematorium - Norfolk	The Grange West Rudham King's Lynn Norfolk NR	01485 528141	www.peacefulpets.co.uk
Equine Crematorium - Yorks.	The Bungalow Near Bank Shelley Huddersfield Yorkshire HD8 8LT	01924 840752	
FACTS Health Centre (Aids)	23-25 Weston Park Crouch End London N8 9SY	020 8348 9195	
Federation of British Cremation Authorities	41 Salisbury Road Carshalton Surrey SM5 3HA	020 8669 4521	
Foreign & Commonwealth office (deaths overseas)	Consular Division King Charles Street London SW1A 2AH	020 7008 0186	www. fco.gov.uk
Foundation for the Study of Infant Deaths	Artillery House (FIDS) 11/19 Artillery Row London SW1P 1RT	0870 787 0554	support@sids.org.uk
Funeral Directors - local	Yellow pages / Telephone book		
Funeral Ombudsman Scheme	26-28 Bedford Row London WC1R 4HL	020 7430 1112	
Funeral Standards Council	30 North Road Cardiff CF1 3DY	029 2038 2046	
Greenfield Coffins - Cardboard in colours	UNIT 6/7 Lakes Road Braintree Essex CM7 3SS	01376 327074 Fax 01376 342975	
H M Coroners Office	Yellow pages / Telephone book		
H M Inspector of Anatomy (Department of Health)	Wellington House 133-155 Waterloo Road London SE1 8UG	020 7263 4130	
Heaven on Earth (funerals / purpose built coffins)	18 Upper Maudlin Street Bristol BS2 8DJ	0117 926 4999	www.Heavenonearthbristol.co.uk heaven.earth@virgin.net
Help the Aged - Senior Line		9-5 Mon-Fri 0808 800 6565	
Help the Aged - Senior Line - N. Ireland		0808 808 7575	

Home office (Coroner's Section Room 972)	Constitutional Policy Directorate 50 Queen Anne's Gate London SW1H 9AI	0870 000 1585 020 7273 2888/3574	
Hospice Information Service	St Christopher's Hospice 51-59 Lawrie Park Rd Sydenham London SE26 6DZ	020 8778 9345	www.hospiceinformation.info
Hymn Technology	9 South End Croydon CR0 1BE		
Independent Funerals Advice Service IFAS	44 Swain Street Watchet Somerset TA23 0AG	01984 632285	
Inheritance Tax Help line		0845 302 0900	
Inland Revenue web site			www.inland revenue.gov.uk
Intercultural Therapy Centre	278 Severn Sisters Road Finsbury Park London N4 2HY		
Jewish Bereavement Counselling Service	P.O. Box 6748 London N3 3BX	020 8349 0839	
Justine Burgess of Hatfield (funeral directors)	Alfred House The Common Hatfield AL10 OND	01707 262122 Fax 01707 274006	
Law Society Gazette	50-52 Chancery Lane London WC2AA 1SX	020 7242 1222	
Lesbian & Gay Bereavement Project	Vaughan M Williams Centre Colindale Hospital London NW9 5GH	020 7403 5969 7.00-10.30 pm 020 8455 8894 Off weekdays	
Local Cemeteries & Crematoria	Yellow pages / Telephone book		
Local Hospitals	Yellow pages / Telephone book		
Local Probate Office - ask Registrations Office	Yellow pages / Telephone book		
London Association of Bereavement Services	356 Holloway Road London N7 6PN	020 7700 8134 Fax 020 7708 146	
London Gazette	P.O. Box No. 7923 London SE1 5ZH	0870 600 3322	www.Londongazette.co.uk
London Lighthouse (Aids & HIV support)	111-117 Lancaster Road London W11 1QT	020 7792 1200 Text phone 020 7792 2979	
Lymm A W (white Rolls Royce)	Robin Hood House Robin Hood Street Nottingham Notts. NG3 1GF	0115 950 5875	admin@lymn.co.uk

187

Macmillan Cancer Relief Fund & Cancer Line	89 Albert Embankment London SE1 7UQ	0808 808 2020	
Marine Volunteer Reserve (consents)	Mr Greg Darby Newhaven E. Sussex	01892 853500	
Maritime and Coast guard Agency (deaths at sea)	Anchor Court Keen Road Cardiff S. Wales CF24 5JW	029 8876 3444	
Memorial Forests (Life for Life)	Watergrove Nr Rochdale	0161 627 8413	
MIND Nat. Inst. Mental Health	P.O. Box 277 Manchester M60 3XN	0845 766 0163	www.mind.org.uk
Ministry of Agriculture, Fisheries & Food (marine)	3-8 Whitehall Place (2nd floor) Area D London SW1A 2HH	0845 933 5577	www.mceu.gov.uk
Miscarriage Association (incl. ectopic preg)	c/o Clayton Hospital Northgate Wakefield West Yorkshire WF1 3JS	0192 420 0799	
Motor Bike Funerals Ltd.	Essex Lodge 26 East Street Prittlewell Essex SS2 6LH	01702 618315	
Motor Neurone Disease Association	P.O. Box 246 Northampton NN1 2PR	01604 250505	
Motorcycle Funerals Limited (Paul Sinclair)	89 Belvoir Road Coleville Leicester Leicestershire LE67 5AG	01530 834616	
Multiple Sclerosis Society	MS National Centre 372 Edgware Road London NW2 6ND	020 8438 0700	
Narrow boat coffins - Vic Fearn & Co.	Crabtree Mill Hempshill Lane Bulwell Nottingham NG6 8PF	0115 927 1907 Fax 0115 977 1571	
National AIDS Helpline	Healthwise 1st Floor 8 Matthew Street Liverpool L2 6RE	0151227 4150	
National Assembly for Wales	Peir House Cardiff Bay Cardiff S Wales CF100 1DA	029 2082 5111	

National Association of Bereavement Services	20 Norton Folgate London E1 6BD	020 7247 1080 020 7709 9090 (24hrs/ansphone)	
National Association of Funeral Directors	618 Warwick Road Solihull West Midlands B91 1AA	0121 711 1343	info@nafd.org.uk
National Association of Memorial Masons	27a Albert Street Rugby CV21 2SG	01788 542 264	
National Association of Prepaid funeral plans	618 Warwick Road Solihull West Midlands B91 1AA	0121 711 1343	
National Association of Widows	3rd floor, 48 Queens Road Coventry CV1 3ER	024 7663 4848	
National Federation of Spiritual Healers	Old Manor Farm Studio Church St. Sunbury on Thames TW16 6RG	0845 123 2777	
National Secular Society	Bradlaugh House 47 Theobalds Rd. London WC1X 4SP	020 7430 0908	
Natural Burial Company Cardboard Coffins	Suite 1 Devonshire House Bank Street Lutterworth Leicestershire LE17 4AG	01455 550099	
Natural Death Centre	6 Blackstock Mews Blackstock Road London N4 2BT	020 7359 8391 Fax 0207354 3831	ndc@alberyfoundation.org
Organ Donor Register	P.O. Box 14 Patchway Bristol BS34 8ZZ	0845 6060 400	
Overseas Registration Section	Smedley Hydro Trafalgar Road Birkdale Southport PR8 2HH		
Parkinson's Disease Society	215 Vauxhall Bridge Road London SW1V 1EJ	020 7931 8080	
Paws to rest	Coombes View Nun Close Armathwaite Carlisle CA4 9TJ	016974 72232	www.appcc.org.uk
Peace Funerals - wicker coffins - body bags	Gleadless Mount Sheffield S12 2LN	0114 253 0505	

Peoples Dispensary for Sick Animals (PDSA)	Whitechapel Way Priorslee, Telford Salop TF2 9DQ	0800 917 2509	
Pet Bereavement Support Group	c/o The Blue Cross Shilton Road Burford Oxfordshire OX18 4PF	0800 096 6606	www.havenfunerals. com
Phoenix International (Steve Thomas)	c/o Haven Funerals 13 The Broadway London W3 8HR	0800 783 4044	
Probate Help Line (incl. Inheritance Tax) IR Capital Taxes	Ferrers House P.O. Box 38 Castle Meadow Road Nottingham NG2 1BB	0845 30 20 900	www.inland revenue.gov.uk
Probate Registry. The (formerly Somerset House)	42-49 High Holborn London WC1V 6NP	020 7947 6000	www.probateser vice.gov.uk
Probate Office from - Registration Office	Yellow pages / Telephone book Eng. & Wales	0870 241 0109 Northern Ireland (028 9023 5111)	
Rainbows (Catholic charity)	Cheadle Hulme 11 Madison Avenue SK8 5DF	0161 488 4470	
Registration Office - Births/marriages/deaths	Yellow pages / Telephone book		
Roadpeace - for traffic accidents	PO Box 2579 London NW10 3PW	020 8964 1021 Fax 020 8838 5103	www.roadpeace. org
Royal Society Prevention of Cruelty to Animals	London Regional Office P.O. Box 756 London SE25 5SF	0345 888999	
Saga - services for over 55 year olds	The Saga Building Middleberg Square Folkestone Kent CT20 1AZ	01303 771111	
Samaritans - Local number	Yellow pages / Telephone book	Help Line 08457 90 90 90	
SAWD Ltd. Bamboo Coffins	Highsted Farm Highsted Valley Sittingbourne Kent ME9 0AG	01795 472262 Fax 01795 422633	wainman@sawd .demon.co.uk
SCI Pre-arrangement Ltd	Farringdon House Wood Street East Grinstead RH19 1EW	01342 325005	
Scottish Executive Justice Department	Spur VI, Saughton House Broomhouse Drive Edinburgh EH1 3XD		

Service Corporation International (SCI)	Plantsbrook House 94 The Parade Sutton Coldfield B72 1PH	0121 354 1557	
Shire Horse Hearse - Mr Clayton	Headlands Farm Eaneury, Gayton Nottingham NN7 3JF	01327 830181	
Shrouds (woollen)	Carlisle Cemetery Office Richardson Street Carlisle CA2 6AL	01228 625310	junec@carlisle-city.gov.uk
Society of Allied & Indepd. Funeral Directors	Crowndale House 1 Ferdinand Place London NW1 8EE	020 7267 6777	
Solid brass/hardwood /9" stake pet memorial Shires of Bath	Dept 340 1 Bartlett Street Bath BA1 2QT	08708 50 11 55	
SSAFA Forces Help (ex service people & families)	19 Queen Elizabeth Street London SE1 2LP	020 7403 8783 Fax 020 7403 8815	www.SSAFA.org .uk
Stillbirth & Neonatal Death Society (SANDS)	28 Portland Place London W1N 4DE	020 7436 5881 Fax 020 7436 3715	support@uk-sands.org
Stroke Association	Stroke House 123-127 Whitecross St London EC1Y 8JJ	020 7566 0300	
Support after Murder or Manslaughter (SAMM)	Cranmer House 39 Brixton Road London SW 9 6DZ	020 77735 3838	
Survivors of Bereavement by Suicide (SOBS)	Volsere House 14-18 West Bar Green Sheffield Yorks. S1 2DA	0114 272 5955	sobs.admin@care4free.net www.care4free.net
T. Cribb & Sons (white horse hearse)	Victoria House 10 Woolwich Manor Way Beckton London E6 5PA	020 7476 1855 Fax 0207 476 0371	
Terrence Higgins Trust (Aids or HIV support)	52-54 Gray's Inn Road London WC1X 8JU	020 7831 0330 Help 12-10pm 020 7242 1010	www.tht.org.uk
The Treasury Solicitors' Department (BV)	Queen Anne's Chamber 28 Broadway London SW1H 9JX	020 7210 3000	
UK Passport Agency	Globe House 89 Eccleston Square London SW1V 1PN		
Veterans Agency (for service people)	Norcross Blackpool FY5 3WP	0800 169 22 77 0800 169 34 58 (text phone)	

Vic Fearn & Co Ltd - (designer coffins)	Crabtree Mill Hempshill Lane Bulwell Nottingham NG6 8PF	0115 927 1907 Fax 0115 977 1571	
Victim Support Yellow pages/Telephone	National Office Cranmer House 39 Brixton Road London SW9 6DZ	0845 3030 900	
Vintage Lorry Funerals - David Hall	Kingsfield House Kingsfield Close Bradford on Avon Wiltshire BA15 1AW	01225 865346	hall3@which.net
War Pensions Agency MoD	See local telephone directory	Help line 0800 169 22 77 Fax 01253 332014	
War Widows Association of Gt Brtn (see Veterans)	c/o 48 Pall Mall London SW1Y 5JY	01629 636 374	
Welsh Assembly	Pier Head Street Cardiff Bay Cardiff S. Wales CF100 1DA	029 2082 5111	
White Dove Company (release doves at funerals)	9/11 High Beech Road Loughton Essex IG10 4BN		
White horse hearse (see T Cribb & Sons)			
Wicker Coffins & Body bags	Peace Funerals of Sheffield Gleadless Mount off Ridgeway Road Sheffield S12 2LN	0114 253 0505 0800 093 0505	
Willow Coffins - The SAWD Partnership	Highsted Farm Highsted Valley Sittingbourne Kent ME9 0AG	01795 472262 Fax 01795 422633	
Winston's Wish (children & parents)	Clara Burgess Centre Bayshill Road Cheltenham Gloucester GL50 3AW	01242 515157	info@winstons wish.org.uk
Wood Green Animal Shelters (rehoming animals)	601 Lordship Lane Wood Green London N22 5JG	020 8888 2351	
Woodland burial site - Bucks	Olney Green Burial Ground Yardley Road Olney Bucks MK46 5EH	01234 241808	information@the greenburial company.plc.uk www.thegreen burialcompany. com

Woodland burial site - The Arbory Trust	Bishop Woodford House Barton Road Ely Cambs. CB7 4DX	01284 749974	info@arborytrust.org www.arborytrust.org
Woodland Burial Cemetery	Westall Park Redditch Worcs B96 6JY	01386 792806	
Woodland burial site - Norfolk	Watton Road, Colney Norwich Norfolk NR4 7TY	01603 811556 Fax 01603 811770	

Index